RE-ENVISIONING FAMILY ENGAGEMENT AND LITERACY IN EARLY CHILDHOOD CLASSROOMS

Families are resources that are extremely powerful and important for young learners from minoritized backgrounds, yet such families are often overlooked, silenced, or ostracized. This book presents a much-needed framework for family and community engagement in the early childhood and elementary literacy classroom that embraces and foregrounds students' unique cultural backgrounds. This book spotlights the families of minoritized learners and the crucial role that they play in building dynamic and inspiring environments for learning. To re-envision the engagement of these families in the early childhood classroom, the book provides an accessible understanding of Yosso's theory of community cultural wealth. Covering key topics such as children's literature and digital tools, the book features strategies for implementing culturally responsive classroom practices to create positive home–school partnerships. Each chapter highlights one type of capital in community cultural wealth—aspirational, linguistic, familial, social, navigational, and resistant—and gives teachers guidance on working with and supporting the efforts of families both inside and outside of the classroom.

This book is an essential resource to inform current and future early childhood educators on how to gain deeper understandings of what families—especially from Communities of Color—already *are* doing for the education of their children, and how best to support them.

Julia López-Robertson is Professor of Education at the University of South Carolina, USA.

Melissa Summer Wells is Associate Professor of Education at the University of Mary Washington, USA.

RE-ENVISIONING FAMILY ENGAGEMENT AND LITERACY IN EARLY CHILDHOOD CLASSROOMS

"Porque así ya conocemos"

Julia López-Robertson and Melissa Summer Wells

NEW YORK AND LONDON

Designed cover image: © Getty Images

First published 2024
by Routledge
605 Third Avenue, New York, NY 10158

and by Routledge
4 Park Square, Milton Park, Abingdon, Oxon, OX14 4RN

Routledge is an imprint of the Taylor & Francis Group, an informa business

© 2024 Taylor & Francis

The right of Julia López-Robertson and Melissa Summer Wells to be identified as the authors of this work has been asserted in accordance with sections 77 and 78 of the Copyright, Designs and Patents Act 1988.

All rights reserved. No part of this book may be reprinted or reproduced or utilised in any form or by any electronic, mechanical, or other means, now known or hereafter invented, including photocopying and recording, or in any information storage or retrieval system, without permission in writing from the publishers.

Trademark notice: Product or corporate names may be trademarks or registered trademarks, and are used only for identification and explanation without intent to infringe.

ISBN: 9781032375816 (hbk)
ISBN: 9781032375809 (pbk)
ISBN: 9781003344377 (ebk)

DOI: 10.4324/9781003344377

Typeset in Bembo
by KnowledgeWorks Global Ltd.

CONTENTS

Author Biographies vi
Acknowledgments vii

1 Al Principio: Knowing Teachers, Knowing Families 1

2 Porque así Ya Conocemos: Re-envisioning Family Engagement and Literacy in Early Childhood Classrooms 17

3 Sueños for Our Children's Future: Aspirational Capital 35

4 Language from El Corazón: Linguistic Capital 50

5 The Richness of Familia: Familial Capital 69

6 Together in Comunidad: Social Capital 86

7 Making Mapas: Navigational Capital 102

8 Sí Se Puede: Resistant Capital 121

9 Conclusion: Voces in Action: Using Community Cultural Wealth to Engage in Action 139

Appendix A: Analysis of CCW Themes in Selected Children's Literature 158
Index 175

AUTHOR BIOGRAPHIES

Julia López-Robertson is Professor of Education at the University of South Carolina, USA. She earned her B.S. from Northeastern University (Boston, MA) in elementary education, her M.A. in Bilingual/Multicultural Education from the University of Arizona, and her Ph.D. in Language, Reading, and Culture also from the University of Arizona. A former early childhood bilingual classroom teacher (17 years), her research focuses on the intersections among language, race, ethnicity, and culture as they relate to the teaching and learning of English Learners and their families, and in preparing teachers for diverse classrooms.

Melissa Summer Wells is Associate Professor of Education at the University of Mary Washington, USA. She earned her B.A. from Furman University (Greenville, SC) in elementary education and music before completing her M.A. in early childhood education at Furman University. She completed her Ph.D. at the University of South Carolina (Columbia, SC) in the Language and Literacy program. She taught in the public schools of South Carolina for eight years as a third-grade teacher, kindergarten teacher, and elementary literacy coach before assuming her current position at the University of Mary Washington in 2017. Her current teaching and research interests involve family engagement, critical theory, literacy, arts integration, and culturally responsive pedagogy.

ACKNOWLEDGMENTS

Our work would not have been possible without the support of several key individuals. First of all, we are immensely grateful to the families, children, and educators who welcomed us into their spaces to listen, learn, and build new possibilities for family engagement together. Thank you for sharing **confianza** with us and inspiring us to re-envision asset-based ways of engaging families. We would also like to thank the editorial team at Routledge for helping us take our work and shape it into this book.

We are who we are because of the loving support of our own families and networks.

Julia López-Robertson
Melissa Summer Wells

I am forever grateful to my husband, JR, for his constant love and support and to my sons, Tomás and Pedro, for encouraging me with, '**Mami, ya termina eso**'/*Mami, finish already*. My deepest admiration and love to all the Latina mothers and to the teachers who have kindly shared their teaching spaces and families with me and who always include me in their projects. To the memory of my parents, Lázaro and Ana Rosa López, who like the Latino families in this book persevered and taught me by example that there are no obstacles we cannot overcome. Finally, to Melissa, thank you for joining me in this journey, I am always in awe of your attention to detail and the speed with which you work. We had a few obstacles of our own, but we did it!

Julia López-Robertson

I am thankful for the circles of people who love and support me and made this work possible. Throughout my life, my family has shaped me into the educator I am today, one who is willing to question, advocate, and dream. I am especially grateful to my husband, Robert, who patiently took over many responsibilities to make sure I could focus on finishing this project, while our rescue beagle, Snickerdoodle, snoozed in her bed behind my desk chair. I am thankful for Julia's ongoing support of my development as a scholar and teacher educator. Finally, I need to thank Ariya's mother, whom you'll meet in Chapter 1. You taught me that resistance is an act of love. Thank you for calling me out and causing me to challenge inequities in educational spaces.

Melissa Summer Wells

1
AL PRINCIPIO
Knowing Teachers, Knowing Families

"Our families can't…"

"Our families don't have…"

"Our families aren't involved…"

"Our families don't care…"

We truly hope you have never heard sentences like the ones above uttered in any educational setting. But we have. And we suspect you have too. You might have even used some of these phrases yourself, years ago or even yesterday.

For our young learners from minoritized cultures and backgrounds, families are resources that are extremely powerful and important, yet they are often ignored, silenced, or ostracized. Framed around Yosso's (2005) concept of community cultural wealth (CCW), this book moves critical theories into accessible practice for early childhood educators. Our goal is for readers to take away a deeper understanding of the CCW families share with our youngest learners and classrooms and how to build more productive, positive, and enduring home–school partnerships.

Al principio, we share our **cuentos** before addressing the importance of knowing teachers and families as we re-envision family engagement and literacy in early childhood through the lens of CCW. The chapter closes with an analysis of the book framework.

Our Cuentos

As educators, we revel in the power of **cuentos**. Stories entertain, educate, and reveal (Bishop, 1990). They take us to varied places: to great lands of imagination, to carefree summer days of childhood, to fascinating lives of others. Sometimes, however, stories take us to unexpected places that shape our identities in unexpected ways (Short, 2012).

Throughout this book, we will share stories of how we re-envision family engagement and literacy in early childhood classrooms, based on the work we have done with families throughout our careers as educators. First, though, it is important for us to explain who we are. Here are our own **cuentos** of how we arrived at the places we are today, invested in the work we invite you to join us in doing.

Julia's Cuento

If you tell what she says, I'll get you when you get home.

Those are the words my older brother firmly whispered to me as I left the house with my mother. We were on our way to parent–teacher conferences and I remember it like it was yesterday. I was a good student: I always did my homework and behaved well. My brother, not so much. My mother trusted me to tell her what the teacher said about my brother, and the teacher, I suppose, trusted me too. But what choice did she have? Our school did not have a translator. I did not know it at the time, but I possessed a highly sought-after commodity: language. I served my family and teachers as a translator, and more specifically, I was a language broker. The commodity I was dealing was language: the ability to communicate in Spanish and English. My brother handed me quite an ethical dilemma: tell the truth and face his wrath or lie to my mother. I did not lie to my mother.

My parents, a Colombian mother and Cuban father, were uneasy about sending us to the public school. As immigrants, they were completely unfamiliar with the American educational system and felt more comfortable sending my siblings and me to our much smaller local Catholic school. We knew all the children in school since we all came from the same town. I remember there were a lot of Anglo, a few African American, and a growing number of Latino[1] children in our school and neighborhood. As the years progressed, the number of Anglo families in our school declined, while the number of Latino families was steadily rising. When I taught in this school several years later, my first-grade classroom of 25 students had only one Anglo child my first year, and none my second and final year. Our school reflected national demographics; the Latino population was steadily increasing. Also mirroring national demographics, our school was not prepared to work with Spanish-speaking children or families, ever since the time I was a student.

As a student, I never saw myself in my schools—anywhere—nor do I recall anything ever being sent home in Spanish. The only way my family knew what was going on in school is when my siblings or I would talk about school or translate notes that were sent home. I remember one note that was about an informational meeting for Brownies; the dates and times as well as some information was on the flyer. When my mother asked what it was about, I remember being confused because brownies were food—a soft cookie, a dessert, I described to her, not a person. Needless to say, I never became a Girl Scout. But I did become a teacher.

My first teaching job was as a first-grade teacher in the Catholic school I attended. I recall my principal handing me a milk crate full of teacher's editions of math, phonics, spelling, and religion books. It was heavy, literally and figuratively. I had a brief moment of freaking out (this was followed by several moments of freaking out over the course of my teaching career) when it hit me that I had to teach these subjects. How in the world was I going to teach all these subjects? She must have seen the panic on my face and matter-of-factly patted me on the back and said, "You'll be fine." Off I went.

In a few short weeks, it would be me and my 25 first graders together all day every day. And so, it began. I had 1 Anglo boy, 3 Haitian children, 1 African boy, 2 African American children, and 18 Latino children in my class. In addition to reading, writing, mathematics, and science, I taught art, music, physical education (PE), and religion (I drew heavily on my upbringing and schooling in Catholic school). A few weeks into the school year, I noticed that my teaching was not effective because I was not meeting milestones, particularly in the language arts. I was unclear why this was happening, as I spent so much time planning.

Even then I loved reading aloud and sharing stories with children and I also loved when they told me stories. I recall this exact day because it was life-changing for me. After a read aloud, one of my girls was a little confused about some of the details and sought clarification, asking her question in Spanish. I was about to respond when another Spanish-speaking student replied to the question and offered further details, which provided clarification and also speculation about the topic of the story—in Spanish. What ensued left me with my mouth open; the children (by now they were basically all talking) engaged in a discussion about the story which was connected to our unit of study—in Spanish. Their lively discussion provided me with information about their knowledge of the topic and also indicated points where there was some confusion. More importantly, it demonstrated that they were more confident sharing their growing knowledge in Spanish. From that day forward, I became a bilingual teacher; I was not trained as one, but the children made me one.

Becoming a bilingual classroom teacher was not how I envisioned my career. I had never been taught by a Spanish-speaking teacher and I never spoke Spanish in school. I was a part of a group that the Archdiocese created for teachers interested in learning about whole language and the role culture played in teaching, the Intercultural Training and Resource Center (ITRC). At the ITRC, we read professional books, discussed pedagogy, and had access to a variety of teaching materials—my favorite were picture books from other countries. It was at the ITRC that I came across the first picture book I had ever seen written in Spanish—a bilingual picture book, *Mr. Sugar Comes to Town/La visita del Señor Azúcar* (Rhomer & Gomez, 1989). I checked out the book and read it to my class often; they loved it! We read it, acted it out, and eventually made a bilingual big book for our class. The book and our engagements helped me understand the role of culture and language in teaching. Teaching and talking in Spanish with my first two classrooms of children helped me see the necessity of building on one's first language and the important role of language in classrooms. I come to this book from my personal experiences, some noted above, and a desire for all children and families to feel welcome, safe, and respected in their schools.

Melissa's Cuento

My path to this topic has followed a twisting and complicated path. When I began my career as a public school teacher in 2009, I was absolutely petrified of parents. I was afraid they would uncover me as the first-year teacher fraud that I was. I was afraid they would doubt my authority as a classroom teacher. I was afraid that they would question every instructional move I made. When it was time for parent–teacher conferences, anxiety would rule my life for the entire week. I was definitely not seeing my families as the educational partners that now I know they are. In fact, in trying to protect my role as a teacher by asserting my instructional authority, I was making my job *more* difficult. Of course, when one of my third graders came into my classroom one day and announced, "My mom saw you helping with the car line, and she says you look like you should be in high school," that didn't exactly help my already-existent imposter syndrome.

Despite this initial fear, I have the parent of a kindergarten student to thank for the most transformative moment of my entire teaching career. It was my third year teaching, and my first year teaching kindergarten instead of third grade. I had a rocky start with one child in particular. Ariya[2] was constantly getting in trouble: she would wind up in conflict with her peers over toys, "talk back" to adults, and conveniently not hear directions, even when they were given multiple times. These patterns unfortunately resulted in many "sad faces" going home on Ariya's daily behavior sheet. After a few weeks, her mom wrote me a note back, saying she would no longer sign the behavior sheet because she viewed her signature as agreement that her child was bad, and she did not think her child was bad. This comment gave me pause: I did not believe that a child's choices on a given day at school reflected their potential as a whole, but I realized how the structure of the behavior sheet could mistakenly imply that. I was at a loss as the behaviors continued, so we scheduled a conference with Ariya, her mom, the assistant principal, and myself. In this conference, Ariya's mom delivered the words that forever changed my life as an educator:

*The reason why you don't like my child is because **you're racist**.*

After this statement, the assistant principal promptly ended the conference. Aryia and her mother left the room while I sat in shock, holding back tears.

Those words haunted me for weeks. I thought I had been raised to be tolerant, accepting, anything but *racist*. But I quickly realized that Ariya's mom wasn't wrong. Ariya was Black. I am White. I grew up in a predominantly White neighborhood. All but one of my childhood friends were White. All of my teachers were White, except my third-grade teacher. The books I read in school and beyond featured characters that looked like me and shared many of my experiences. I can turn on the TV to find commercials, newscasters, and sitcoms that relate to my White culture. Whiteness had surrounded me my entire life, yet I had never noticed it. Now, I was bringing that culture of Whiteness into my classroom. So are the 80% of teachers in the United States who are White (Loewus, 2017). And while being White doesn't make you racist[3] automatically, being White does mean you are socialized into certain cultural norms, expectations, and behaviors. These norms influence how we approach a lot of different things as people and as teachers. Take my interactions with Ariya, for example. Were the ways she was negotiating with her peers for toys and her social interactions with adults truly problematic, or were they just *against the norms of Whiteness* with which I was familiar?

Ariya's mom opened my eyes to the inequitable situations our children and families of color face in schools. Many times, these situations are created unintentionally. Schools often create policies against the backdrop of the White culture that remains largely invisible to those who live within it. Requiring families to show ID to get into the school building seeks to prevent dangerous intruders from compromising the safety of our schools, but it also means that families without a government-issued ID face challenges if they wish to eat lunch with their child. Sending home all school newsletters in English sends a message to families who don't speak English. Addressing all families as "parents" leaves out the grandmother who is the primary caregiver for her grandchildren.

My **cuento** won't end with "happily ever after." I am working every single day to realize the invisible privileges granted to me as a White woman, a White teacher. I have made this my mission throughout being a third-grade teacher, kindergarten teacher, elementary literacy coach, and now, a teacher educator.

I have a lot of work left to do, but I am writing this book to invite you to join me in this journey. When we know better, we do better. I don't want first-year teachers to be afraid of their students' families, like I was. I certainly don't want any teachers to be called racist in a parent–teacher conference. My hope is that this book will help you see the ways your own culture—White or otherwise—influences your educational contexts on a daily basis, and that you can begin to see beyond your own cultural norms to see the incredible ways our students' families support their learning.

Re-envisioning Family Engagement and Literacy: Knowing Teachers, Knowing Families

"Our families *can*…"

"Our families *have*…"

"Our families *are engaged*…"

"Our families *do* care…"

When we re-envision family engagement in early childhood settings, we hear these rewritten counternarratives. When we begin with assets—with what families *can* and *do*—we find new possibilities. This work involves deeply knowing teachers and families.

We come to this work with a variety of experiences in a variety of geographic locations across the United States: the Northeast, the Southeast, and the Southwest. As educators, teacher educators, and stakeholders in our local educational contexts, we've held multiple roles as we've worked with families. The voices and stories we share with you throughout this book are drawn from those contexts, which fall into three overarching configurations: family engagement through classroom teaching; family engagement through special events; and family engagement through focused affinity groups.

Family Engagement through Classroom Teaching

As former elementary educators, we both engaged families directly through classroom activities. As an elementary literacy coach, Melissa worked with an early childhood educator (Kadence, who identified as White) to gather data as families engaged in digital learning communities, which were private groups for classroom families only hosted on Class Dojo's Class Story and a private group on Flickr. The goal for the digital learning communities was twofold: to invite families into the classroom virtually while also encouraging families to share artifacts of learning in their own lives. Students, families, and teachers engaged in the digital learning community by posting media or responding to media posted by others, and then they reflected on the experience at the end of the year. All of these engagements were based on classroom teaching, instead of special school-wide events.

Family Engagement through Special Events

In addition to the day-to-day opportunities for family engagement within individual classroom spaces, we also have had opportunities to engage families through special events, such as school-wide family literacy nights. One example of school-wide family literacy nights arose out of Julia's collaboration with Pilar, a Latina classroom teacher, who worked very hard to create and maintain relationships with her families. She suspected that something was not right with her families' engagement as attendance at school events began to falter, even though there was 100% attendance at the first few school events. Concerned with this recent turn of events, Pilar invited the families to school one evening for an informal meeting.

We had one goal that evening, to meet with families and listen as they expressed questions and/or concerns. We decided to begin the evening with a read aloud in Spanish simply as a way to create a shared experience. We chose to read *Viva Frida* (Morales, 2015), a beautifully illustrated book about Mexican artist Frida Kahlo. We engaged the six mothers and their children who joined us that evening in a discussion about the book where they marveled at the illustrations and shared some questions about Frida Kahlo. We then asked the children to think about and draw their favorite part of the story while we met with the mothers.

We gathered with the mothers in the shared space in between all the classrooms while the children worked in the classroom (we could see all of them from where we sat) as we did not want the children to participate in this part of our meeting. We restated our goals: to listen to their questions and concerns. There were a few moments of silence as it seemed the mothers were gathering the courage to speak up. While it was difficult for us to remain silent, we resisted the urge to prompt and encourage dialogue, instead providing wait time. The conversation began with a clarifying question about school policies, library book checkout, and lunch procedures. Another mother expressed concerns about the lack of understandable information they received: **"Toda la información que recibo es en inglés. Todavía no se leer en inglés"**/*All the information I receive is in English. I do not know how to read English yet.* The other mothers agreed and added that even though they had noted in the registration forms that they preferred communication in Spanish, everything was in English. Finally, and in exasperation, Hilda noted, **"Nos ignoran"**/*We are* *ignored.* This statement opened the floodgates as the mothers shared examples of incidents where they felt devalued and insignificant. All the mothers added, **"Si nos tratan a nosotras así, ¿qué aran con nuestros niños?"**/*If they treat us like this, what do they do with our children?*

As a result of this meeting, Pilar and Julia organized special events aimed at building relationships with Latinx families. We hosted a few gatherings, where families were encouraged to share their language and culture with other families, and literacy nights. Even though our events were focused on Pilar's classroom (we felt it more manageable to work on a smaller scale), attendance at school events rose. The relationship with the Latinx families continued to develop and then COVID hit. Since returning to school full time, we noticed that families were again feeling disconnected, so while we are at the beginning of our relationship, we are not at the starting point. We are building on our prior experiences and the families are in the driver's seat.

Family Engagement through Focused Affinity Groups

Finally, some of our work with families has emerged out of organic spaces where focused affinity groups formed, like at Sunnyside Elementary. The principal at Sunnyside Elementary felt that the Latinx families' needs were not being fully met by the school and, upon learning about the "cultural misrepresentations and microaggressions" (López-Robertson & Haney, 2016, p. 105) they experienced, asked that Julia and her teacher-partner create a space where Latino families could feel welcomed and a sense of belonging in the school community. Julia and her teacher-partner, Ms. Jones, met weekly with a group of Latina mothers where they engaged in activities that centered the mothers' language, literacy, and ways of knowing, as resources and assets.

We recruited Latinx families while at a Family Night; we explained that our goal was to involve them actively in the school community and shared our vision to create "a space where language, literacy, stories, and lived experiences could be supported" (Early, 2017, p. 177) and were the foundation to all the work we did. On the first day, we had three mothers arrive. After a few minutes of talking, they suggested Friday afternoon from 12:30 to 2:00 was the best time to meet. They had two concerns regarding child care: would they have to return at dismissal time and what about the younger siblings who were not school-aged? The principal had agreed to let the younger siblings come to school as a part of our group and for the school-aged children to be dismissed to our room, giving them time to participate in our literacy engagements with their mothers and younger siblings. Each of the meetings began with a read aloud, conducted in Spanish since we centered the work on our mothers' language and literacy (only one English book was read aloud because we had a particular goal in using it). This was followed by a discussion of the book where mothers asked questions and shared connections to life experiences. Additionally, we engaged the mothers and children in a variety of activities related to the read aloud: art activities, a school ABC book, and family stories.

Our weekly meetings also served as a space where the mothers could bring school- and community-related questions. We discussed advanced courses, bus schedules, and school policies and procedures. The principal was "deliberate in the manner in which she strengthened the active participation of Latina families" (López-Robertson & Haney, 2021, p. 74) and approved our requests to take the mothers and their children on field trips. The goals of the trips were to familiarize the families with the community so that they could see their place in the community and to learn about the resources available to them. We met for about five years, during which time our goals never changed; we wanted our families to recognize the strengths they possessed and to come to a place where their language, literacy, stories, and lived experiences were the foundation of all work.

Book Framework

The stories and experiences contained in this book are the results of years of personal experience and research. When conducting research with families, it can be challenging to honor families' voices while also preserving the anonymity of their identities. We changed the names of the family members, students, and teachers referenced in this book. We relied upon transcripts, notes, and artifacts gathered with families' approval to form the data sets we present throughout this book.

In all the settings in which we worked, our groups overwhelmingly consisted of Latina mothers. Distortions of Latina mothers are based on the premise that "because [Latina] women who are poor and uneducated are not often seen as resources within the household, schools do not often validate their life experiences or draw on their multiple funds of knowledge" (González, 2005, p. 71). We share their stories respectfully, and in doing so "make explicit the multiple identities that these women, as mothers, as socializers of children, and as key personages in the lives of school-age children, have actively fashioned for themselves in the face of overwhelming adversity and suffering" (González, 2006, p. 211).

One of our goals throughout the book is to help readers see what the different forms of CCW (Yosso, 2005) look like in classrooms and schools. CCW acknowledges strengths and "reframes deficit perspectives of Communities of Color" (Pérez Huber, 2009, p. 711) in areas such as aspirational capital, linguistic capital, familial capital, social capital, navigational capital, and resistant capital. We will explain CCW in greater depth in Chapter 2.

Episodes and Counternarratives

Each chapter contains "episodes" or vignettes to illustrate each of the different aspects of CCW in actual classroom contexts. It is important for us to include the voices of families, to provide a counternarrative (Solórzano & Bernal, 2001; Solórzano & Yosso, 2001) to the stereotypically held views of communities of color as not interested in their children's schooling. It is too often the case that the voices of families of color are not present in the research; we include their voices and gratefully acknowledge their participation in the work. We share their stories with permission and respect.

We draw from research in higher education and mathematics teacher education to define an episode. Mentoring episodes and the notion of high-quality connections originated to examine workplace interactions and were adapted by Schwartz and Holloway (2014) as they sought to understand the relevance of mentoring in graduate education. The researchers offer that high-quality connections positively impact learning and boost engagement and suggest that as a relational practice, teaching and learning facilitates people's growth in "relation to others rather than through isolated individual effort" (p. 39). In mathematics teacher education, Nemirovsky et al. (2005) draw from Shulman's (1991, 1992) seminal work on the importance of classroom-based teaching cases as a tool for teacher preparation. They suggest that cases provide teachers the opportunity to engage with, discuss, and later reflect on a variety of detailed teaching situations: these are not full case studies, rather they are "contextual, local, and situated" (Shulman, 1992, p. 28) teaching and learning experiences. Following this, we define an episode as a teaching experience where the participants (teachers, researchers, students, families) are engaged together, working to achieve the same goal in a co-created contextually based experience.

In addition, these episodes and vignettes also serve another vital purpose as counternarratives. Also known as counterstories, these pieces serve four main functions in education: they "build community among those at the margins of society"; "challenge the perceived wisdom of those at society's center"; "nurture community community cultural wealth, memory, and resistance"; and "facilitate transformation in education" (Yosso, 2006, pp. 14–15). Therefore, counternarratives are **cuentos** that interrupt the status quo, center the experiential knowledge of people of color, and humanize their creators. It is important to note that counternarratives are not meant to be monolithic; they do not represent the experience of an entire group of people, but rather just the experience of the storyteller within a specific context.

You will notice that we feature families' voices throughout this text as we share their **cuentos**. Many times, these voices are in Spanish. Like García-Sánchez and Orellana (2019), we present the families' original voices in their home languages in bold text first, followed by the English translation in italic text. We believe this conventional approach provides literal, physical weight to our families' words, especially when those words demonstrate multilingualism. More traditional conventions, such as putting the non-English language in italics, highlights the language's "otherness" and situates English as the "norm." We desire to interrupt that norm and re-situate families' languages as the norm.

Children's Literature

Another central element in the framework of this book is children's literature, again aligning with our belief in the power of **cuentos**. Each chapter will share multiple examples of children's literature: one featured earlier in the chapter, and then a list of picturebooks near the end of each chapter aligned with each element of CCW in their corresponding chapters. The feature picturebook is sometimes a piece of literature that came up in our work with families, and other times it is a particularly powerful example of the element of CCW being discussed.

The list of picturebooks near the end of each chapter is not exhaustive, but was curated strategically. We began by researching picturebooks on specific award lists for children's literature (both the award winners and the honor books) between 2018 and 2022:

- Américas Award (honors authors, illustrators, and publishers whose books portray Latin America, the Caribbean, or Latinx cultures in the United States)
- Tomás Rivera Mexican American Children's Book Award (honors authors and illustrators who create literature depicting the Mexican American experience)
- Pura Belpré Award (honors Latinx authors whose work centers the Latinx experience)
- Coretta Scott King Award (honors African American authors whose work centers African American culture alongside human values)
- Stonewall Book Award (honors literature focusing on LGBTQ+ communities and experiences)
- Schneider Family Book Award (honors books that portray the experiences of people with disabilities)
- Middle East Book Award (honors books that contribute meaningfully to the understanding of the Middle East, specifically Afghanistan, Algeria, Bahrain, Egypt, Iran, Iraq, Israel, Jordan, Kuwait, Lebanon, Libya, Morocco, Oman, the Palestinian Territories, Qatar, Saudi Arabia, Syria, Tunisia, Turkey, the United Arab Emirates, and Yemen)
- American Indian Youth Literature Award (honors books by and about Native American and Indigenous people in North America; for picturebooks,

both the author and the illustrator must be connected to an Indigenous community)
- Caldecott Medal (honors artists of American picturebooks)
- Newbery Medal (honors authors of American children's literature)

Many of the books on these lists are considered multicultural picturebooks, or books that "highlight the lives of people from marginalized and underrepresented groups in the United States" (Short, 2016, p. 5). CCW itself prioritizes reframing the assets communities of color possess, and therefore we felt that the award lists above provided the most opportunities to view CCW in action within the pages of picturebooks.

We then located read-aloud videos of the books to view and code for elements of CCW independently before coming together to triangulate our analysis. One challenge we faced with this method was that lesser-known books, such as those who received the Middle East Book Award or the American Indian Youth Literature Award, did not have read-aloud videos available, thus further limiting access to books that center voices that are already limited within the realm of children's book publishing. Books that featured animal or inanimate objects as main characters were excluded from our analysis because these types of characters steer away from portrayals of diverse experiences and critical conversations, and "can reinforce 'colorblind' notions" (Boutte et al., 2008, p. 953). In fact, the Cooperative Children's Book Center (Tyner, 2018) found that picturebook characters were four times more likely to be a dinosaur than an American Indian child. For these reasons, we felt that highlighting picturebooks with human characters aligned most strongly with exemplifying elements of CCW.

While each chapter includes a list of books we analyzed and felt had the strongest representations of the corresponding capital within CCW, the reality is that each form of capital frequently interrelates with other forms of capital. Appendix A contains a comprehensive list of all the children's literature recommended throughout the book and indicates if we perceived that a text addressed many capitals of CCW simultaneously. However, these are not the only books to feature elements of CCW, and we encourage you to read other picturebooks with a critical eye toward their portrayals of CCW.

Outline of Chapters

Throughout the rest of this book, we will look at each of the aspects of Yosso's (2005) theory of CCW in the context of classroom practice. Each chapter will include structures to facilitate transfer of the information to your own educational contexts: **cuentos** from the field, which will show how we learned with and through families through multiple episodes; tips for planning critically informed instruction and developing meaningful, dialogic relationships with families; lists of children's literature that serve as windows, mirrors, and sliding glass doors (Bishop, 1990) for all students and families; and technology tools that can engage families in humanizing, dialogic ways.

Chapter 2, "**Porque así ya conocemos**: Re-envisioning Family Engagement in Early Childhood Classrooms," explains the difference between family involvement and family engagement, problematizes traditional unidirectional home–school relationships that result in monologic discourse instead of dialogue (Bakhtin, 1981), and provides a basic introduction to critical race theory (CRT) in education, including Yosso's model of CCW and its comparison to other cultural wealth models.

The remaining chapters will investigate CCW and the intersection with family engagement in early childhood settings. As noted above, each chapter will also include vignettes and episodes of actual engagement with families, suggestions for next steps for instruction and home–school partnerships, relevant children's literature, and featured technology for family engagement.

- Chapter 3: "**Sueños** for Our Children's Future: Aspirational Capital"
- Chapter 4: "Language from **el corazón**: Linguistic Capital"
- Chapter 5: "The Richness of **familia**: Familial Capital"
- Chapter 6: "Together in **comunidad**: Social Capital"
- Chapter 7: "Making **mapas**: Navigational Capital"
- Chapter 8: "**Sí se puede**: Resistant Capital"

Finally, Chapter 9, "Conclusion: **Voces** in Action—Using Community Cultural Wealth to Engage in Action" provides a summary framework for engaging in critical action that builds dialogic, humanizing relationships (Freire, 1970) that recognize and honor students' and families' CCW. This framework, however, is not a recipe of prescriptive elements and steps to take. It is a framework for knowing students and families deeply, for crafting strength-based counternarratives, and for taking critically informed action that designs equitable spaces for families to serve as experts and meaningful contributors to their children's learning experiences, both in and out of school.

Al Principio

As we get started, we see many spaces and places where this work is important. Teachers, you are in the trenches with students and families on a daily basis, and we recognize the important role you play in partnerships with families. Instructional coaches, family liaisons, and administrators, you often have the responsibility to plan large-scale efforts that support family engagement. Front office staff, you are the first people our students and families encounter as they enter the doors of schools. Preservice teachers, you are in the midst of learning how our educational system functions, and we invite you to consider how your relationships with families can support your work as future teachers, even before you have a classroom to call your own. Graduate students, you are returning to gain additional knowledge that may not have been part of your initial coursework. Families, perhaps you are looking for ways to advocate for yourselves and your children. There is space for each of you in this book.

Getting started isn't always easy, however. Our project faced a lot of ups and downs, and even some complete shutdowns and restarts. Amidst relocations, job changes, policy and program changes, funding changes, a global pandemic, and more, we had to change our partnerships and structures multiple times. Knowing this is important because as we forge meaningful relationships with families that center their rich backgrounds, experiences, and knowledge, this work is rarely linear with a clear beginning, middle, and end.[4] In fact, if we are too focused on what we expect to happen, we might completely miss incredibly valuable learning opportunities.

Let's begin!

Notes

1 Latino/a and/or the country of origin is used when the person/s self-identify as such. The term Latinx promotes gender inclusivity and is used when speaking of peoples with roots in Spanish-speaking countries who live in the United States and who may or may not speak Spanish. The discussion of terminology goes beyond the scope of this book; we offer this brief note to clarify our use of terms. For a more complete discussion, see Salinas and Lozano (2019).
2 All names of people and places throughout this book are pseudonyms.
3 There are different types of racism: individual racism, systemic racism, and institutional racism. Usually, when someone is accused or accuses others of being racist, this is individual racism at play. However, systemic and institutional racism are also prevalent, even in school settings, and can be much harder to interrupt without intentional actions.
4 Even though many early childhood literacy activities highlight the importance of naming the beginning, middle, and end of a story, this "traditional" linear narrative structure is very much White/Westernized. Other cultures prioritize other narrative traditions. We will talk more about cultural interpretations of storytelling in Chapter 4.

References

Bakhtin, M. (1981). *The dialogic imagination: Four essays by M. M. Bakhtin*. (M. Holquist, Ed.). University of Texas Press.
Bishop, R. S. (1990). Mirrors, windows, and sliding glass doors. *Perspectives, 6*, ix–xi.
Boutte, G. S., Hopkins, R., & Waklatski, T. (2008). Perspectives, voices, and worldviews in frequently read children's books. *Early Education & Development, 19*(6), 941–962. doi: https://doi.org/10.1080/10409280802206643.

Early, J. S. (2017). *Escribiendo juntos:* Toward a collaborative model of multiliterate family literacy in English only and anti-immigrant contexts. *Research in the Teaching of English, 52*(2), 156–180.

Freire, P. (1970). *Pedagogy of the oppressed.* Continuum.

García-Sánchez, I. M., & Orellana, M. F. (Eds.). (2019). *Language and cultural practices in communities and schools: Bridging learning for students from non-dominant groups.* Routledge.

González, N. (2005). *I am my language: Discourses of women and children in the borderlands.* University of Arizona Press.

González, N. (2006). *Testimonios* of border identities: "Una mujer acomedida donde quiera cabe. In D. D. Delgado Bernal, C. A. Elenes, F. E. Godinez, & S. Villenas (Eds.), *Chicana/Latina education in everyday life: Feminista perspectives on pedagogy and epistemology* (pp. 197–213). Suny Press.

Loewus, L. (2017, August 15). *The nation's teaching force is still mostly White and female.* Education Week. https://www.edweek.org/teaching-learning/the-nations-teaching-force-is-still-mostly-white-and-female/2017/08

López-Robertson, J. & Haney, M. J. (2021). Toward culturally sustaining pedagogy: Engagements with Latina mothers through Latino/Latina children's literature. In K. Nash, C. Glover, & B. Polson (Eds.), *Toward culturally sustaining teaching: Early childhood educators honor children with practices for equity and change* (pp. 61–81). National Council of Teachers of English/Routledge.

López-Robertson, J. & Haney, M. J. (2016). Making it happen: Risk-taking and relevance in a rural elementary school. In S. Long, M. Souto-Manning, and V. Vasquez (Eds.). Courageous leadership: Administrators taking a stand for social justice in early childhood education, practice and promise. New York, NY: Teachers College Press. Pp. 102–112.

Pérez Huber, L. (2009). Challenging racist nativist framing: Acknowledging the community cultural wealth of undocumented Chicana college students to reframe the immigration debate. *Harvard Educational Review, 79*(4), 704–730.

Nemirovsky, R., DiMattia, C., Ribeiro, B., & Lara-Meloy, T. (2005). Talking about teaching episodes. *Journal of Mathematics Teacher Education, 8*(5), 363–392.

Salinas, C., & Lozano, A. (2019). Mapping and recontextualizing the evolution of the term Latinx: An environmental scanning in higher education. In E. G. Murrillo (Ed.), *Critical readings on Latinos and education: Tasks, themes, and solutions* (pp. 216–235). Routledge.

Schwartz, H. L., & Holloway, E. L. (2014). "I become a part of the learning process": Mentoring episodes and individualized attention in graduate education. *Mentoring & Tutoring: Partnership in Learning, 22*(1), 38–55.

Short, K. G. (2012). Story as world making. *Language Arts, 90*(1), 9–17.

Short, K. G. (2016). A curriculum that is intercultural. In K. G. Short, D. Day, & J. Schroeder (Eds.), *Teaching globally: Reading the world through literature* (pp. 3–24). Stenhouse.

Shulman, L. S. (1991). Ways of seeing, ways of knowing: Ways of teaching, ways of learning about teaching. *Curriculum Studies, 23*(5), 393–395.

Shulman, L. S. (1992). Towards a pedagogy of cases. In J. H. Shulman (Ed.), *Case study methods in teacher education* (pp. 1–30). Teachers College Press.

Solórzano, D. G., & Bernal, D. D. (2001). Examining transformational resistance through a critical race and LatCrit theory framework: Chicana and Chicano students in an urban context. *Urban Education, 36*(3), 308–342.

Solórzano, D. G., & Yosso, T. J. (2001). Critical race and LatCrit theory and method: Counter-storytelling. *International Journal of Qualitative Studies in Education*, *14*(4), 471–495.

Tyner, M. (2018). *CCBC 2017 multicultural statistics*. CCBlogC. http://ccblogc.blogspot.com/2018/02/ccbc-2017-multicultural-statistics.html

Yosso, T. J. (2005). Whose culture has capital? A critical race theory discussion of community cultural wealth. *Race Ethnicity and Education*, *8*(1), 69–91.

Yosso, T. J. (2006). *Critical race counterstories along the Chicana/Chicano educational pipeline*. Routledge.

Children's Literature Cited

Morales, Y. (2015). *Viva Frida*. Scholastic.

Rhomer, H., & Gomez, C. (1989). *Mr. Sugar comes to town/La visita del Señor Azúcar* (E. Chagoya, Illus.). Children's Book Press.

2
PORQUE ASÍ YA CONOCEMOS

Re-envisioning Family Engagement and Literacy in Early Childhood Classrooms

Sitting across the table from the mother of a student in a second-grade classroom, Melissa, the classroom teacher, a mother, and her daughter were debriefing the use of two digital tools—Flickr and Class Dojo's "Class Story" feature—as a way to keep families engaged with classroom events and allow them to share updates from home with the class too. Near the end of their time together, Melissa asked the mother if she thought it was important or not for families to be able to post pictures and videos for others in the class to view. She replied:

> **Yo pienso que sí, es importante porque así ya conocemos de otras culturas de las personas que tal vez nostros no lo hacemos, como méxicanos es diferente? Yo pienso que sí. Es importante.** / *I think that yes, it is important because we already know about other cultures of people that maybe don't do it like us, like how Mexicans are different? I think so. It is important.*

This mother went on to explain how in Mexico, Christmas isn't as important as el Día de los Tres Reyes, or Three Kings' Day, on January 6, and that there is a holiday called el Día del Niño, or The Day of the Child, which celebrates children each year on April 30. The classroom teacher admitted that she had never heard of el Día del Niño.

Porque así ya conocemos: *because we already know.* In that moment, this mother was talking about one way of knowing, of knowing the cultures from her homeland of Mexico. This mother knew she had much knowledge and community cultural wealth (CCW) (Yosso, 2005) to share with the school; all that she needed was a space to speak and be heard. How much more did she

DOI: 10.4324/9781003344377-2

already know—do the families of our students already know—if we the teachers, if we the institution of school, could just create spaces to listen and to learn with and from each of our families?

In this chapter, we will explore the foundational principles of this book. To re-envision family engagement and literacy in early childhood classrooms, we will begin with a survey of common, more "traditional" practices with family engagement and family–school communication before offering possibilities for overarching strategies to foster meaningful family–school partnerships. Then, we will present the theoretical framework that underlies the book, including a critical overview of literacy instruction and an introduction to the theory of CCW (Yosso, 2005), explaining how it differs from other theorizations of capital.

Re-envisioning Family Engagement and Literacy in Early Childhood Classrooms

Meaningful engagement with families has long been a goal in early childhood classrooms. In the following sections, we will investigate the differences between family involvement and family engagement; approaches to family–school communication; strategies to foster home–school knowledge exchanges; and considerations when engaging families with technology.

Family Involvement versus Family Engagement

Throughout this book, we have chosen to use the word *family*. A report from Generations United (2022) indicated that almost 3% of children living in the United States live apart from their parents and that nearly two-thirds of those are being raised by grandparents. Foster parents, relatives, or other caring adults may also be raising children who are not biologically theirs; therefore, in an effort to be inclusive of the variety of family structures we find in schools and society, throughout this book we will use *family* instead of parents, unless we are quoting another speaker who used a different term.

Family involvement and family engagement are related but distinct concepts. Traditionally, parent involvement suggests that parents do things *for* the school: participate in school book fairs, send items in to bake sales, or help with fundraising efforts. Ferlazzo (2011) suggests that in schools, family involvement "leads with its mouth—identifying projects, needs, and goals and then telling parents how they can contribute" (p. 12). The school is the one leading the connection with the child and their parents; the school knows what it wants and has also predetermined which students and parents can provide what they have identified as a need.

Family engagement is more about relationship-building where the school "leads with its ears," asking and listening as families share their dreams, aspirations, and worries (Ferlazzo, 2011, p. 12). Engagement also considers the families' role in identifying and offering suggestions for solving issues; there is more sense of a relationship. The National Association for Family, School, and Community Engagement (NAFSCE) defines family engagement as

- "a shared responsibility in which schools and other community agencies and organizations are committed to reaching out to engage families in meaningful ways and in which families are committed to actively supporting their children's learning and development";
- "continuous across a child's life and entails enduring commitment but changing parent roles as children mature into young adulthood"; and
- "cut[ting] across and reinforc[ing] learning in the multiple settings where children learn—at home, in prekindergarten programs, in school, in after school programs, in faith-based institutions, and in the community" (NAFSCE, n.d. para. 1).

From these elements, we see the importance of family engagement being a shared, life-long endeavor: it involves schools, families, and communities sharing a mutual goal of academic success for children.

An important issue to keep in mind is the mismatch between school expectations and family expectations when it comes to minoritized families. Some minoritized families may have little to no experience with American public schools and as such do not understand the cultural expectation for them to participate in their children's learning. Rather than explain the expectations, too often they "are made to feel unwelcome in schools and are belittled and critiqued when they try to intervene on behalf of their children's education" (Villenas & Deyhle, 1999, p. 433). When working with all families, and minoritized families specifically, schools need to ensure that they are clear about engagement expectations from the start.

If you are interested in learning more about family engagement, we recommend the following resources.

- "Introduction to Family Engagement in Education" is a massive open online course (MOOC) available through Harvard featuring Dr. Karen Mapp, who is a noted researcher on family engagement. Learn more here: https://online-learning.harvard.edu/course/introduction-family-engagement-education
- *Involving Latino Families in Schools* (Delgado Gaitan, 2004)
- *Families with Power: Centering Students by Engaging with Families and Community* (Cowhey, 2022)
- *Partnering with Immigrant Communities: Action through Literacy* (Campano et al., 2016)
- *New Ways to Engage Parents: Strategies and Tools for Teachers and Leaders, K-12* (Edwards, 2016)

Approaches to Family–School Communication

When thinking about the ways schools traditionally communicate with families (maybe even from your own experience as a student), what are some common formats and venues? Here are some of the ideas that come to mind:

- Newsletters (print or digital)
- Phone messages via phone trees/automated calling
- Digital messages via platforms like Remind or Class Dojo
- Notes in daily folders
- Personalized phone calls home
- Parent–teacher (family) conferences

If we look at the main goals of each of those forms of communication, who is positioned as the "owner" or sharer of knowledge and information, and who is positioned as the recipient? Overall, the school holds the information and relays it to the families. This could be considered a one-way flow of information, as shown in Figure 2.1.

This unidirectional flow of communication can be due to several different factors. First and foremost, if the school is viewed as the center of learning, then families are expected to support the school's efforts. One cause of this view can be attributed to high-stakes standardized testing. Because so much emphasis is placed on these tests and passing them, schools want to control the preparation that students receive to pass these tests. Teachers, not families, tend to be the ones with the official credentials and awareness of the standards; families often do not have this same professional background to support students' learning for performance on standardized tests. Another way this power dynamic plays out is that schools often get to control what counts as knowledge. For example, even though students use school literacy practices informally at home (such as reading books, writing paragraphs and essays, and demonstrating comprehension), teachers often do not recognize home literacies practiced at school, such as jump rope rhymes, digital media practices, faith literacies, or pop culture references. There is a need for greater reciprocity between school and home learning (Compton-Lilly & Gregory, 2013).

Therefore, the school is positioned as the entity with the most power, and the school then uses this power to bestow information upon families. This model closely resembles what Freire (1970) called the banking model of

FIGURE 2.1 Unidirectional information flow of school–family communication.

FIGURE 2.2 Multidirectional information flow of school–family communication.

education. In the banking model, teachers are viewed as the possessors of the knowledge, and the students are viewed as the empty vessels into which this knowledge is poured—like how a piggy bank is empty, and its one purpose is to hold the coins that others put into it. The challenge with this kind of a model, both in the context of classroom teaching and in school–home communication, is that it does not recognize what families and students already bring with them. No student or family member is an empty vessel; every human being brings with them their own sets of experiences, background knowledge, and strengths.

There is an alternative, however. What if we could make Figure 2.1 look like Figure 2.2 instead?

This version of the diagram can be explained through several different theories. First, Bakhtin's (1981) theory of dialogism finds its roots in—you guessed it—dialogue. When you imagine what is involved with dialogue, you probably would mention open communication among two or more people. Bakhtin builds on this idea with three specific features of dialogism. First is addressivity. The idea behind addressivity is that any spoken or written event responds to what has already happened in the past and plans for the future imagined audience. Basically, addressivity *addresses* the past as it moves into the future. Think about a recent dialogue you've had: you probably referenced some prior shared event or experience before the conversation went in a new direction. That experience was addressivity in action. The second feature of dialogism is answerability, which is the ethical obligation to respond. A dialogue does not work well if one person is doing all of the talking and never letting other parties respond; that would be considered a monologue. In any true dialogue, all parties have to respond to each other. The third feature of dialogism is heteroglossia, which speaks to Bakhtin's belief that language exists in multiple speech varieties that continually evolve. There is no one way to "do" language or have a dialogue. Beyond the surface structures of languages and dialects (such as English, African American Language, Southern English, Ecuadorian Spanish, Honduran Spanish—this list could continue for the rest of this book), there are also cultural norms of communication (body language, eye contact, personal space, to name a few). Heteroglossia recognizes the way that language expressions coexist and inform each other. Have you ever found yourself spending time with a coworker or friend who uses different speech patterns or expressions than you do, and suddenly you realize that you've adopted one of their key phrases? That is heteroglossia in action.

Where do Bakhtin's features of dialogism fit into the multidirectional flow of information between schools and families? For addressivity, communication should address the prior experiences of both schools and families, not just of schools. Families have a wide range of experiences and skills that might be unintentionally overlooked or excluded. For answerability, both schools and families have the ethical responsibility to respond to each other and their needs. In traditional unidirectional home–school communication, the families are expected to respond to the needs of the school more than the school is expected to respond to the needs of the family. For example, if the school sends home a letter about upcoming standardized testing, the expectation is that the family will respond by making sure their child is at school on time, well-rested and fed, in order to perform to their highest ability on this high-stakes test. True answerability that serves the needs of both groups might look more like this: the school hosts a family literacy night, and prior to this night, a survey is sent to families (translated for families who speak Spanish, or Pashto, or Ukranian) asking them what questions they have about literacy or supporting their child's literacy development, and then planning interactive sessions for the event around these questions. Heteroglossia could be embodied in the front office, with informational brochures translated into families' home languages, or the encouragement of families to come and share read alouds in their home language, or the encouragement of educators to attend a community cultural celebration. In just these few examples, you can see how the theory of dialogism can transform home–school communication into a rich experience that honors the needs and experiences of both families and schools.

Another key theory that informs multidirectional communication between families and schools is called funds of knowledge (Moll et al., 1992). This work began with working-class, Mexican communities in Tucson, Arizona. Researchers partnered with teachers to go to students' homes and identify and document varying forms, or funds, of knowledge in students' homes. Some key outcomes of this work included **confianza** and the interruption of deficit narratives. **Confianza** is the mutual trust that teachers built with families during this project. Families demonstrated an incredible level of trust of the teachers in their own homes, and teachers began to have increased trust in the funds of knowledge families possessed. As a result of this **confianza**, deficit narratives were interrupted. When schools ignore students' funds of knowledge from home, deficit-based instruction can result (Vélez-Ibáñez & Greenberg, 1992). Once educators and families could focus on what *was* present in students' funds of knowledge at home, they did not have to focus instead on what *wasn't* happening.

Strategies to Foster Home–School Knowledge Exchanges

Recognizing the funds of knowledge that students and families bring with them is an important start to humanizing, dialogic family engagement. Sometimes it can seem daunting to make changes to traditional communication practices, especially in settings where the information flow has been predominantly from school to home. As we look toward re-envisioning family engagement and literacy in early childhood settings, here are a few strategies you can try.

- *Family journals*: Family journals can take a variety of forms. One example is to fill backpacks with materials—like a book translated in the family's home language and/or English, audio recordings of a book in a home language and/or English, and a blank family response journal that families can use to engage in reading together and record responses in open-ended journals. (For more information, see Rowe & Fain, 2013.)
- *Photo stories*: Originating from the PhOLKS (Photographs of Local Knowledge Sources) project, photo stories allow students to take photographs as a lens into their out-of-school lives. Children can use devices with photo-taking capabilities at home (such as tablets or phones) or take-home cameras on a rotating basis to photograph family members or things that are important to them, and then create writings based on these photographs. Family members can also provide narrations to accompany photographs. (For more information, see Allen et al., 2002.)
- *Community visits*: It sounds simple, but sometimes we can learn the most when we do something as simple as leave our own educational contexts. Attend community events and schedule home visits. These kinds of activities often reveal prior assumptions educators may hold about families and students and can break stereotypes about home visits being used to judge families. (For more information, see Cowhey, 2022; López-Robertson et al., 2010, also discussed how she scheduled home visits for her students every year.)
- *Literacy digs*: Flint (2008) conceptualized "literacy digs" as proactive searches for expressions of literacy in students' and families' contexts. Literacy digs can involve home or community visits, pictures of environmental print at home, and other culturally relevant literacy practices. Miller (2010) challenged educators to use approaches like literacy digs to be "willing to look beyond their own definitions of literacy to consider all of the students they teach as uniquely, culturally, and socially literate beings" (p. 245). (For more information, see Flint, 2008.)
- *Co-developed family events*: Instead of using preprogrammed family engagement, educators can plan opportunities to involve families beyond thematic "nights." Educators can build meaningful relationships with families while

involving families in students' learning by asking for advice, offering more than one way for families to participate, and avoiding regulating literacy activities (i.e., by telling families there is only one way to complete a reading/writing activity). This grassroots style of family engagement (i.e., Cowhey, 2022) is vital because it begins with the families' interests and needs. (For more information, see Allen & Kinloch, 2013.)

- *Critiquing family engagement opportunities*: Make sure events are planned intentionally to build deep relationships and/or support student learning. Hosting an event that invites families to share cultural memoirs and artifacts will foster much stronger relationships with families than an annual Muffins with Moms event. Additionally, even an event that seems to be culturally relevant to the non-critical eye can be problematic. For example, are family events that celebrate families' diverse backgrounds framed in meaningful contexts based on families' interests and needs, or are they superficial, one-and-done events the school plans to "check the box" of family engagement and diversity? It can be hard to move away from long-standing traditions or critically analyze events, but re-envisioning family engagement to be more engaging and culturally responsive can create powerful new traditions. Successful family engagement is linked to student learning, is welcoming and inclusive of many cultures, and is respectful of families' funds of knowledge. (For more information, see Allen, 2008, and Henderson & Mapp, 2002.)

Considerations When Engaging Families with Technology

When used intentionally, technology offers exciting opportunities to extend family engagement into virtual spaces. The increasing popularity and accessibility of smartphones plays a substantial role. In 2021, the Pew Research Center found 85% of Americans owned a smartphone, a dramatic increase from the 35% who did in 2011. Users who are "smartphone-dependent," meaning their primary form of internet access is through a smartphone, are more likely to be younger adults, be from lower income backgrounds, have a high school education or less, and be not identify as White (Pew Research Center, 2021). These demographics are significant because these are the same populations who, given historic definitions of the "digital divide," have been labeled as being the least likely to have access to technology. The increasing accessibility through technology—especially through smartphones—means that it can be a powerful tool for engaging families.

Here are some considerations when choosing how to engage families through technology, based on our own work in the field (Wells, 2017):

- Start with your purpose. Just because a tech tool is new and exciting does not mean that it will work for your purposes. What do you need a tech tool to do to meet your needs? Do not pick a tech tool just because it looks "fun"!

- Pick platforms that are dialogic. While communication of key announcements with families is important, a platform that simply allows educators to push out messages to families is not a dialogic space. Check for responsivity: can family members respond and contribute as well?
- Pick platforms with established histories. Technology changes frequently, and while it is tempting to pick up the next new technology, it can also be quite frustrating if that platform is phased out within a year or two. Pick a tried-and-true platform that has the potential to be around for many years.
- Protect privacy. Consider if a tech tool requires an account with a log-in, or if it only operates by linking to personal social media accounts. Respect that some families will not want their social media connected to other platforms.
- Consider accessibility. In a digital world, accessibility takes many different forms. Does a tech tool work across devices, or will it only work on a laptop? Does a tech tool work with all platforms, or is it only accessible on Apple devices? Does a tech tool only work as an app downloaded to a device, or is there a web-based client families can choose to use instead? (Avoid requiring app-only interfaces, since sometimes families might not have enough space on their device left to download the app, which will then prevent them from participating.) Does a tech tool require data or internet access, or is it available offline too? Does a tech tool support multilingual users, or does it only support English?
- Meet with families to demonstrate what the platform can do. Don't assume that everyone will know how to use a tech tool. Instead, explicitly teach digital literacy skills to students and families. It's also quite possible that families have prior experience with this platform and can help other families—and even you!—learn about its features.

Technology can provide innovative ways to engage families. Maintaining open communication with families about what is working and what technological difficulties are arising will ensure that these digital tools are used effectively.

Theoretical Framework

Rather than approaching our work from a lens where *we* know what families and children need, through our work we seek to build on their ways of knowing, and focus on their "repertoires of practice—the ways of engaging in activities stemming from participation in a range of cultural practices, as well as the learning that occurs in the development of those repertoires" (Gutiérrez & Johnson, 2017, p. 251). Together we take a critical sociocultural approach (Freire & Macedo, 1987; Vygotsky, 1978) and build on Freire and Macedo's (1987) view of teaching and learning as a "relationship of learners to the world" (p. viii). We recognize that learning is heavily influenced by social, cultural, and political forces (Nieto, 2009) and believe that children's lived experiences must be made a part of school learning for them to be able to "transform their lived experiences into knowledge and use the already acquired knowledge as a process to unveil new knowledge" (Macedo, 2000, p. 19). We consider families to be children's first teachers and view them as capable, competent, and active contributors to their children's learning. We view their funds of knowledge (González et al., 2005) and "meaning-making processes as crucial to their learning and ours" (López-Robertson, 2017, p. 8), as well as starting points for our teaching.

Freire's (1970) emancipatory learning theory encourages educators to view families from an asset-based lens where they are the experts with valuable knowledge from which we, the educators, are to learn. We seek to create an environment where our families become "agents who can intervene and advocate on behalf of their children, and who can make adaptations and resist barriers to education" (Baquedano-López et al., 2013, p. 150). Schools can aid in achieving this goal by creating curriculum that is culturally relevant. Historically, American education has focused on curriculum and teaching practices that benefit White, middle-class, English-speaking students (Long et al., 2013) and is "designed to benefit few and disenfranchise most" (Davila & Bradley, 2010, p. 40). Instead, numerous scholars (i.e., Delpit, 2012; Gay, 2010; Howard, 2010; Ladson-Billings, 2009; Paris & Alim, 2017) advocate for culturally relevant and culturally sustaining pedagogy. While most mainstream teaching caters to mainstream students socialized into mainstream cultural norms, culturally relevant pedagogy embraces the unique sets of experiences and understandings that all students bring to the classroom by "teach[ing] *to and through* their personal and cultural strengths, their intellectual capabilities, and their prior accomplishments" (Gay, 2010, p. 26). Gay (2010) described culturally responsive teaching as validating, comprehensive, multidimensional, empowering, transformative, and emancipatory, while being anchored in four pillars of practice: (1) teacher attitudes and expectations; (2) cultural communication in the classroom; (3) culturally diverse content in the curriculum; and (4) culturally congruent instructional strategies.

At the heart of culturally relevant pedagogy lies the recognition of the contributions of *all* students, not just those from mainstream cultures. Such a focus allows teachers to focus not on what students cannot do, but rather what they *can* do. However, socialization into institutions, including public education, often results in colorblindness, or the refusal to acknowledge differences based on skin color (Gay, 2010; Howard, 2010). While mainstream cultures may see colorblindness as a positive trait, this practice actually results in "dismissing one of the most salient features of the child's identity" (Ladson-Billings, 2009, p. 36). Therefore, teachers—especially White teachers—must not ignore color

(Paley, 2000). Rogoff (2003) added that "we need to understand the coherence of what people from different communities do, rather than simply determining that some other group of people do not do what 'we do'" (p. 17). Therefore, before we can help children develop strong self-concepts, we must be aware of our own identity profiles and how these identities impact our teaching (Gay, 2010; Harro, 2000).

In critical race theory (CRT), the lived experiences of minoritized groups are storied and validated by centering "the research, pedagogy, and policy lens on Communities of Color and call[ing] into question White middle-class communities as the standard by which all others are judged" (Yosso, 2005, p. 82). Often, the approaches in this field defy traditional epistemological approaches, such as using stories as a method of research (i.e., Bell, 1992; Delgado, 2000; Solorzano & Yosso, 2002). In Chapter 1, we introduced four uses of counterstories in educational spaces (Yosso, 2006) to interrupt deficit norms and rehumanize individuals from marginalized communities. Solorzano and Yosso (2002) identify five basic elements of CRT in education:

1. The intercentricity of race and racism—that racism is permanent and is more than classism.
2. Challenging dominant ideology—problematizing colorblindness, objectivity, neutrality, and meritocracy as a "camouflage for the self-interest, power, and privilege of dominant groups" (p. 26).
3. Commitment to social justice—working to empower minoritized groups and eliminate oppressive structures.
4. The centrality of experiential knowledge—using stories to legitimize the lived experiences of people of color.
5. The transdisciplinary perspective—connecting racist themes in different historical and contemporary contexts.

In education, CRT serves an important role by critiquing deficit theorizing. Yosso (2005) asserted that "one of the most prevalent forms of contemporary racism in U.S. schools is deficit thinking" (p. 75). This deficit thinking against students and families of color usually embodies itself in two assumptions: (1) that minority students enter school without "normative cultural knowledge and skills" (p. 75), and (2) that parents do not support or value their children's education. When these assumptions interact with instruction, banking models of education become the relied-upon method of teaching, so as to "fill up" students with this supposedly missing knowledge. Educators who practice this deficit theorizing believe that the system of school is not flawed, but rather the families and community are and must change. García and Guerra (2004) found that deficit assumptions in school usually begin with overgeneralizations about family backgrounds.

Literacy Instruction: A Critical Lens

In early childhood education, certain approaches to literacy—such as read alouds and shared reading of predictable texts—may be considered to be universal, but it is important to contextualize the history of common literacy practices and whose communities they honor and silence. Holdaway (1979) first translated the at-home bedtime story, an experience shared between a parent and a child based within a shared text, into the now-common classroom practice of shared reading. Other researchers confirmed the positive influence of adults and children reading side by side at home (i.e., Butler, 1998; Doake, 1985; Teale, 1984; Teale & Sulzby, 1986). These studies, however, are not without limitations; as Miller (2010) noted, most "researched in [W]hite, middle class contexts" (p. 247). Therefore, much of the research that has shaped common early childhood literacy practices did not consider the literacy practices of *all* our students and families.

In addition, materials for literacy instruction are often limited in cultural scope. Gangi (2008) found Whiteness overrepresented in children's literature textbooks, booklists, order forms, and award lists, and she highlighted the lack of multicultural literature represented in many common published literacy resources and assessments (see Table 2.1). Therefore, even the resources that early childhood educators access to plan and assess literacy have potential for underlying cultural bias.

As we consider traditionalized approaches to literacy instruction, a critical lens is necessary. "Literacy" is not the bias-free, neutral skill our curriculum frameworks would like us to believe it is. Instead, we must actively pursue materials that are windows, mirrors, and sliding glass doors for *all* children (Bishop, 1990) and critically consider whose literacy traditions are validated or ignored in the ways we define literacy in early childhood settings.

Community Cultural Wealth

Specific to our work is Yosso's (2005) notion of CCW, which is built on an asset-based lens where families and children are seen as holders and creators of knowledge (Delgado Bernal, 2002). Yosso identified six forms of capital:

- Aspirational capital, which envisions hopes and dreams for the future;
- Linguistic capital, which refers to the skills resulting from communication in multiple languages or discourses;
- Familial capital, which acknowledges the significance of family history, culture, and memory;
- Social capital, which consists of networks of people as well as resources in the community;

TABLE 2.1 Multicultural Children's Literature in Professional Literacy Textbooks

Name of Professional Literacy Textbook	Multicultural Children's Literature Represented
Guided Reading: Good First Teaching for All Children (Fountas & Pinnell, 1996)	Of 2,500 recommended leveled book titles 10 authors of color
Words Their Way (Bear, Invernizzi, Templeton, & Johnston, 2004)	Of the 49 children's books recommended in this text, none are authors/illustrators of color. Also, 43 pages of pictures in this text are of White children
Mosaic of Thought (Keene & Zimmerman, 1997)	The entirety of this text recommends fewer than five multicultural books
Strategies that Work (Harvey & Goudvis, 2000)	In chapters about teaching specific comprehension strategies, few books by authors of color are mentioned (only two in Visualizing chapter; none in other chapters) Appendix B does have some high-quality multicultural literature
Informal Reading Inventory/IRI (Roe & Burns, 2007)	In Appendix A (which helps teachers find books for students based on their tested levels), no books about/by people of color are on the pre-primer level, two are on the primer level, two are on the first level, and one is on the second level
Developmental Reading Assessment/ DRA (Beaver, 1997)	Of the 20 storybooks in this assessment, no children of color are in the pictures

Source: Adapted from Gangi (2008, pp. 32–34).

- Navigational capital, which looks at the skills required to navigate social institutions, especially those built upon mainstream norms and values; and
- Resistant capital, which recognizes the skills used to challenge inequality.

Each chapter that follows will focus on one form of capital as we delve into vignettes and episodes from our work with families; resources, including children's literature and digital tools; and strategies for aligning classroom practice and family engagement opportunities with families' preexisting CCW. While we present each form of capital in its own chapter, it is also important to note that the "CCW framework is not static" (Pérez Huber, 2009, p. 712) and all the forms of capital connect and relate to one another.

The forms of capital embedded in CCW are not the same as previous theorizations of capital. Bourdieu (Bourdieu & Passeron, 1977) framed capital as part of a hierarchical society that desired social replication, based on data he gathered about social class inequalities in France in the 1960s (Goldthorpe, 2007).

In his conceptualization of capital, Bourdieu believed that middle- and upper-class families had valuable capital, which could be transmitted and reproduced through family or schooling. He specifically focused on economic capital (material wealth), social capital (access to informal and formal social networks), and cultural capital (access to cultural knowledge and artifacts privileged by society and dominant groups). Bourdieu's theory of capital has been used for deficit theorizing to explain why People of Color have lower academic and social outcomes than White people (Yosso, 2005). Bourdieu's conceptualization of capital frames schools as sites of assimilation of "high" culture and contributes to deficit-oriented beliefs that schools help "disadvantaged" students whose backgrounds do not give them the knowledge, skills, and capital they "need" (Valenzuela, 1999). Yosso (2005) explicitly challenged Bourdieusian cultural capital theory (Bourdieu & Passeron, 1977) with the creation of the theory of CCW; therefore, the social capital Yosso (2005) describes should not be confused with Bourdieu's conceptualization of social capital (Bourdieu & Passeron, 1977).

With its focus on CCW (Yosso, 2005), we believe this book fills a gap between theory and practice that Acevedo and Solorzano (2021) named:

> We see the need for scholars to collaborate with practitioners and showcase the importance of using CCW as an approach to facilitate learning in various PK-20 contexts. CCW represents a tool to implement research, praxis, and policies that challenge ongoing overt and covert institutional and individual attempts to marginalize Communities of Color.
>
> *(p. 12)*

Communities of color are bombarded with negative images from the media that tell them they have nothing to offer their children because, for example, they are poor; do not speak English; and are not citizens of this country. These "daily indignities take a toll on the integrity and livelihood of people of color" (Villenas & Deyhle, 1999, p. 414) and soon, some begin to believe it. Approaching family engagement through the lens of CCW can help families recognize and understand that they indeed possess skills, knowledge, and strategies that can help their children succeed in school. We also work to help schools recognize and value the multiple and diverse ways of knowing families possess in order to help "sustain the lifeways of communities who have been and continue to be damaged and erased through schooling" (Paris & Alim, 2017, p. 1).

Conclusion

In this chapter, we have outlined some key theories and approaches that guide our work as we re-envision family engagement in early childhood classrooms. We envision opportunities for family engagement that center multidirectional, multimodal communication. We envision opportunities for family engagement that are responsive to students' and families' strengths, interests, and needs. We envision opportunities for family engagement that acknowledge the CCW families bring to—and beyond—educational contexts. And it all begins with families.

As the mother in the conversation featured at the beginning of this chapter so beautifully said, "**porque así ya conocemos**" / *because we already know*. We hope the strategies in the following chapters will support you in recognizing and honoring what our students' families already know.

References

Acevedo, N., & Solorzano, D. G. (2021). An overview of community cultural wealth: Toward a protective factor against racism. *Urban Education*. https://doi.org/10.1177/00420859211016531

Allen, J. (2008). Family partnerships that count. *Educational Leadership*, *66*(1), 22–27.

Allen, J., Fabregas, V., Hankins, K. H., Hull, G., Labbo, L., Lawson, H. S., Michalove, B., Piazza, S., Phia, C., Sprague, L., Townsend, S., & Urdanivia-English, C. (2002). PhOLKS lore: Learning from photographs, families, and children. *Language Arts*, *79*(4), 312–322.

Allen, J., & Kinloch, V. (2013). Create partnerships, not programs. *Language Arts*, *90*(5), 385–390.

Bakhtin, M. (1981). *The dialogic imagination: Four essays by M. M. Bakhtin* (M. Holquist, Ed.). University of Texas Press.

Baquedano-López, P., Alexander, R. A., & Hernández, S. J. (2013). Equity issues in parental and community involvement in schools: What teacher educators need to know. *Review of Research in Education*, *37*(1), 149–182.

Bear, D. R., Invernizzi, M., Templeton, S., & Johnston, F. (2004). *Words their way: Word study for phonics, vocabulary, and spelling instruction* (3rd ed.). Prentice Hall.

Beaver, J. (1997). *Developmental reading assessment*. Celebration Press.

Bell, D. (1992). *Faces at the bottom of the well: The permanence of racism*. Basic Books.

Bishop, R. S. (1990). Mirrors, windows, and sliding glass doors. *Perspectives*, *6*, ix–xi.

Bourdieu, P., & Passeron, J. (1977). *Reproduction in education, society and culture*. Sage.

Butler, D. (1998). *Babies need books: Sharing the joy of books with children from birth to six* (Rev. ed.). Heinemann.

Campano, G., Ghiso, M., & Welch, B. J. (2016). *Partnering with immigrant communities: Action through literacy*. Teachers College Press.

Compton-Lilly, C., & Gregory, E. (2013). Conversation currents: Learning from families and communities. *Language Arts*, *90*(6), 464–472.

Cowhey, M. (2022). *Families with power: Centering students by engaging with families and community*. Teachers College Press.

Davila, E. R., & Bradley, A. A. (2010). Examining education for Latinas/os in Chicago: A CRT/LatCrit approach. *Educational Foundations*, *24*, 39–58.

Delgado, R. (2000). Storytelling for oppositionalists. In R. Delgado & J. Stefancic (Eds.), *Critical race theory: The cutting edge* (pp. 60–70). Temple University Press.

Delgado Bernal, D. (2002). Critical race theory, Latino critical theory, and critical raced-gendered epistemologies: Recognizing students of color as holders and creators of knowledge. *Qualitative Inquiry, 8*(1), 105–126.

Delgado Gaitan, C. (2004). *Involving Latino families in schools: Raising student achievement through home–school partnerships.* Corwin.

Delpit, L. (2012). *"Multiplication is for white people": Raising expectations for other people's children.* The New Press.

Doake, D. (1985). Reading-like behavior: Its role in learning to read. In A. Jaggar & M. T. Smith-Burke (Eds.), *Observing the language learner* (pp. 82–98). NCTE.

Edwards, P. (2016). *New ways to engage parents: Strategies and tools for teachers and leaders, K–12.* Teachers College Press.

Ferlazzo, L. (2011). Involvement or engagement? *Educational Leadership, 68*(8), 10–14.

Flint, A. S. (2008). *Literate lives: Teaching reading and writing in elementary classrooms.* Wiley.

Fountas, I. C., & Pinnell, G. S. (1996). *Guiding reading: Good first teaching for all children.* Heinemann.

Freire, P. (1970). *Pedagogy of the oppressed.* Continuum.

Freire, P., & Macedo, D. (1987). *Literacy: Reading the word and the world.* Bergin & Garvey.

Gangi, J. M. (2008). The unbearable whiteness of literacy instruction: Realizing the implications of the proficient reader research. *Multicultural Review, 17*(1), 30–35.

García, S. B., & Guerra, P. L. (2004). Deconstructing deficit thinking: Working with educators to create more equitable learning environments. *Education and Urban Society, 36*(2), 150–168.

Gay, G. (2010). *Culturally responsive teaching: Theory, research, and practice* (2nd ed.). Teachers College Press.

Generations United. (2022). *Together at the table: Supporting the nutrition, health, and well-being of grandfamilies.* https://www.gu.org/resources/state-of-grandfamilies-report-2022/

Goldthorpe, J. H. (2007). "Cultural capital": Some critical observations. *Sociologica, 2*(2), 1–23. doi: https://www.rivisteweb.it/doi/10.2383/24755.

González, N., Moll, L. C., & Amanti, C. (Eds.). (2005). *Funds of knowledge: Theorizing practices in households, communities, and classrooms.* Lawrence Earlbaum Associates.

Gutiérrez, K. D., & Johnson, P. (2017). Understanding identity sampling and cultural repertoires: Advancing a historicizing and syncretic system of teaching and learning in justice pedagogies. In D. Paris & H. S. Alim (Eds.), *Culturally sustaining pedagogies: Teaching and learning for justice in a changing world* (pp. 247–260). Teachers College Press.

Harro, B. (2000). Cycle of socialization. In M. Adams, W. J. Blumenfeld, R. Castañeda, H. W. Hackman, M. L. Peters, & X. Zúñiga (Eds.), *Readings for diversity and social justice* (pp. 15–21). Routledge.

Harvey, S., & Goudvis, A. (2000). *Strategies that work: Teaching comprehension to enhance understanding.* Stenhouse.

Henderson, A. T., & Mapp, K. L. (2002). *A new wave of evidence: The impact of school, family and community connections on study achievement.* Southwest Educational Development Laboratory.

Holdaway, D. (1979). *The foundations of literacy.* Ashton Scholastic.

Howard, T. C. (2010). *Why race and culture matter in schools: Closing the achievement gap in America's classrooms.* Teachers College Press.

Keene, E., & Zimmerman, S. (1997). *Mosaic of thought: Teaching comprehension in a reader's workshop.* Heinemann.

Ladson-Billings, G. (2009). *The dreamkeepers: Successful teachers of African American children* (2nd ed.). Jossey-Bass.

Long, S., Volk, D., Baines, J., & Tisdale, C. (2013). "We've been doing it your way long enough": Syncretism as a critical process. *Journal of Early Childhood Literacy*, *13*(3), 418–439. doi: http://doi.org/10.1177/1468798412466403.

López-Robertson, J. (2017). Diciendo cuentos/Telling stories: Learning from and about the community cultural wealth of Latina mamás through Latino children's literature. *Language Arts*, *95*(1), 7–16.

López-Robertson, J., Long, S., & Turner-Nash, K. (2010). First steps in constructing counternarratives of young children and their families. *Language Arts*, *88*(2), 93–103.

Macedo, D. (2000). Introduction. In P. Freire (Ed.), *Pedagogy of the oppressed* (pp. 11–27). Continuum Press.

Miller, E. T. (2010). An interrogation of the "if only" mentality: One teacher's deficit perspective put on trial. *Early Childhood Education Journal*, *38*, 243–249. DOI 10.1007/s10643-010-0423-z.

Moll, L. C., Amanti, C., Neff, D., & González, N. (1992). Funds of knowledge for teaching: Using a qualitative approach to connect homes and classrooms. *Theory into Practice*, *31*, 132–141.

NAFSCE (n.d.). *Family engagement defined*. National Association for Family, School, and Community Engagement. https://nafsce.org/page/definition

Nieto, S. (2009). *The light in their eyes: Creating multicultural learning communities* (2nd ed.). Teachers College Press.

Paley, V. (2000). *White teacher* (3rd ed.). Harvard University Press.

Paris, D., & Alim, H. S. (Eds.). (2017). *Culturally sustaining pedagogies: Teaching and learning for justice in a changing world*. Teachers College Press.

Pérez Huber, L. (2009). Challenging racist nativist framing: Acknowledging the community cultural wealth of undocumented Chicana college students to reframe the immigration debate. *Harvard Educational Review*, *79*(4), 704–730.

Pew Research Center (2021, April 7). Mobile fact sheet. https://www.pewresearch.org/internet/fact-sheet/mobile/#panel-d40cde3f-c455-4f0e-9be0-0aefcdaeee00

Roe, B. D., & Burns, P. C. (2007). *Informal reading inventory: Preprimer to twelfth grade* (7th ed.). Houghton Mifflin.

Rogoff, B. (2003). *The cultural nature of human development*. Oxford University Press.

Rowe, D., & Fain, J. G. (2013). The family backpack project: Responding to dual-language texts. *Language Arts*, *90*(6), 402–416.

Solorzano, D., & Yosso, T. J. (2002). Critical race methodology: Counter-storytelling as an analytical framework for education research. *Qualitative Inquiry*, *8*(1), 23–44.

Teale, W. H. (1984). Reading to young children: Its significance to literacy development. In H. Goelman, A. Oberg, & F. Smith (Eds.), *Awakening to literacy* (pp. 110–121). Heinemann.

Teale, W. H., & Sulzby, E. (1986). *Emergent literacy: Writing and reading*. Ablex.

Valenzuela, A. (1999). *Subtractive schooling: US-Mexican youth and the politics of caring*. SUNY Press.

Vélez-Ibáñez, C. G., & Greenberg, J. B. (1992). Formation and transformation of funds of knowledge among U.S.-Mexican Households. *Anthropology & Education Quarterly*, *23*(4), 313–335. doi: http://doi.org/10.2307/3195869.

Villenas, S., & Deyhle, D. (1999). Critical race theory and ethnographies challenging the stereotypes: Latino families, schooling, resilience and resistance. *Curriculum Inquiry*, *29*(4), 413–445.

Vygotsky, L. S. (1978). *Mind in society: The development of higher psychological processes*. Harvard University Press.

Wells, M. S. (2017). "Porque hací ya conocemos": *Dialogic ways of knowing in critical coaching and digital learning communities*. Publication No. 10264497. (Doctoral dissertation, University of South Carolina). ProQuest Dissertations Publishing.

Yosso, T. J. (2005). Whose culture has capital? A critical race theory discussion of community cultural wealth. *Race Ethnicity and Education*, *8*(1), 69–91. doi: http://doi.org/10.1080/1361332052000341006.

Yosso, T. J. (2006). *Critical race counterstories along the Chicana/Chicano educational pipeline*. Routledge.

3
SUEÑOS FOR OUR CHILDREN'S FUTURE

Aspirational Capital

Julia read *Soñadores* (Morales, 2018) in Spanish to the families gathered in Pilar's classroom. The families loved the book: the illustrations, the message, and the fact that it was Yuyi Morales' own immigration story. After the read aloud, Pilar asked the families, "**¿Cuáles son sus sueños para sus niños?**" *What are your dreams for your children?* Pilar and Julia shared their dreams to begin the conversation and then the families shared theirs. Below are **sueños** two families shared.

Irma: **Mi sueño es que mis chamacos salgan adelante en el mundo. Quiero que sean felices y que estudien para que no tengan que trabajar tan fuerte como nosotros sus padres. Quiero que sepan que aquí pueden hacer lo que desean.** / *My dream is for my children to get ahead in the world. I want them to be happy and to study so that they will not have to work as hard as we [their parents] did. I want them to know that here [United States] they can do what they desire.*

Pati: **Me gustaría que fuese a la universidad. Yo no pude, y quiero que ella tenga la oportunidad. En este país, es posible. Ella puede estudiar lo que quiera y puede ser profesional. Así también me puede ayudar cuando sea viejita.** / *I would like for her to go to the University. I was unable to go, and I want her to have the opportunity. In this country, it is possible. She can study what she wants, and she can be a professional. That way she can help me when I am older.*

As seen in these excerpts, the families held aspirations for their children to be successful in the United States and they equated success with continuing

DOI: 10.4324/9781003344377-3

their schooling and attending the university. Irma also noted that she wanted her children to know that in this country (the United States), one can do what they desire, while Pati offered that her desire was for her daughter to study as she was unable to do in her home country. These families' **sueños** for their children's bright futures are examples of aspirational capital.

In this chapter, we will examine the first aspect of community cultural wealth—aspirational capital. How do we incorporate families' aspirations for their children in early childhood education? How do we also acknowledge the barriers that sometimes stand between families and their dreams?

Aspirational Capital

Aspirational capital addresses the ability "to maintain hopes and dreams for the future, even in the face of real and perceived barriers" (Yosso, 2005, p. 77). Having high expectations for the future, especially children's futures, is an example of aspirational capital. While sometimes these dreams might not seem attainable, they provide families with hope. Although families may work in low-paying jobs and face obstacles linked to their sociocultural and sociopolitical histories (Nieto, 2009), these dreams and belief in these dreams irrespective of circumstance teach children the "resilience and resistance that has characterized the lives of all indigenous peoples since 1492" (Villenas & Deyhle, 1999, p. 422).

Families have ample experience with aspirational capital well before their children enter our classrooms. Immigrant families risk everything to leave their homeland in pursuit of opportunities that they did not and/or will not have in their home country. Naturally, families—both immigrant and U.S. born—have high hopes and dreams for their children's future; this is not something that we (teachers) need to teach them (Delgado Bernal & Alemán, 2017).

Cuentos from the Field: Aspirational Capital in Action

Before families can share their dreams and aspirations with educators, we must first develop **confianza**. **Confianza** is a shared trust between families and educators that "is reestablished or confirmed with each exchange and leads to the development of long-term trusting relationships" (González et al., 1993, p. 3). It takes time to develop trusting relationships with families of color in particular because of the way they have been historically and sometimes continue to be devalued by schools (e.g., Delgado-Gaitan, 2001; McLaren & Jaramillo, 2014). To uncover the wealth of knowledge that has been ever present in families' lives, we must engage in critical conversations built upon **confianza**. **Confianza** does not develop overnight; building this trusting relationship with families takes time, effort, and mutual respect. The episodes that follow exemplify the spaces where families' aspirational capital emerged in our own experiences in early childhood contexts.

Episode One: Sueños para nuestros niños / Dreams for Our Children

The opening vignette took place during the second family event held in November in Pilar's classroom at Mountainview Elementary School. Pilar communicated regularly with the families through a variety of formats, including weekly newsletters, phone calls, and the class webpage. Julia had met a few families at Pilar's first school event (Open House) and her weekly visits were featured in the newsletter, so the families who had not met her were familiar with who she was.

As we noted in Chapter 1, the Latinx families had expressed concerns and general feelings of being overlooked at school, so Pilar invited the families to school one evening for an informal meeting to solve the problem together. There were four mothers and one father (one married couple) in attendance. Pilar welcomed everyone and we sat together at a few of the tables. We had refreshments and some snacks available; Pilar offered the families a snack, introduced Julia, and told them our plans for the evening. She explained that we were there to listen to their questions and concerns and that we would begin with a story as a way to **"sentirse más cómodo"**/*feel more comfortable.* Irma noted, **"Hay sí, todos los días la niña me cuenta de los libros que leen"**/*Oh yes, everyday my daughter tells me about the books you read.* Victoria added, **"Y también se ven en la 'newsletter' que manda"**/*And we also see them in the newsletter you send.*

As noted in the introduction to the chapter, Julia read *Soñadores* by Yuyi Morales (2018), a much loved author in Pilar's class; the children engage in a weekly read aloud—almost a Readers' Theatre—of *Niño Wrestles the World*, also written by Morales (2013). During the read aloud, the families excitedly shared connections they were making to the illustrations, the author's words, and their lived experiences which were similar to those in *Soñadores*. Maite laughed as she shared a memory while pointing to the illustration in the book where Yuyi Morales and her son are swimming in the fountain in the park.

> **Había un calor ese día, la niña no aguantó y se metió en la fuente. Estaba tan a gusto hasta que nos dijeron que no se podía hacer eso. Bueno, lo disfrutamos un poco.** / *It was so hot that day, my daughter could not stand it and she jumped into the fountain. She was enjoying herself so much until we were told that we could not do that. Well, we enjoyed ourselves a little.*

We all laughed at the image and shared understanding of seeking relief from the sometimes unbearable summer heat! After a few minutes, Pilar asked,

"¿Cuáles son sus sueños para sus niños?"/ *What are your dreams for your children?* In the opening vignette we shared Irma and Pati's, and below we share other families' dreams.

Pablo:	**En mi país soy arquitecto. Me encantaría si yo pudiera estudiar para hacerlo aquí también. Se que no es posible así que le digo a los niños que estudien. Me dijo la mayor que quiere estudiar ingeniería, no es arquitectura, pero es mejor de lo que hago.** / *In my country I am an architect. I would love to be able to study and be one [architect] here [United States] too. I know it is not possible so I tell the children that they must study. The oldest told me she wanted to study engineering, it is not architecture, but it is better than what I do.*
Victoria (Pablo's wife):	**Es importante que estudien para salir adelante. Aunque no somos nosotros que vamos a estudiar, ellos nos ayudan. Su éxito es nuestro éxito.** / *It is important that they [the children] study so that we can get ahead. Even though we are not the ones who will study, they will help us. Their success is our success.*
Maite:	**Yo también quiero que estudien. En México, yo no tuve carrera, pero siempre quise ir a la universidad. Mi prima Laura fue a DF a estudiar y me sentía tan orgullosa de ella. Yo quiero eso para mis niños.** / *I also want them to study. In Mexico, I did not have a career but I always wanted to go to the University. My cousin Laura studied in Mexico City, and I felt so proud of her. I want that for my children.*

Pablo shared that he was an architect in his home country and lamented that he was unable to pursue the career in the United States. Later he shared that there was simply too much for him to do to become an architect here; "**Para empezar, necesito aprender inglés para la entrada a la universidad y no hay tiempo**" / *To begin with, I need to learn English in order to gain entrance to the university and there is no time.* Since it is not possible for Pablo to study, he encourages his children to do so. He told us, tongue in cheek, that his oldest daughter wanted to pursue engineering, not architecture, and that it was fine because it was better than what he does—Pablo is a roofer.

Victoria, Pablo's wife, added that their children's attainment of an education will help everyone in the family because their success is our success. This is a common sentiment shared among many immigrant groups: the notion that the collective will succeed with an individual's success. Even though Maite did not have the opportunity to attend the university or have a career as she noted, she is proud of her cousin, Laura: an example that the success of one is shared by all. Laura's accomplishment serves as an example for Maite's children; they are able to see that one of their family members attended the university and has a successful career. Laura's example helps Maite's children see that it is possible for them to pursue higher education.

It is important to note that regardless of our families' income, career, or vocation, all want their children to pursue higher education. Like other immigrant families, these families emphasized the importance of academic achievement to achieve social mobility (Gonzalez et al., 2022). In spite of the obstacles our families and children will face in the pursuit of an education, a significant one being that "policies and practices reflect the fact that society, educational leaders, and many teachers often do not see Brown kids as college bound" (Delgado Bernal & Alemán, 2017, p. 47), our families are committed. We have to work to interrupt this; our families, as seen in the excerpts, have the aspirations for their children to pursue a university education.

Episode Two: Advocacy as Aspirational Capital

Families often reveal their dreams for their children through conversations—sometimes at unexpected times and in unexpected places—so listening is key. In her setting, Melissa noticed families expressing their aspirational capital by advocating for their children's needs. After all, for us to achieve our dreams, we need the appropriate support and conditions to excel.

One way families advocated for meeting their children's needs was as young scholars. For example, Eda's mother came to an end-of-year conference and explained, **"Mi hija ha dice que si ella se sienta aquí, no puede ver [el pizarrón] muy bien**" / *My daughter told me if she sits here, she can't see the board well.* This mother recognized the importance of being able to see the board in order to succeed in school, and while she worked with the eye doctor to figure out the issue, she also advocated for Eda to have a new seat closer to the board where she could still see and participate. After making sure this instructional need for her daughter was met, she proudly explained how much Eda loved reading:

> **Es que ella se la pasa leyendo todo el tiempo. Andamos en el carro anda leyendo. Temprano a veces así anda leyendo la noche cuando ya le pagó la luz. Y con la lámpara está leyendo.** / *She spends all her time reading. We go in the car and she's reading. Sometimes she's reading at night when I've turned off the light. And with the flashlight, she's reading.*

Kadence, her teacher, affirmed that Eda was an incredible reader. Even in these small moments, we can work with families to nurture aspirational capital. So many of our students—especially students of color—are receiving constant messages of what skills they don't have, or what they need to work on. These small reminders of what is going well—what gifts our students do have, because *all* of our students have gifts—can help families' dreams for their children's future continue to grow.

Sometimes families may feel uncomfortable asking the teacher for certain updates or accommodations for their child, and in listening to our families, we realized the important role technology plays. Our families in particular preferred Class Dojo as a communication venue. Eda's first communication with Kadence about Eda's eyesight was via a message in Class Dojo. Another family in an end-of-year conference expressed concern about a grade their child received on a report card several weeks before, saying that they felt "disconnected" not knowing their child was struggling and wanting more updates—potentially using platforms like Class Dojo—throughout the year. Beyond the messages, though, the families we talked to also loved the Class Story feature of Class Dojo. Class Story allows the teacher to post photographs of students in a secure online setting that only families in the class can access. When we asked which media was their favorite, families would frequently laugh and say something to the effect of, "Well, the ones my child was in!" Again, as families dream of their children's futures, they want to share in the moments that contribute toward their growth. Inviting families to share in these moments—both digitally and in real life—can help teachers attend to families' aspirational capital.

As Kadence, the classroom teacher noticed, "The families want their children to go farther in their lives and to gain more knowledge." Teachers and families can form powerful partnerships to make progress toward these dreams and aspirations.

FEATURED CHILDREN'S LITERATURE WITH ASPIRATIONAL CAPITAL

Morales, Y. (2018). *Soñadores/Dreamers* (Y. Morales, Illus.). Neal Porter Books.

In this gorgeously illustrated text, author and illustrator Yuyi Morales follows a mother and her son as they immigrate into the United States. They face challenges learning to navigate an unknown country, but also encounter celebrations—like discovering the magic of a local library. Morales's own immigration into the United States with her son inspires much of the story. The book was released simultaneously as a separate Spanish book, *Soñadores*, and an English book, *Dreamers* (Américas Award, 2019 Commended; Pura Belpré Award, 2019 Illustration Award; Tomás Rivera Mexican American Children's Book Award, 2019 Winner).

Applying Aspirational Capital

Hopes and dreams are exciting celebrations to share within and beyond classroom spaces. However, they are often not obtained without navigating barriers, sometimes significant ones. Below, we will offer some ideas for applying aspirational capital when working with students and families.

Classroom Strategies to Honor Aspirational Capital

- Brainstorm hopes, dreams, and aspirations with students, both short-term and long-term. During a morning meeting, a turn-and-talk activity could invite students to respond to sentence stems like the following:
  - My hopes and dreams for myself are…
  - My hopes and dreams for my family are…
  - My hopes and dreams for my friends are…
  - My hopes and dreams for my class are…
  - I hope that I can learn…
  - I hope that I can do…

  While hopes and dreams can be school related, they do not have to be! Following any of these prompts with an additional sentence stem, "I can start to make this happen by…" gives students practice with not only naming hopes and dreams, but also starting to strategize how to achieve them. These activities can be done at any point in the year, but may be particularly powerful when forming a new classroom community at the beginning of the year.
- Create a digital wall of hopes and dreams. Students can contribute drawings, audio, text, or photographs that capture one of their hopes and dreams, which can be shared on a platform like Google Jamboard or Padlet. Families can then comment on students' hopes and dreams—or even add their own.
- Tie in discussions of hopes and dreams during various cultural observations of new years or new beginnings. In some cultures, the new year begins January 1. For example, Mexico's Año Nuevo is observed on January 1. One common tradition is to eat 12 grapes, making wishes for each month that follows in the year ahead, when midnight strikes. Other cultures observe the new year during the transition between winter and spring. Chinese New Year, celebrated with the occurrence of the new moon in late January or February, marks the beginning of spring. Tet, the Vietnamese New Year, is also celebrated in late January or February, and centers respect for ancestors amidst a celebration of new year. Nowruz, also known as the Iranian or Persian New Year, is usually celebrated around March 21 and directly translates to "new day." One popular tradition during Nowruz is

to assemble the Haft-sin table with seven things that begin with the letter "sin" (which translates to the English "S"): sabze (grains), samanu (sweet pudding), senjed (Persian olive), serke (vinegar), sib (apple), sir (garlic), and somāq (sumac, a dark red spice). On April 13, Songkran, the Thai New Year, uses water to wash away the old and celebrate the new. In India, the new year begins in November during Diwali, the Hindu Festival of Lights. The five-day celebration honors Lakshmi, the Goddess of Wealth, and celebrates wealth in various forms and future prosperity. On the fourth day, the new year officially begins. Most importantly, ask students and families about their traditions. Celebrate not only the cultural backgrounds present in your classroom, but also those *not* present as a way to teach children about all kinds of cultures and celebrations. Carefully research holidays to portray them meaningfully and without essentializing them.

- Invite varied guests to talk to students about their roles and lives, and constantly interrupt stereotypes. When we only ask our African American boys if they want to become basketball stars when they grow up, we are feeding into stereotypes and limiting what they see as possible for the future. Visitors can show possibilities for the future that children might not have seen yet.
- Listen and build **confianza**. It takes great bravery to share personal hopes and dreams, even for young children. With trust comes honesty and vulnerability. Instead of retrofitting our dreams for our students, it is important that we listen critically and closely to honor the futures *they* envision for themselves.

Family Strategies to Honor Aspirational Capital

- Brainstorm hopes, dreams, and aspirations with families, both for their children and for themselves. This work can occur in multiple settings: during beginning-of-the-year events when families and children come together; during family conferences throughout the year; during family events where multiple families work together to brainstorm and discuss; or in any other configuration that meets your families' needs. One graphic organizer that Julia used with her families is shown in Figure 3.1.
- In conferences, focus on celebrating what is going well and on planning for future dreams and goals. Sometimes, conferences can be hyper-focused on what a child is missing or needs to "fix." This can quickly dehumanize students and families alike, even if the teacher has the best intentions of offering the child opportunities for growth. Once families have shared aspirations for their child, find ways to incorporate them into learning experiences in the classroom and beyond. Celebrate together with multidirectional communication about the child's growth in specified areas in a variety of contexts.

Sueños for Our Children's Future: Aspirational Capital   43

FIGURE 3.1   Julia used this organizer to brainstorm hopes, dreams, and gifts with families.

- Support families with their own aspirations, especially when barriers present themselves. Two related strategies, mental contrasting and WOOP (Oettingen et al., 2009), may be of interest during conferences or family events. With mental contrasting, individuals can compare and contrast both the positive and negative implications of a future goal or aspiration. Most significantly, anticipating challenges that lie ahead can help make strategic plans of how to respond when those challenges do arise, thus maintaining momentum toward meeting a goal or aspiration. WOOP asks individuals to consider four areas: wish (visualizing an aspiration), outcome (brainstorming the ideal outcome of the aforementioned wish), obstacles (the challenges they will face while pursuing the aspiration), and planning (making a plan for how to respond when the aforementioned obstacles are encountered). Again, do not assume that families need to learn about mental contrasting and WOOP—follow their leads and offer as a suggestion if needed.
- Listen and build **confianza**. Yes, listening to build trust is important for both students and families! Structure opportunities to listen to families both in person and in digital spaces. Families may prefer to share their hopes and dreams using modalities and spaces with which they are more comfortable, which may not be the school setting for some families. Consider hosting "listening tours" in the community (at the local library or even at a local fast food joint that is easily accessible for families) or using digital tools (ranging from direct messaging to video calls, see Table 3.1 later in this chapter). Some families may prefer to share their hopes and dreams directly, and others may feel more confident in a group with other families or community members present. Listen to your families and their needs and structure opportunities accordingly.

Conclusion

As we saw in the chapter, all families have dreams and aspirations for their children; this is not something that must be taught in school. For families to feel safe sharing these dreams and aspirations, teachers and schools must work to develop a trusting relationship, **confianza,** with families. It takes time to build this **confianza,** but it is not impossible.

Dreams, however, are often obtainable only after overcoming great challenges. Families utilize their many forms of capital, including their support networks, to help them with challenges they may face in reaching their dreams. Our schools must become sites of possibilities that recognize families as capable and knowledgeable contributors to their children's education and value their lived experiences. We find that listening—one of the seemingly easiest things to do—is a very significant way to begin to build a relationship with families. Listening to families—focused and careful listening, without interruption—signals that we care and want to support them in reaching their goals and aspirations.

Additional Resources

Children's Literature

The following 12 award-winning picturebooks address themes related to aspirational capital. For a complete list of picturebooks and other areas of community cultural wealth these books may contain, see Appendix A.

Carmela Full of Wishes (de la Peña, 2018)

It's a big day for Carmela: her birthday, and the day when she finally will go to the laundromat with her big brother. During the trip to the laundromat, she sees a dandelion and dreams of many aspirations: her dad being home with his immigration paperwork complete, her mom staying in a fancy hotel bed instead of always having to make them for guests, the bad things she can turn her mean brother into. Her wishes are almost crushed before she can make them, but then her brother shows her a new source of wish-making. Through her wishes, Carmela demonstrates aspirational capital; additionally, this book does not present a rose-colored vision of dreams, but rather presents them alongside very real challenges Carmela and her family face in their lives (Américas Award, 2019 Commended Title).

Dancing Hands: How Teresa Carreño Played the Piano for President Lincoln (Engle, 2019)

Music was a source of hopes and dreams for Teresa Carreño throughout her life, starting when her mom sang her lullabies and her dad played piano. Music brought her peace, which was especially important when she and her family had to leave their home in Venezuela due to the revolution. Teresa used her musical talent to ground herself in her new home, the United States, and eventually became so famous as the "Piano Girl" that President Lincoln invited her to play at the White House (Pura Belpré Award, 2020 Illustration Award Winner).

A Drop of the Sea (Chabbert, 2018)

Ali's great-grandmother thinks that all of her dreams have come true except for one: seeing the sea. The challenge now is that her aging body no longer can make the journey to see the sea. So, Ali finds a different way to work around barriers and make her wish come true. This book demonstrates how love and creativity work together to realize aspirations (Middle East Book Award, 2019 Picture Book Winner).

Maybe Something Beautiful: How Art Transformed a Neighborhood (Campoy & Howell, 2016)

Based on the true story of the Urban Art Trail in California, this book joyfully portrays how a community used art to make a tired, aging city less gray. Through aspirations and paint, the people took to heart that "the world is your canvas," and they dreamed—and created—a new, colorful community (Tomás Rivera Mexican American Children's Book Award, 2017 Winner).

Tomorrow (Kaadan, 2018)

The war in Syria means Yazan's world is changing. He misses seeing his friends and going to the park to play. So, he takes his hopes and dreams into his own hands and brings the park to his bedroom until it's safe to go outside to play again (Middle East Book Award, 2019 Picture Book Honorable Mention).

Bowwow Powwow: Bagosenjige-niimi'idim (Child, 2018)

Windy Girl enjoys listening to Uncle's stories about traditions from the past. After attending a powwow, Windy falls asleep and dreams of a special bowwow powwow, featuring some very special four-legged dancers. This book teaches traditions but also the powerful whimsy of dreams. It is presented bilingually in English and Ojibwe. The author and illustrator identify as Red Lake Ojibwe, and the translator is a member of the Lac La Croix First Nation (American Indian Youth Literature Award, 2020 Picture Book Winner).

Brick by Brick (Sheffield, 2020)

A little boy reveres his papi and his important skill: bricklaying. While his father builds with bricks, the boy builds with books. At the end, papi reveals a special surprise: he has built the "always house" the family has dreamed of. This story shows how dreams are built through hard work and commitment, using tools like bricks—and books. It incorporates translanguaging between Spanish and English (Américas Award, 2021 Commended Title).

Seven Special Somethings (Khorram, 2021)

It's almost Nowruz, the Persian New Year, and the Haft-sin table is already filled with the seven special things that start with "S" that will bring them happiness in the new year. After the items are accidentally knocked over, Kian finds seven new special somethings that he can add to the Haft-sin table before the family comes together to celebrate. This book demonstrates aspirational capital by highlighting one cultural tradition to celebrate the hopes that come with a new year (Middle East Book Award, 2021 Honorable Mention).

Maryam's Magic (Reid, 2021)

As a child in Iran, Maryam Mirzakhani loved stories, but did not love math at first. Then, she started to see the stories built into math, and she used her unique perspective to change the field. This true story shows how the aspirations of the real-life Maryam—the first woman and first Iranian to win the prestigious Fields Medal in mathematics—followed her dreams of combining two loves: stories and math (Middle East Book Award, 2021 Honorable Mention).

Classified: The Secret Career of Mary Golda Ross, Cherokee Aerospace Engineer (Sorell, 2021)

This true story follows Mary Golda Ross in her life-long journey to fuse her passions for math and her Cherokee heritage. She worked hard, often as the only woman in her classes and her job, to become a designer of top-secret airplanes and spacecraft at Lockheed Aircraft Corporation. In addition, she mentored other women and Indigenous people who wanted to become engineers like her. This book shows how Mary followed her aspirations to change the realm of aerospace engineering as an Indigenous woman. The author identifies as Cherokee and the illustrator identifies as Métis (American Indian Youth Literature Award, 2022 Picture Book Honor Book).

The Me I Choose to Be (Tarpley, 2021)

Aspirations begin with the power of self-love, which is captured beautifully in this book through the recurring refrain: "My creativity and curiosity flow without end, and if I meet an obstacle, I just begin again. I am a planet, a limitless galaxy, and I am the me I choose to be" (Coretta Scott King Book Award, 2022 John Steptoe Award for New Talent, Illustrator).

Magnificent Homespun Brown: A Celebration (Doyon, 2020)

In this jubilant, playful book, a series of narrators join together to celebrate the different hues and manifestations of brown. This book's celebration-focused, lyrical narrative portrays aspirations of the beauty and intrinsic potential of all kinds of brown skin (Coretta Scott King Book Award, 2021 Illustrator Honor Book).

Digital Tools

TABLE 3.1 Digital Tools: Aspirational Capital

Tool	Description
Padlet (https://padlet.com/)	Padlet is a platform that creates a digital "bulletin board" to which sticky note-like posts can be added. The posts support a variety of multimodal forms: text, images, videos, links, and more. It is platform and device agnostic and can be used in a web browser or as an app. Boards can be set to use specific configurations, such as a grid (posts automatically appear evenly spaced rows of boxes), a shelf (columns), or grid (free-form). Settings can allow for other users to comment on posts or react to them with a heart emoji, star, or upvoting. Privacy preferences can be set to private, password-protected, secret, or public to control who has access to the Padlet. The password-protected option would allow families to access the Padlet within the classroom community. Boards can also be saved as PDFs, images, or Excel spreadsheets to create a long-lasting artifact. The free account includes three Padlet boards, which could be remade. Accessing more than three Padlet boards requires an upgrade to a paid plan. Only the creator of the Padlet needs to create an account; other users can access the Padlet without having to log in.
Jamboard (https://jamboard.google.com/)	Jamboard is a digital whiteboard available through Google Suite. Similar to Padlet, it allows users to post multimodal ideas and responses, including formats like sticky notes, images, text boxes, shapes, and a pen for freeform writing or drawing. Jamboard allows for multiple "frames," similar to slides in a presentation, instead of one continuous digital wall like Padlet. The creator of the Jamboard needs a Google account, but it can be shared to allow anyone with the link or specific users' accounts to view or edit.

References

Delgado Bernal, D., & Alemán, E., Jr. (2017). *Transforming educational pathways for Chicana/o students: A critical race feminista praxis*. Teachers College Press.

Delgado-Gaitan, C. (2001). *The power of community: Mobilizing for family and schooling*. Rowman & Littlefield Publishers.

González, N., Moll, L. C., Floyd-Tenery, M., Rivera, A., Rendón, P., Gonzales, R., & Amanti, C. (1993). *Teacher research on funds of knowledge: Learning from households* (Educational Practice Report 6). UC Berkeley: Center for Research on Education, Diversity and Excellence. https://escholarship.org/uc/item/5tm6x7cm

Gonzalez, L. C., Ramirez, B. R., Burciaga, R., Pérez Huber, L., & Solorzano, D. G. (2022). Latino educational (in)opportunities: Causes, consequences, and challenges to unequal opportunities to learn. In E. G. Murillo, Jr., D. Delgado Bernal, S. Morales, L. Urrieta, Jr., E. R. Bybee, J. S. Muñoz, V. Sáenz, D. Villanueva, M. Machado-Casas, & K. Espinoza (Eds.), *Handbook of Latinos and education: Theory, research, and practice* (2nd ed., pp. 383–400). Routledge.

McLaren, P., & Jaramillo, N. E. (2014). Critical pedagogy, Latino/a education, and the politics of class struggle. In A. Darder & R. D. Torres (Eds.), *Latinos and education: A critical reader* (2nd ed., pp. 69–84). Routledge.

Nieto, S. (2009). *The light in their eyes: Creating multicultural learning communities* (3rd ed.). Teachers College Press.

Oettingen, G., Mayer, D., Timur Sevincer, A., Stephens, E. J., Pak, H. J., & Hagenah, M. (2009). Mental contrasting and goal commitment: The mediating role of energization. *Personality and Social Psychology Bulletin, 35*(5), 608–622.

Villenas, S., & Deyhle, D. (1999). Critical race theory and ethnographies challenging the stereotypes: Latino families, schooling, resilience and resistance. *Curriculum Inquiry, 29*(4), 413–445.

Yosso, T. J. (2005). Whose culture has capital? A critical race theory discussion of community cultural wealth. *Race Ethnicity and Education, 8*(1), 69–91.

Children's Literature

Campoy, I., & Howell, T. (2016). *Maybe something beautiful: How art transformed a neighborhood* (R. López, Illus.). Clarion Books.

Chabbert, I. (2018). *A drop of the sea* (R. N. Guridi, Illus.). Kids Can Press.

Child, B. J. (2018). *Bowwow powwow: Bagosenjige-niimi'idim* (J. Thunder, Illus.). Minnesota Historical Society Press.

de la Peña, M. (2018). *Carmela full of wishes* (C. Robinson, Illus.). G.P. Putnam's Sons.

Doyon, S. C. (2020). *Magnificent homespun brown: A celebration* (K. Juanita, Illus.). Tilbury House Publishers.

Engle, M. (2019). *Dancing hands: How Teresa Carreño played the piano for President Lincoln* (Rafael López, Illus.). Atheneum Books for Young Readers.

Kaadan, N. (2018). *Tomorrow* (N. Kaadan, Illus.). Lantana Publishers.

Khorram, A. (2021). *Seven special somethings* (Z. Faidhi, Illus.). Dial Books.

Morales, Y. (2013). *Niño wrestles the world* (Y. Morales, Illus.). Roaring Brook Press.

Morales, Y. (2018). *Soñadores/Dreamers* (Y. Morales, Illus.). Neal Porter Books.

Reid, M. (2021). *Maryam's magic* (A. Jaleel, Illus.). Balzer + Bray.

Sheffield, H. W. (2020). *Brick by brick* (H. W. Sheffield, Illus.). Nancy Paulsen Books.
Sorell, T. (2021). *Classified: The secret career of Mary Golda Ross, Cherokee aerospace engineer* (N. Donovan, Illus.). Millbrook Press.
Tarpley, N. A. (2021). *The me I choose to be* (R. & K. Bethencourt, Illus.). Little, Brown and Company.

4

LANGUAGE FROM EL CORAZÓN

Linguistic Capital

On a Friday afternoon, a group of mothers gathered to read and talk about picturebooks with Julia and the school's literacy coach at the weekly mothers' group. After an hour together and an initial discussion of the book, *Pepita Talks Twice/Pepita habla dos veces* (Lachtman, 1995), their children joined them to engage with the book and other literacy-related activities. Our goal in using this read aloud was to highlight the value of maintaining home languages. Two of the mothers shared the following:

> **¿Cómo no entienden lo bueno que es poder hablar dos idiomas? ¿Por qué no ven que es importante?** / *How do they not understand how good it is to speak two languages? Why do they not see that it is important [to be bilingual]?*

> **¿Si en nuestros países, en donde no hay las abundancias que hay aquí, realizan lo que es ser bilingüe, porque aquí no? No lo entiendo.** / *If they realize the importance of being bilingual in our countries, where there are not the abundances that there are here, how is it not recognized here? I do not understand.*

The mothers wondered why their children's school does not see the value in their children's ability to communicate in Spanish and English. Their children, like many other emergent bilinguals, come to school with the ability to communicate in two languages, yet this skill is often not recognized or valued (López-Robertson, 2021; Luna & Martinez, 2013; Reyes et al., 2016; Suárez-Orozco & Suárez-Orozco, 2001). Furthermore, rather than build upon their skills with language, children's bilingualism is viewed through a deficit lens and as something that needs to be overcome and eradicated in a "push to produce English monolinguals" (Moll, 2011, p. x).

Twenty-five years ago, Valdés (1996) offered that "schools validate the culture of the ruling class and at the same time fail to legitimatize the forms of knowledge brought to school by groups not in power" (p. 19). In spite of the fact that a quarter century has passed, Tinajero et al. (2022) note that

> In a nation in which relatively few educational policy makers or practitioners can speak or write a language other than English, skills and knowledge in Spanish are often proscribed by mainstream educators who have adopted subtractive approaches to schooling, characterizing diverse learners' native languages and cultures as "barriers" to learning, rather than assets.
>
> *(Tinajero et al. 2022, p. 403)*

How do we foster an asset-based view of the linguistic abilities many children and families possess so that, as the mothers noted above, linguistic abilities are valued and viewed as important in schools?

In this chapter, we will look at the significance of linguistic capital. How do we leverage multilingual families' assets within and beyond early childhood spaces? How can we validate additional literacy practices that sometimes get overlooked, such as storytelling?

Linguistic Capital

Linguistic capital refers to "the intellectual and social skills attained through communication experiences in more than one language and/or style" (Yosso, 2005, p. 78). Language is "what we speak, hear, read, or write in everyday life" (García & Wei, 2014, p. 6). Language is a gift (López-Robertson, 2014) that is given to children, yet many families who speak languages in addition to English must make a difficult decision to bestow the gift of language upon their children or not. There are numerous reasons behind the decisions families make regarding the gift of language: parents weigh the influence of society, the attitudes others have toward language, and in many cases their personal experiences. While language policy in schools and/or society cannot dictate what families do in their own homes with regard to language use, Dixon and Wu (2014) found that "policies can encourage or discourage the family's use" (p. 422) of their home language. Additionally, Zentella (2005) offers that the choice to keep the home language or to focus on the language of power (frequently English) is influenced by the "information and opportunities [families] are given and their ability to counteract the damaging language ideologies shaped by the market value of English, English-only campaigns, and a legacy of linguistic purism and linguistic insecurity that is erasing Spanish" (p. 10). As educators, we must provide support to families to continue using their home language—the language of their **corazones**/*hearts*—with their children.

Cuentos from the Field: Linguistic Capital in Action

As a part of ongoing weekly meetings with Julia, a group of mothers engaged in a read aloud and discussion of *Pepita Talks Twice/Pepita habla dos veces* (Lachtman, 1995), a story about Pepita, a young bilingual child who is tired of speaking twice, in both Spanish and English. Pepita helps her community and family by drawing on her bilingual skills. She helps by speaking on the phone for her neighbor: Pepita listens to her neighbor and translates what she says from Spanish to English for the person on the phone. Pepita also helps her **tía** by translating from Spanish to English. One day, Pepita decides that she has had enough; she is tired of talking twice and decides that she will only speak English. Pepita's family wonders how she will communicate with her grandmother when she visits as she does not speak English. At the end of the story, Pepita realizes the value in her bilingualism when she saves the family dog Lobo from an oncoming car.

Following the read aloud, the mothers engaged in a discussion about the book and any connections they made to the book. The following episodes all emerged as a result of discussions based on this story.

Episode One: Bilingualism Is an Asset

After reading *Pepita Talks Twice/Pepita habla dos veces* (Lachtman, 1995), Pati shared that a daughter of one of their friends had recently gotten a job and her bilingualism was attributed to her being chosen from among other candidates.

> **La hija de Rafaela habla muy bien español e inglés y le acaban de ofrecer un trabajo porque es bilingüe. Rafaela me contó que la razón que la escogieron es porque sabe hablar español. Bueno tiene su licenciatura, pero el hablar español fue lo que dio la ventaja. Que bien que reconocieron lo bueno que es ser bilingüe. Felicidades a la hija de Rafaela.** / *Rafaela's daughter speaks Spanish and English very well and she was just offered a job because she is bilingual. Rafaela told me that the reason she [her daughter] was chosen [for the job] is because she knows how to speak Spanish. Well, she does have her degree [bachelor's], but speaking Spanish gave her [Rafaela's daughter] the advantage. How good that her bilingualism was recognized. Congratulations to Rafaela's daughter.*

Later in the discussion, Maite suggested that "**¡La persona bilingüe vale por dos!**"/*A bilingual person is worth two [people]!*

Suárez-Orozco and Suárez-Orozco (2001) point out that language is a "marker of identity and an instrument of power" (p. 135). For both Pepita and the daughter of Pati's friend, their abilities with language "uniquely positioned them to take part in a multiliterate community, drawing from their unique languages, cultures, and perspectives" (Early, 2017, p. 161); their bilingualism was viewed as an asset.

Episode Two: Desire to Learn English

As the discussion about *Pepita Talks Twice/Pepita habla dos veces* (Lachtman, 1995) continued, the mothers expressed their desire to learn English with statements such as "**Yo quiero aprender inglés. Como no, es nuestro país ahora y hay que saber hablar inglés**" / *I want to learn English. Of course, this is now our country, and we must know how to speak English.* Marta told a story of being in line at the grocery store and not understanding the cashier because she spoke too quickly. Marta asked the cashier to repeat herself which was met with a sneer. Marta offered:

> **Yo quiero hablar inglés. Yo sé lo importante que es poder hablar inglés. Es que no tengo tiempo. Ofrecen clases en la biblioteca, pero no tengo como llegar. Y ya saben que el autobús es imposible, en lo que llega uno, ya hay que dar vuelta y venir a recoger los niños de la escuela.** / *I want to speak English. I know how important it is to speak English. I do not have the time. They offer classes in the library, but I do not have a way to get there. And you know how impossible the bus is, by the time I get there, I would have to turn around and come back to pick up the children from school.*

Families recognize the importance of learning English; they want to learn how to communicate in their new country, but it is not easy. Access is an important factor, for many families there may only be one car in the home, perhaps the courses are offered at inconvenient times, and childcare is another consideration. Pati wondered about her younger children, "**¿Quién los cuida en lo que estamos en las clases?**" / *Who would watch them while we were in class?* All of the mothers agreed that it is not about wanting to learn English because "**tenemos las ganas**"/*we have the desire.*

Among the many challenges that immigrants to the United States will face, "learning the language and culture of the host country may be the most radical" (Dixon & Wu, 2014, p. 414), but that does not mean that they do not want to learn English or participate in the culture. Learning English is important to the families; as Pati noted, **"Saber inglés es tener poder. Igual para los niños que para nosotros, hay que aprender."** / *To know English is to have power. It is the same for the children and us, we need to learn.*

As sites of socialization, schools need to understand that "immigrant students' everyday language practices outside of school can be powerful tools for academic language development" (García-Sánchez, 2019, p. 139). Schools need to work to ensure that families and children are made to feel welcome as they are, they do not need to change. Schools must also understand that all families have something to contribute and knowing English is not a requisite for anything. As Hilda noted, **"Yo no sé inglés, pero es no es decir que no voy a contribuir; yo trabajo, pago impuestos, y ayudo en mi comunidad."** / *I do not know English, but that does not mean that I cannot contribute; I pay taxes and help my community.*

Schools and institutions "need to make a child's home, family, and community a central part of the curriculum" (Ada & Zubizarreta, 2001, p. 236) and keep in mind that issues like childcare for younger siblings and transportation limit a family's ability to access the resources that may be present in school. Families want the opportunity and need to have access to programming. These mothers (like many others) have the desire to learn English; rather than exclude them, schools need to take into consideration the many hurdles that some may have to face and work with them to find ways of enacting learning spaces that are accessible to them.

Episode Three: Maintaining Home Languages while Learning English

A concern that many of the mothers expressed was the notion that learning English means losing their home language, Spanish. Their children are surrounded by English in school, on the television, and even in the books they read and check out from the library. While the mothers understand and believe that the children must learn English, they worry that they will lose the ability to communicate with family members. One mother noted, **"No deben perder el español para aprender el otro"** / *[The children] should not lose Spanish to learn the other [English].* Victoria emphatically offered:

> **Hay que mantener nuestro idioma. Como dices, no van a poder hablar con sus abuelitos y otra familia. Que tristeza me da pensar que no podrían hablar con mis padres. Hay que seguir hablándoles en español para que no se les olvide. Y al mismo tiempo aprender inglés. No tiene que ser uno o el otro; los dos juntos.** / *We need to maintain our language. Like you said, they [children] will not be able to talk with their grandparents or other family. It makes me sad to think that they would not be able to speak with my parents. We need to keep talking to them in Spanish so that*

they do not forget. And at the same time learn English. It does not have to be one or the other, it can be both together.

Victoria's sentiment is in line with Delpit (2000) who believes that "acquiring the ability to function in a dominant discourse need not mean that one must reject one's home identity and values" (p. 249). Language is a part of who we are and connects us to our community and family. It is not necessary to replace one language with the other; languages can and do coexist.

In fact, emergent bilingual students seeking to make meaning from teaching and learning are engaging in translanguaging, "an approach to language pedagogy that affirms and leverages students' diverse and dynamic language practices in teaching and learning" (Vogel & García, 2017, p. 1). Translanguaging engages emergent bilinguals (both children and adults) in drawing from and fluidly using their complete linguistic repertoire as they seek to make meaning and communicate with others (García & Wei, 2014).

Maite added, **"No entiendo esta pelea, español o inglés. Ya basta, déjenlos que hablen ambos. No le hace daño saber los dos. Estoy cansada ya"** / *I do not understand this fight, Spanish or English. Enough, let them speak both. It will not harm them to know both. I am tired [of the Spanish vs. English].* Maite's frustration at the Spanish versus English issue is evident and shared by the mothers. Indeed, it does not harm the children to speak both languages; it is possible for children to succeed in school speaking both Spanish and English. Children should not be limited in the tools that they are allowed to use to make sense of instruction; rather, if they have more than one language at their disposal, educators must "acknowledge and validate students' home language without using it to limit students' potential" (Delpit, 2000, p. 249).

Episode Four: Language Brokers

The mothers spoke about the similarities between their experiences and those in the book, *Pepita Talks twice/Pepita habla dos veces* (Lachtman, 1995), and connected to their children acting as Pepita in their lives. Irma talked about a recent event; she entered the bank and the Spanish-speaking teller with whom she always interacts was not working that day. She ended up asking the monolingual English-speaking teller to speak to her daughter, Yvette, who would then translate for her. Irma explained that she felt bad for putting her young daughter in that situation but was so appreciative that she was able to help her.

Victoria suggested that the mothers look at the situation in another way and find the positive:

Ellos se sienten que están haciendo algo para ayudarnos. La niña se siente orgullosa que puede traducir. Me dijo que quiere ser abogada

para ayudar gente como nosotros que no sabemos inglés. Dice que no quiere que la gente sufra por no saber el idioma. / *They [the children] also feel that they are doing something to help us. My daughter feels proud to be able to translate. She told me that she wants to be an attorney to help people like us who do not know English. She says she does not want people to suffer because they do not know the language.*

Victoria noted that the children's ability to translate for their families was a skill that they should be proud of: **"La niña se siente orgullosa"** / *She feels proud*. Indeed, bilingualism is a skill to be proud of; emergent bilingual children gain knowledge from strategically using language and literacy in a variety of social contexts, including homes, communities, churches, and schools (Moll & González, 1994). Through engagement in language and literacy events, emergent bilinguals "not only develop their literacy abilities but also accumulate various forms of knowledge (e.g., numerical, digital, multimodal) that become essential to their survival" (Reyes et al., 2016, p. 14). Using their bilingual abilities, emergent bilinguals learn to use language as a commodity to help their families—they act as language brokers.

Language brokers is a term used to describe children of immigrants "who interpret and translate between culturally and linguistically different people and mediate interactions in a variety of situations including those found at home and school" (Tse, 1996, p. 226). Being a language broker is an important role, as we saw above, and yet most families and teachers do not know about this valuable skill. Reynolds and Orellana (2019) offer:

> These language and literacy brokering practices are ubiquitous, normative, and integrated into many everyday household tasks, and they are consequential for learning and development, including of the kinds of things that schools value. But they are rarely recognized or built on in school.
>
> *(p. 199)*

Language brokering requires knowledge of more than the language; as language brokers, children and youth manipulate social, cultural, linguistic, and practical knowledge to help their families communicate and navigate life in a new language and land.

Families are often unaware of language brokering and the knowledge of language it requires from their children because, as one mother said, **"solo es algo que hacemos"**/*it is just something we do*. Language brokering is a skill that needs to be valued and built upon in school as it is vital to some families' survival. Teachers should encourage emergent bilinguals' experimentation "with the two languages at their disposal" (Reyes, 2012, p. xv).

> **FEATURED CHILDREN'S LITERATURE WITH LINGUISTIC CAPITAL**
>
> Lachtman, O. D. (1995). *Pepita talks twice/Pepita habla dos veces* (A. P. Delange, Illus.). Arte Público Press.
>
> Pepita lives at the intersection of two worlds: one Spanish-speaking and one English-speaking. Pepita often gets asked to help people navigate between those two worlds, and she becomes frustrated with all the requests to help translate. But one day, Pepita realizes that speaking two languages is indeed a gift—even a life-saving gift. This bilingual (Spanish/English) book celebrates the gift of "talking twice"—speaking two languages.

Applying Linguistic Capital

To create a classroom environment that recognizes students' and families' linguistic capital, here are strategies to use both in the classroom and when engaging families. First, we will focus on one common occurrence in early childhood classrooms with strong ties to linguistic capital: storytelling.

Linguistic Capital and Storytelling

Instead of framing linguistic capital from an English-centric standpoint, community cultural wealth validates the strengths of students and families who experience a variety of communicative systems (including artistic systems), many of which revolve around stories. When children arrive at school, they bring with them years of language socialization (Zentella, 2005) with the language of their homes and communities and with ways of using language that are specific to their communities. For example, by kindergarten many Latino children have usually already experienced community traditions of storytelling. According to Yosso (2006), storytelling offers children a variety of academic benefits: they learn memorization, how to pay attention to details, how to take dramatic pauses, how to capture an audience, how to change the tone of voice to add interest, and how to play with language to see what makes people laugh and what scares them.

In early childhood settings, stories are common. We read them. We tell them. We listen to them. Stories are an important part of many lives and cultures, and the traditions governing stories can vary greatly. When considering linguistic capital, educators should be aware of diverse storytelling traditions and how to celebrate them in the classroom and beyond.

Teachers in the United States are usually more familiar with linear, or topic-centered, stories. In this form of storytelling, a main topic is established, and then setting, characters, and plot support that main topic with a clear beginning, middle, and end (Trumbull & Pacheco, 2005). Boutte et al. (2008) highlight that while this form of storytelling is often the invisible norm, this focus on "storylines and events proceed[ing] in a linear and sequential manner as opposed to a cyclical or circular way of being" can "easily shadow dimensions of Black culture" (p. 951).

Another kind of storytelling is episodic, or topic-associating stories. In this form of storytelling, various smaller tales or anecdotes are combined without a clear beginning, middle, or end (Cazden, 1999; Heath, 1983). Episodic stories, which may also be called circular stories, allow the speaker to connect multiple distinct ideas, which is impossible in a linear storytelling structure (Boutte, 2007). Many cultures, including African American oral storytelling traditions, use this episodic structure (Delpit, 1998). Heath (1983) compared storytelling in one African American community and one White community and found stories and judgments of "good" or "bad" stories differed greatly. For example, "[The White] community allows only stories which are factual and have little exaggeration; the [African American community] uses reality only as the germ of a highly creative fictionalized account" (p. 184). Similarly, Michaels and Cazden (1986) found that young White children told "topic-centered" narratives focused on a single event, while young Black children told "episodic" narratives with different scenes and longer trajectories.

Many cultures have specific storytelling traditions. Vietnamese storytelling traditions focus more on characters than plot (Söter, 1988). Arabic storytelling repeats significant elements (Sa'Adeddin, 1989). If teachers are used to linear stories and their structures, they may misunderstand story traditions from different cultures as incorrect or deficient, when in fact they are completely different—and entirely valid—structures for storytelling.

These cultural differences in storytelling approaches can surface during daily learning structures such as circle time. If you have ever had a child whose story about their day yesterday starts "veering off" into fictionalized events, it could be that this child comes from a storytelling tradition that prioritizes episodic storytelling where these fictionalized events are not detours but are actually central to the storytelling process. Cazden (1988) noted that adults responded more positively to children's stories when they shared the child's cultural background. When listening to a Black child's episodic narrative and a White child's topic-centered narrative, the White adults thought the Black child's story was "incoherent" and that the child was less academically competent, whereas Black adults found the same story "well-formed" and "interesting." Having an awareness of different storytelling traditions can help educators interrupt deficit-based assumptions. Just because a story doesn't follow the storytelling structure you grew up with does not mean it is "wrong"!

In addition, "[teachers] should recognize that the linguistic form a student brings to school is intimately connected with loved ones, community, and personal identity" (Delpit, 1998, p. 19). How we tell and use stories is rooted in our cultural backgrounds, often most strongly with our families. As we create space for our families' linguistic capital in our classrooms, storytelling is an aspect we should not overlook.

Classroom Strategies to Honor Linguistic Capital

- Incorporate translanguaging in books or morning messages. Translanguaging occurs when multilingual speakers weave aspects of multiple languages into one linguistic act, such as reading or writing. Instead of saying one complete thought in one language and then repeating it in another—which would be considered translation—translanguaging seamlessly combines multiple linguistic features. Translanguaging supports linguistic capital by normalizing that communication can occur meaningfully in multiple languages. Choosing books that translanguage—meaning they insert words in varying languages in the midst of other languages, such as English—gives students important practice with using context clues to figure out meanings of unknown words. Furthermore, writing morning messages that insert words from different languages celebrates linguistic capital.
- Give children role-playing opportunities with different dialects and languages. As Delpit (1998) notes, "Playing a role eliminates the possibility of implying that the child's language is inadequate and suggests, instead, that different language forms are appropriate in different contexts" (p. 20). Create authentic opportunities for role-playing to avoid perpetuating stereotypes.
- Complete contrastive analysis. Contrastive analysis allows for multiple linguistic systems to be directly compared or analyzed. Based on the work of multiple scholars (Boutte & Johnson, 2013; Wheeler, 2008; Wheeler & Swords, 2006; Whitney, 2005), here are a few suggestions for using contrastive analysis in early childhood settings:
    - Engage in linguistic scientific inquiry. Collect samples of student speech, analyze them for patterns, name the rule, test the rule, and listen for the pattern/rule in future interactions.
    - Write with intention for different audiences. In a morning message, how might linguistic choices differ for speakers of African American Language, Spanish, Pashto, or other languages?

TABLE 4.1 Example of Contrastive Analysis Chart

African American Language	*Standardized English*	*Spanish*
There <u>ain't nothing</u> left.	There's <u>nothing</u> left.	<u>No</u> hay <u>nada</u>.
I <u>don't</u> want <u>nothing</u>.	I <u>don't</u> want anything.	<u>No</u> quiero <u>nada</u>.
I <u>don't</u> see <u>nobody</u>.	I <u>don't</u> see anyone.	<u>No</u> veo a <u>nadie</u>.
I <u>didn't</u> do <u>nothing</u>.	I <u>didn't</u> do anything.	<u>No</u> hago <u>nada</u>.

- Compare and contrast Standardized English with other language varieties. Color coding certain syntactical features—like where negative words function in sentences to highlight that double negatives are actually not "errors" in languages other than English—can help make this process more concrete for early childhood students. The example chart in Table 4.1 shows what this would look like in practice. The three columns contain the same sentences in African American Language, Standardized English, and Spanish, with the negative words underlined (they can be written in a different color as well). This coding reveals that while English has a rule against double negatives in a sentence, it actually is a legitimate syntactical structure in the African American Language and Spanish sentences.
- Ask families to share stories! Turn these stories into a class anthology that students can take turns "checking out" to read with their families. Invite storytellers into the classroom to share a story live during class.
- Sing songs in different languages. Try to get someone who speaks the language, such as a family or community member, to sing the song. Display the lyrics in the actual language to read as you sing along, and work hard to make your pronunciation as close to the expert speaker's as possible. It may help to ask the expert speaker to record the song so that you can keep practicing!
- Include linguistic capital in lessons. For example, if you are doing a unit on maps or geography, the <u>Native-Land.ca project</u> (https://native-land.ca/) displays various Indigenous languages and where they are spoken. Slate (Blatt, 2014) analyzed languages reported in the U.S. Census data and created maps to show the most common languages in all 50 states, if you'd like more ideas of languages to learn with your students.

Family Strategies to Honor Linguistic Capital

- Encourage families to continue speaking home languages. Sometimes families mistakenly believe that continuing to speak their home languages will hurt their child's ability to learn English, but this is actually not the case

at all. Reading skills in home languages transfer to additional languages (Páez & Rinaldi, 2006).
- Remind families that at-home literacy activities can include multiple modalities and multiple languages. Invite families to share the ways they are using reading, writing, and language skills in diverse linguistic systems in their daily lives so that children can see firsthand the variety of ways their families enact their linguistic capital.
- Educate families on the actual benefits of multilingualism. Multilingual people have strong thinking skills (Cummins, 2007); can focus, remember, and make decisions better (Bialystok, 2001); and can learn other languages with greater ease (Jessner, 2008).
- Provide multilingual lists of children's books for families. Children's books can incorporate multiple languages in a variety of ways. Sometimes a text is predominately in English with a few words in other languages sprinkled throughout, which can be a form of translanguaging. Other books have the same text written in English and another language, serving as a direct translation that can be more accessible for families with linguistic capital in languages other than English. The Diverse Book Finder website has a list of multilingual texts that can be a great starting point (https://diversebookfinder.org/content/second-language/).
- Translate materials for families. Whenever possible, educators and schools should provide documents in families' home languages. This action sends a clear message to families that they are valued members of the school community whose linguistic capital is honored and respected. Having a school-based translator is ideal, but not all schools have access to this resource. Digital tools that can assist with translation are provided later in this chapter.
- Work with front office staff on welcoming multilingual families. Front office staff are often the first school representatives multilingual families encounter. Just as classroom teachers can't be expected to be proficient in all of their students' home languages, front office staff likely will not have the linguistic diversity necessary to communicate in all families' home languages. Some strategies that front office staff can use are providing brochures of FAQs about the school in multiple languages; learning key phrases that are used frequently; and using visuals. Also, consider recruiting front office staff from community members. These community members often speak the language (or languages) of the community in which they live, and they may already know many of the families attending the school, which increases trust. Most importantly, remind front office staff of the importance of patience and a smile, which are understood in all languages!

Conclusion

At the opening of the chapter we wondered: how do we foster an asset-based view of the linguistic abilities many children and families possess so that linguistic abilities are valued and viewed as important in schools? Schools must recognize that (1) families possess knowledge and ways of making meaning of the world that are valuable and vital to their children and community and (2) their children are immersed in learning these ways of knowing and making meaning daily. An important way of knowing that many minoritized children possess is the ability to communicate in more than one language. Schools need to view bilingual children and their families as competent language learners as evidenced through the language brokering that children do for their families and teachers. Schools must be intentional in our work with children and families and build curriculum that centers the multiple ways of knowing and making meaning our children and their families possess. After all, language is an act of love that joins the **corazones**/*hearts* of children and families.

Additional Resources

The following seven award-winning picturebooks address themes related to linguistic capital. For a complete list of picturebooks and other areas of community cultural wealth these books may contain, see Appendix A.

Children's Literature

Fuego Fueguito/Fire, Little Fire/Tit, Titchin **(Argueta, 2019)**

Through poetry and vivid illustrations, this book explores the importance of fire in glyphs and codices from central Mexico's Indigenous groups. This book supports linguistic capital by including bilingual poems in English and Spanish on each page, and then the entire poem is translated into Nahuatl, an endangered Indigenous language from El Salvador, at the end of the book (Américas Award, 2020 Commended Title).

Soldier for Equality: José de la Luz Sáenz and the Great War
(Tonatiuh, 2019)

This book captures the story of José de la Luz Sáenz, a Mexican American who fought not only in the U.S. Army during World War I, but also fought prejudice against Mexican Americans in the United States by creating the League of United Latin American Citizens (LULAC), the oldest and largest Latinx civil rights organization. Luz spoke English and Spanish, and then he learned French during the war. His linguistic capital landed him an impressive position in the

Intelligence Office in Europe during the war, where he received, translated, and relayed messages (Américas Award, 2020 Commended Title; Pura Belpré Award, 2020 Honor Book).

Salma the Syrian Chef (Ramadan, 2020)

Salma and her mom are Syrian refugees now living in Vancouver, though her Papa remains in Syria. Her mom works long hours and takes English classes, and Salma worries that her mom misses Syrian food. Salma works with adult translators in the Welcome Center to try to find ingredients and spices from Syria in her new home in Vancouver; however, many of them do not know Arabic. Salma demonstrates her linguistic capital by translating ingredients in Arabic into her new language of English, and when she doesn't know the English names, she draws pictures for her adult translators so that they can teach her the English words (Middle East Book Award, 2020 Picture Book Winner).

We Are Grateful: Otsaliheliga (Sorell, 2018)

This text, written primarily in English but with Cherokee terms incorporated throughout, invites readers to journey through the four seasons and express gratitude for different traditions, experiences, or natural elements. When Cherokee words are introduced, they are written with a pronunciation guide, the actual Cherokee script, and a definition at the bottom of the page. The author identifies as Cherokee (American Indian Youth Literature Award, 2020 Picture Book Honor Book).

Child of the Flower-Song People: Luz Jiménez, Daughter of the Nahua (Amescua, 2021)

This book follows the life of real-life Luz Jiménez, who was a Nahua girl living in Mexico in the early 1900s until the Mexican Revolution forced her and her family to leave her village and move to Mexico City. Throughout her life, she resisted attempts to assimilate her culture and her Nahuatl language (Américas Award, 2022 Winner; Pura Belpré Children's Author Award, 2022 Honor Title).

ABC El Salvador (Ayala, 2021)

Written bilingually in Spanish and English, this book follows Xiomara and Kevin, a brother and sister, as they learn about El Salvador's culture and traditions, one for each letter of the alphabet. The alphabet also includes letters unique to the Spanish alphabet, including ch, ll, and ñ. At the end, a glossary explains all of the vocabulary introduced in the book. This book demonstrates linguistic capital because it centers the Spanish alphabet and vocabulary instead of focusing on solely the English alphabet (Américas Award, 2022 Commended Title).

Isabel and Her Colores Go to School **(Alessandri, 2021)**

Isabel has to conquer two fears at the same time: going to a new school and learning a new language. As she watches and learns how both of these new systems function, she learns that she can communicate through colors in her artwork. The book aligns with linguistic capital because it utilizes translanguaging between Spanish and English throughout, and also models how multimodal communication is an asset (Américas Award, 2022 Commended Title).

Digital Tools

Before we look at a few digital tools related to linguistic capital (Table 4.2), remember that the burden of translation should not always fall on families and

TABLE 4.2 Digital Tools: Linguistic Capital

Tool	Description
Google Translate (https://translate.google.com/)	Since launching in 2006, Google Translate has been a popular free translation service. Users can translate from one language directly into another, with over 110 languages to choose from (including Spanish, Arabic, Chinese, and Pashto). Text to translate can be input either by voice or by typing into the provided box, which harnesses linguistic capital by allowing users to choose whether to use their oral or written linguistic skills. The site also supports translation of entire documents in multiple formats (including Word documents, PDFs, PowerPoints, and Excel sheets). Google Translate is available as both a web-based format and an app for Apple and Android devices, which allows it to function across platforms and devices. The mobile version has additional features, such as "Snap," which allows users to take pictures of signs and menus and have them instantly translated; "Write," which allows users to use their touchscreen to write characters that are not accessible on traditional keyboards; and an offline mode to allow for translations without internet, though this feature requires downloading a specific language in the app, so it does require internet initially as well as storage space on a mobile device.

(Continued)

TABLE 4.2 (Continued)

Tool	Description
Class Dojo (https://www.classdojo.com/)	Since Class Dojo initially launched in 2011 as a digital behavior management system, it has added many other features. Private messaging launched in 2014, and translation capabilities debuted in 2015. Families can translate private messages into over 30 languages by tapping on the message and selecting their home language. Class Dojo is available both as a web-based client and as a downloaded app for both Apple and Android devices, and users can select their preferred language in both spaces.
Talking Points (https://talkingpts.org/)	Talking Points is a free multilingual messaging app. It fosters communication in over 145 languages, higher than other tools on the market. To achieve high-quality translations, Talking Points uses a mixture of AI and human translators. Families can send and receive messages via texting or an app.

speakers of languages other than English. Whenever possible, educators and schools should translate documents into languages their families can access instead of sending home materials in English and expecting families to use digital tools and other resources to translate them into their home language.

Ideally, a school-based translator is available to assist with translation responsibilities or to check over translations educators create, since machine-based translations are not going to be perfect (but they are definitely getting much better!).

References

Ada, A. F., & Zubizarreta, R. (2001). Parent narratives: The cultural bridge between Latino parents and their children. In M. Reyes & L. Halcón (Eds.), *The best for our children: Critical perspectives on literacy for Latino students* (pp. 229–244). Teachers College Press.

Bialystok, E. (2001). *Bilingualism in development: Language, literacy, and cognition.* Cambridge University Press.

Blatt, B. (2014, May 13). *Tagalog in California, Cherokee in Arkansas: What language does your state speak?* Slate. https://slate.com/culture/2014/05/language-map-whats-the-most-popular-language-in-your-state.html

Boutte, G. S. (2007). Teaching students who speak African American language. In M. E. Brisk (Ed.), *Language, culture, and community in teacher education* (pp. 47–70). Lawrence Erlbaum Associates.

Boutte, G. S., Hopkins, R., & Waklatski, T. (2008). Perspectives, voices, and worldviews in frequently read children's books. *Early Education & Development, 19*(6), 941–962.

Boutte, G., & Johnson, G. (2013). Do educators see and honor biliteracy and bidialectalism in African American language speakers? Apprehensions and reflections of two grandparents/professional educators. *Early Childhood Education Journal*, 41(2), 133–141.

Cazden, C. B. (1988). *Classroom discourse*. Heinemann.

Cazden, C. B. (1999). The language of African American students in classroom discourse. In C. T. Adger, D. Christian, & O. Taylor (Eds.), *Making the connection: Language and academic achievement among African American students* (pp. 31–52). Center for Applied Linguistics and Delta Systems Co.

Cummins, J. (2007). Pedagogies for the poor? Realigning reading instruction for low-income students with scientifically based reading research. *Educational Researcher*, 36(9), 564–572.

Delpit, L. (1998). What should teachers do? Ebonics and culturally responsive instruction. In T. Perry & L. Delpit (Eds.), *The real Ebonics debate: Power, language, and the education of African-American children* (pp. 17–26). Beacon Press.

Delpit, L. (2000). Acquisition of literate discourse: Bowing before the master. In M. A. Gallego & S. Hollingsworth (Eds.), *What counts as literacy? Challenging the school standard* (pp. 241–251). Teachers College Press.

Dixon, L. Q., & Wu, S. (2014). Home language and literacy practices among immigrant second-language learners. *Language Teaching*, 47(4), 414–449.

Early, J. S. (2017). *Escribiendo juntos:* toward a collaborative model of multiliterature family literacy in English only and anti-immigrant contexts. *Research in the Teaching of English*, 52(2), 156–180.

García, O., & Sánchez, M. T. (2022). The making of the language of US Latinxs: Translanguaging tejidos. In M. T. Sánchez & O. García (Eds.), *Transformative translanguaging espacios: Latinx students and their teachers rompiendo fronteras sin miedo* (pp. 19–44). Multilingual Matters.

García-Sánchez, I. M. (2019). Centering shared linguistic heritage to build language and literacy resilience among immigrant students. In I. M. García-Sánchez & M. F. Orellana (Eds.), *Language and cultural practices in communities and schools: Bridging learning for students from non-dominant groups* (pp. 139–160). Routledge.

García, O., & Wei, L. (2014). *Translanguaging: Language, bilingualism and education*. Palgrave Macmillan.

García-Sánchez, I. M. (2019). Centering shared linguistic heritage to build language and literacy resilience among immigrant students. In I. M. García-Sánchez & M. F. Orellana (Eds.), *Language and cultural practices in communities and schools: Bridging learning for students from non-dominant groups* (pp. 139–160). Routledge.

Heath, S. B. (1983). *Ways with words: Language, life, and work in communities and classrooms*. Cambridge University Press.

Jessner, U. (2008). *Teaching third languages: Findings, trends, and challenges*. Université de Lausanne. https://doi.org/10.1017/S0261444807004739

López-Robertson, J. (2021). *Celebrating our cuentos: Choosing and using Latinx literature in elementary classrooms*. Scholastic Publishers.

López-Robertson, J. (2014). My gift to you is my language: Spanish is the language of my heart. In B. Kabuto & P. Martens (Eds.), *Linking families, learning, and schooling: Parent–researcher perspectives* (pp. 80–91). Routledge.

Luna, N. A., & Martinez, M. (2013). A qualitative study using community cultural wealth to understand the educational experiences of Latino college students. *Journal of Praxis in Multicultural Education*, 7(1), 2. https://doi.org/10.9741/2161-2978.1045

Michaels, S., & Cazden, C. B. (1986). Teacher–child collaboration on oral preparation for literacy. In B. Schieffelin & P. Gilmore (Eds.), *The acquisition of literacy: Ethnographic perspectives* (pp. 132–154). Ablex.

Moll, L. C. (2011). Foreword. In M. L. Reyes (Ed.), *Words were all we had: Becoming biliterate against the odds* (p. x). Teachers College Press.

Moll, L. C., & González, N. (1994). Lessons from research with language-minority children. *Journal of Reading Behavior*, 26(4), 439–456.

Páez, M., & Rinaldi, C. (2006). Predicting English word reading skills for Spanish-speaking students in first grade. *Topics in Language Disorders*, 26(4), 338–350.

Reyes, I. (2012). Biliteracy among children and youths. *Research Reading Quarterly*, 47(3), 307–327.

Reyes, I., DaSilva Iddings, A. C., & Feller, N. (2016). Building relationships with diverse students and families: A funds of knowledge perspective. *Journal of Early Childhood Literacy*, 16(1), 8–33.

Reynolds, J. F., & Orellana, M. (2019). Transliteracy practices by youth in new immigrant communities. In I. M. García-Sánchez & M. F. Orellana (Eds.), *Language and cultural practices in communities and schools: Bridging learning for students from non-dominant groups* (pp. 195–212). Routledge.

Sa'Adeddin, M. A. A. M. (1989). Text development and Arabic-English negative interference. *Applied Linguistics*, 10(1), 36–51.

Söter, A. (1988). The second language learner and cultural transfer in narration. In A. Purves (Ed.), *Writing across languages and cultures* (pp. 177–205). Sage.

Suárez-Orozco, C., & Suárez-Orozco, M. M. (2001). *Children of immigration*. Harvard University Press.

Tinajero, J. V., Munter, J. H. & Araujo, B. (2022). Best practices for teaching Latino English learners in U.S. Schools. In E. G. Murrillo, Jr., D. Delgado Bernal, S. Morales, L. Urrieta, Jr., E.R. Bybee, J. S. Muñoz, V. Sáenz, D. Villanueva, M. Machado-Casas, & K. Espinoza (Eds.), *Handbook of Latinos and education: Theory, research and practice* (2nd ed., pp. 401–421). Routledge.

Trumbull, E., & Pacheco, M. (2005). *The teacher's guide to diversity: Building a knowledge base, volume II: Language*. Brown University. https://www.brown.edu/academics/education-alliance/sites/brown.edu.academics.education-alliance/files/publications/tgd_language.pdf

Tse, L. (1996). Who decides?: The effect of language brokering on home-school communication. *The Journal of Educational Issues of Language Minority Students*, 16, 225–234.

Valdés, G. (1996). *Con respeto: Bridging the distances between culturally diverse families and schools: An ethnographic portrait*. Teachers College Press.

Vogel, S., & García, O. (2017). Translanguaging. *Oxford Research Encyclopedia of Education*. https://oxfordre.com/education/view/10.1093/acrefore/9780190264093.001.0001/acrefore-9780190264093-e-181.

Wheeler, R. S. (2008). Becoming adept at code-switching. *Educational Leadership*, 65(7), 54–58.

Wheeler, R. S., & Swords, R. (2006). *Code-switching: Teaching Standard English in urban classrooms*. National Council of Teachers of English.

Whitney, J. (2005). Five easy pieces: Steps toward integrating AAVE into the classroom. *The English Journal*, 94(5), 64–69.

Yosso, T. J. (2005). Whose culture has capital? A critical race theory discussion of community cultural wealth. *Race Ethnicity and Education*, *8*(1), 69–91. http://doi.org/10.1080/1361332052000341006

Yosso, T. J. (2006). *Critical race counterstories along the Chicana/Chicano educational pipeline.* Routledge.

Zentella, A. C. (2005). *Building on strength: Language and literacy in Latino families and communities.* Teachers College Press.

Children's Literature

Alessandri, A. (2021). *Isabel and her colores go to school* (C. Dawson, Illus.). Sleeping Bear Press.

Amescua, G. (2021). *Child of the flower-song people: Luz Jiménez, daughter of the Nahua* (D. Tonatiuh, Illus.). Abrams Books for Young Readers.

Argueta, J. T. (2019). *Fuego fueguito/Fire, little fire/Tit, titchin* (F. U. Alcántara, Illus.). Piñata Press.

Ayala, H. (2021). *ABC El Salvador* (E. Gómez, Illus.). Lunas Press Books.

Lachtman, O. D. (1995). *Pepita talks twice/Pepita habla dos veces* (A. P. Delange, Illus.). Arte Público Press.

Ramadan, D. (2020). *Salma the Syrian chef* (A. Bron, Illus.). Annick Press.

Sorell, T. (2018). *We are grateful: Otsaliheliga* (F. Lessac, Illus.). Charlesbridge.

Tonatiuh, D. (2019). *Soldier for equality: José de la Luz Sáenz and the Great War* (D. Tonatiuh, Illus.) Abrams Books for Young Readers.

5
THE RICHNESS OF FAMILIA
Familial Capital

Samantha and Justina, two Spanish-speaking first graders, were engaged in a conversation while drawing a response to the book, *In My Family/En mi familia* (Garza, 2000). They were talking about their families, where they lived, and who lived with them. Samantha asked Justina about her **abuelita** since she had not seen her in a few days; **abuelita** usually walked Justina to school.

Justina: **Ella de verdad no es mi abuela, pero yo le digo abuelita. Ella me cuida en lo que mi mamá trabaja, desde que yo era muy chiquita. Hay veces que yo duermo en su casa. Yo la quiero mucho como si era mi abuela verdadera.** /
She really is not my grandmother, but I call her grandmother. She takes care of me while my mom is at work since I was little. Sometimes I sleep in her house. I love her like she was my real grandmother.

Samantha: **Eso no importa. Ella te quiere y te cuida. No tiene que tener tu sangre para ser tu familia. ¿Qué más quieres?** /
That does not matter. She loves you and takes care of you. She does not need to have your blood to be your family. What else do you want?

In the excerpt, Justina offered that the older woman was not her grandmother; she just calls her **abuela**. Samantha's matter-of-fact response indicated that **abuela** does not need to have Justina's blood to be her family because what mattered was that she loved her. These young children's conversation provides an idea of what makes a family: someone who loves and takes care of you regardless of whether they have your blood. As families immigrate to the United States or move to other states within the United States, their familial networks expand to include extended family and kin, both chosen and related by blood. Community networks, which we will focus on in the next chapter, can also become like family.

In this chapter, we will examine familial capital. How do we create school environments that honor all families and familial networks and the contributions these make to their children's learning and the school community?

Familial Capital

Familial capital recognizes "those cultural knowledges nurtured among familia that carry a sense of community history, memory, and cultural intuition" (Yosso, 2005, p. 79). As we saw in the opening excerpt, familial capital goes beyond blood ties and extends into networks of extended family-kin. Funds of knowledge (Moll et al., 1992), the cultural and authentic skills and knowledge that are vital to a family's and community's survival and are passed down through the generations, are an example of familial capital. Funds of knowledge recognize the interconnectedness of the social network to which families belong and how "these social relationships facilitate the development and exchange of resources—including knowledge, skills, and labor, that enhance the household's ability to survive or thrive" (González et al., 2005, p. 73). Included in familial capital are the intangibles: life experiences, emotional support and mentoring, and sharing of beliefs.

To help schools comprehend the richness and multiple ways of knowing their students and families possess, we must first work to assist families in realizing that their knowledge is indeed valuable (López-Robertson, 2017); so often minoritized families buy into the narrative that is told about them and it "becomes the reality of their lives" (Villenas & Deyhle, 1999, p. 419). A major component of our work is helping *families* advocate that they are their child's first and continuous teacher and that their cultural knowledge, their ways of making meaning, and their life experiences positively contribute to their children's education and well-being.

Cuentos from the Field: Familial Capital in Action

At the foundation of our work is the belief that families need to feel safe and respected in schools. Often, schools overlook the fact that many of our minoritized families may not have had positive experiences in their own schooling and as such find schools to be unwelcoming. Edwards (2016) talks about the "ghosts" of past schooling and the negative impacts on families' view of schooling for their own children. Edwards writes, "the failure of schools to build or rebuild linkages between home and schools inadvertently encourages parents to maintain their frozen memories or their community's frozen perceptions of what that school was once like" (p. 108). We seek to engage families and create spaces where they can discover the value in their cultural knowledge and ways of making meaning and bring that learning to be valued in schools. The episodes that follow illustrate ways we have seen families enacting their familial capital in early childhood contexts.

Episode One: Engaging Children and Families with Their Cultural Knowledge

Delgado-Gaitan (2001) writes that "culture is the bedrock upon which the classroom curriculum is based, and as such, it is the most critical aspect of family-school relationships" (p. 109). One way to infuse family into the curriculum is through picturebooks. In her picturebooks, *Family Pictures/Cuadros de familia* (Garza, 1998) and *In My Family/En mi familia* (Garza, 2000), Carmen Lomas Garza shares personal stories accompanied by paintings depicting a variety of her family traditions growing up in Kingsville, Texas, a city near the U.S.–Mexico border. The children were drawn to the paintings and to the familiarity of the stories Garza shared; many of them shared their stories of birthday parties with piñatas, cakewalks that we had at school, and retellings of the time their **nana/abuela** killed a chicken for dinner. The excerpt shared at the opening of this chapter was from a discussion the children were having about Garza's Healer/Curandera story in *Family Pictures/Cuadros de familia* (p. 28). The illustration shows a sick woman in bed, a little boy playing with a ball on the bed, and an older woman holding onto branches as she appears to nurse the woman. The children talked a lot about the illustrations and commented on the familiarity of the objects in the bedroom, particularly the picture of **La Virgen de Guadalupe**, which led to a discussion of church materials that they read with their **nanas** once they arrived at home.

Samantha:	**Mi nana tiene una foto como esa en su cuarto y todas las noches le reza a la Virgencita.** / *My grandmother has a similar picture in her bedroom and every night she prays to the Virgin.*
Justina:	**Sí, la mía también. Algunas veces duermo en su casa cuando mi mamá trabaja tarde y ella y yo rezamos a la Virgencita.** / *Yes, mine [grandmother] does too. Sometimes when my mother works late, I sleep at her house and we both pray to the Virgin.*
Samantha:	**Nosotros vamos a la iglesia para rezarle a la Virgencita y luego cuando llegamos a casa, unas veces mi nana me sienta para leer de la biblia y de los libritos de la iglesia.** / *We go to church to pray to the Virgin and then when we get home, sometimes my nana sits me down to read the Bible and the little books from church.*

Justina: **¡Yo también! Los libritos de la iglesia son chiquitos con oraciones que nana me hace leer.** / *Me too! The little books from church are small with the prayers that my nana makes me read.*

Interestingly, when their mothers came to school for open house, they perused the book *Family Pictures*, and they too commented on the Curandera story, noting "**ese cuarto se parece al mío, también hay cuadro de la Virgencita**" / *That room looks like mine, I also have a picture of the Virgin.*

The mothers continued talking about the Curandera page in *Family Pictures/Cuadros de familia* as they engaged in a brief exchange about the Curandera/Healer. Seeking medical attention becomes more difficult when one lacks knowledge of the process, is new to the community, or does not speak English. In this particular community, many of the families had positive experiences with a Curandera/Healer that had been in the community for years and was well-established and highly respected, as Barbara and Susana discuss.

Barbara: **Allá en mi pueblo usábamos mucho la Curandera, ella sabía más de la medicina que muchos de los médicos.** / *In my town we used the Healer a lot, she knew a lot more about medicine than most of the doctors.*

Susana: **Sí, además con el tiempo que uno toma para llegar a la cita, esperar que la vea el médico, ya la Curandera ha llegado, examinado, y repartido la medicina.** / *Yes, and with the time it takes you to arrive at the appointment, and wait to be seen, the Healer has arrived, examined you, and given the medicine.*

Barbara: **Lástima que se quedó allá.** / *Too bad she stayed there [home town in their country].*

Susana: **Pero Barbara, Matilde conoce una señora allá en la Calle Valley que es buenísima. Tiene un jardín lleno de hierbas y quien sabe qué más, pero es buenísima. Martin tuvo un resfriado malísimo, fuimos con ella y al día siguiente se alivió.** / *But Barbara, Matilde knows a woman who lives on Valley Street and she is fantastic. She has a garden full of herbs and who knows what else, but she is fantastic. Martin [Susana's husband] had a very bad cold, we went to see the Healer and the next day he was better.*

Barbara: **No lo sabía. ¿Al rato me la presentas?** / *I didn't know. Will you introduce us?*

Barbara was lamenting that the Curandera her family relied on for many years remained in their hometown. Susana happily shared the news that Matilde (another mother in the community) had introduced her to the Curandera and she had helped her husband, Martin, get over a very bad cold. Susana explained that Martin had been sick for weeks and that they could not afford to go to Urgent Care. She had bumped into Matilde at the laundromat and that was when she learned about the Curandera. Having a Curandera available provides families access to someone who can help them when they are ill; it makes medical attention more accessible and it is from someone who has earned the community's trust.

The mothers continued reading Samantha and Justina's drawn responses to the book, and then noted that reading the Bible and the children's prayer books were a weekly routine that they believe "**sirven para enseñarles a los niños a leer**" / *are useful to teach the children to read*. Both mothers agreed that the books served a dual purpose "**enseñarles a leer y también compartir nuestra religión y fé con ellos en un modo divertido**" / *to teach them how to read and to share our religion and faith with them in a fun way*. Additionally, it was important to both mothers that the books were available in Spanish because this allowed them to actively share their knowledge and stories with their children in "**nuestra idioma**" / *our language*. Schools should value children's "church language and literacy practices by explicitly letting them [children and their families] know that skills acquired in religious institutions are resources and strengths for learning in schools" (Ek, 2005, p. 92).

Episode Two: Creating Networks to Help and Support Each Other

In the opening vignette, two little girls spoke about an **abuela/nana** who was not really a grandmother but someone who loved and cared for a little girl while her mother worked. This is one type of family: one that is created out of necessity and proximity and, as Samantha said in the opening vignette, out of love. As the girls continued talking about the book, *Family Pictures/Cuadros de familia*, Justina turned the book to the page about "Making tamales" (p. 22) and commented that her family was making tamales like the family in the book. "**Mi nana (la que yo le digo nana) cumplió años y tuvimos una fiesta muy grande con toda la familia**" / *My grandmother (the one I call nana) had a big birthday party and the whole family came*. Justina commented that it felt like they were in the kitchen for days cooking tamales but that the mood was very festive and included a lot of people who she called family that, just like the nana, were not family "**de verdad**" / *really*.

> **Estábamos en la cocina de mi nana y llegó una tía con sus niñas, mis primas, y nos pusimos a jugar como el niño en la foto. Mi tía nos dijo que si íbamos a jugar que teníamos que ir afuera. Mi nana le dijo que nos dejará en la cocina porque ella sabía que sus nietas sí iban a ayudar. Ella me dice nieta, aunque no soy. Eso me hace feliz. Mi nana verdadera está muy lejos y por lo menos la tengo**

a ella. Nana me quiere mucho y la familia de ella es mi familia también. Mi mamá está feliz porque tiene quien le ayude. ¡Ella también le dice nana! / *We were in my nana's kitchen and my aunt arrived with her daughters, my cousins, and we started playing like the boy in the picture. My tia told us that if we were going to play that we needed to go outside. My nana told her to leave us in the kitchen because she knew that we [her granddaughters] were going to help. She calls me her granddaughter, even though I am not. That makes me happy. My real nana is far away and at least I have her. She loves me and her family is my family. My mom is happy because she has someone to help her. She also calls her nana!*

In this lengthy excerpt Justina connected to the notion that family does not need to be blood related; she explains that her grandmother is far away and that she is happy to have this **nana** who loves her and includes her as a part of the family. As a part of this familial network, both Justina and her mother feel loved and supported.

Episode Three: Sewing as Familial Capital

Another example of familial networks occurred as a response to a reading of the book *The Best Part of Me: Children Talk about Their Bodies in Pictures and Words* (Ewald, 2002). To engage mothers in recognizing their contributions to their children's learning, mothers were asked to think about their favorite body part and why (López-Robertson & Haney, 2021). The book, *The Best Part of Me*, is a series of photographs and narratives about favorite body parts written by a group of elementary students. One of the mothers, Rosalia, noted that her favorite body part was her hands and she explained that with her hands she provides for her family. She added:

> **Mi mamá me enseñó a coser y aquí trabajo cosiendo ropita para niños y otras cosas. Con el dinerito puedo darles a los niños cosas que necesitan para estudiar cómo la computadora. También le presto a mi comadre para que ella también pueda empezar su negocito para ayudarle a su familia. ¿Si no nos ayudamos unas a otras, pues quién nos va a ayudar?** / *My mother taught me to sew and here I work in sewing children's clothes and other things. With the money I make, I can give my children the tools they need to study, like a computer. I also share my sewing machine with my close friend so that she too can start a business to help her family. If we don't help each other, who is going to help us?*

In the excerpt, Rosalia notes that she is utilizing her sewing skills that she learned from her own mother, a component of her funds of knowledge

(González et al., 2005), to provide her children with school supplies, namely a computer. Like most immigrants who come to the United States, Rosalia came to work hard (Menjívar, 2016) and provide her children with opportunities that she did not have. Additionally, she is also helping her **comadre**, her close friend, by sharing her sewing machine hoping that she too can begin a business to help her own family. Through these networks, families demonstrate a commitment to their communities and extend the meaning of family as not just those to whom we are related by blood or marriage; family are the members of our social networks and communities. In the next chapter, we will focus on how our families build those social networks in order to navigate their communities and other complex social systems.

Episode Four: The Gift of Names

One of the first gifts families give their children is their name. Names are chosen with intention: sometimes they honor a loved one, or perhaps they frame a dream for their child's future (see aspirational capital in Chapter 3). Names often draw upon a family's linguistic capital (see Chapter 4), which may mean that the letter/sound correspondences do not match the phonemic expectations of the teacher's primary language.

One small but significant commitment teachers can make to honor familial capital is to learn student names—including their correct cultural pronunciations and spellings. Some names like Luis, Jesus, and Jessica—even Julia!—have distinct pronunciations in various languages, even if a speaker or reader recognizes the name from their own language. As Magaña (2022) explains, "Learning to say my name is respect, affirmation and acknowledgement of me and my identity. It makes space for me, but also the possibility of connection. If you want people of color to be included, believe they deserve to be seen, then you can say so by correctly pronouncing their name" (para. 27).

After school one day, Kadence, an early childhood teacher, was talking about student names. Kadence quickly observed how names make individuals unique and shared how one student's family chose to use an inventive spelling of a common English for their child's name; however, since some English-speaking listeners recognized this word, they assumed the family simply did not know how to spell it "correctly." Another student with a name that did not align with phonological patterns of Standardized English was frequently misnamed. Kadence reflected, "Teachers call her [the mispronounced name] too. I even catch myself sometimes calling her that because that's just how we talk." While Kadence admitted that this student had not corrected the pronunciation of her own name, another had in a previous year: "She would speak up. She would say, 'No, it's [correct pronunciation].' And most kids won't say anything, they just go with whatever they're called." She also admitted that she thought one child's name was misspelled because the roster did not follow the Standardized English spelling of the name.

At the very end of the school year, Melissa interviewed a student and her mom about their experience in a family learning community in Kadence's class during the year. In the last moments of the interview, the student started whispering to her mom about her last name, which Kadence had been accidentally pronouncing incorrectly all year. The student's mom shared that her name was mispronounced when she was in school all the time as well.

We have all mispronounced students' names, even when we know the importance of names as markers of identity and gifts from families. What if we prioritized learning from students' families in the first days and weeks of school how *they* pronounce their child's name, why *they* chose this name for their precious child? What if we taught young children that sometimes we make mistakes, and it's OK to teach a friend, teacher, or other adult how to correctly pronounce their name? If we did these things in early childhood classrooms, might fewer students as they get older say it is OK to call them the Americanized or mispronounced version of their real names? Children of color should not carry the burden of teaching teachers how to pronounce their names (Cornwall, 2022); it is up to their teachers to shoulder this responsibility.

FEATURED CHILDREN'S LITERATURE WITH FAMILIAL CAPITAL

Garza, C. L. (1998). *Family pictures/Cuadros de familia* (C. L. Garza, Illus.). Lee & Low Books.

In this book, author and painter Carmen Lomas Garza tells of her own childhood growing up in a Mexican American family in Texas through 15 paintings and stories. This book is written in both English and Spanish and is sure to spark many conversations in the classroom and at home about children's own "family pictures." Lee and Low Books has a teacher's guide to accompany this book available on their website (https://www.leeandlow.com/books/family-pictures-cuadros-de-familia).

Applying Familial Capital

We know our families are our children's first teachers, and we can create many opportunities for families to share their expertise and funds of knowledge (Moll et al., 1992) with us. In the strategies below, we offer ideas for honoring familial capital within and beyond the classroom.

Classroom Strategies to Honor Familial Capital

- Explicitly invite students to help you learn their names. Cornwall (2022) suggests phrases like "I really want to be able to pronounce your name the way you want to hear it" or "I'd love to say your name the way your family says it. Can you help me learn to say it?" Practice the pronunciation and check back in with students frequently as you are learning. For additional ideas and resources, check out the "My Name, My Identity" website: https://www.mynamemyidentity.org/.
- Validate all kinds of family structures. Just as Samantha and Justina realized that family members love and care for you regardless of their status as blood relatives, have conversations early and often about inclusive family structures. Cowhey (2022) refers to family as "the constellation of people who love each student" (p. 34). In Melissa's kindergarten class, she used to talk about families as "a circle of people who love us." Beware of referring solely to students' "moms and dads," as this may not align with students' familial structures.
- Write classroom books about family. Early in the year, ask families to share photographs of themselves to use in a class book with predictable text that says, "This is [student name]'s family." If a photograph isn't available, students can illustrate their family so that everyone in the class is included. (Be sure to honor all of the people the child says belong in their family as they illustrate instead of responding with something like "Is that person really in your family?") Print a copy for the classroom library and watch this book become a popular checkout selection! Additionally, use Google Slides to make digital books that you can share with families free of cost, like in Figure 5.1.
- Create a family cookbook. Ask families to share a favorite recipe. Combine these recipes into a class family cookbook. Use it in class to learn concepts like counting, measurement, sequencing, and simple fractions, and share it with families to encourage them to try another family's favorite recipe!

This is Amira's family.

FIGURE 5.1 Creating family books with Google Slides. "Village family" by KX studio is licensed under CC BY 2.0.

If time and resources permit, families can make their dish to share with the class, but be aware of students' allergies and dietary restrictions. (Also, remember that food is just one aspect of culture. While food holds a special place in many family and cultural traditions, avoid reducing a family or culture to just their food!)
- Curate books that portray multiple family structures and the support that characters receive from families. During interactive read alouds, ask questions like "Who was in this character's family? What does this character learn from their family? What were some problems this character faced with their family, and how were those problems resolved?" Relate the books to students' own lives with questions such as "Who is in your family? How are our families the same and different? What is something your family does to help you, and how do you help them?"

Family Strategies to Honor Familial Capital

- To honor a family's naming decision for their child, explicitly ask them for models of pronouncing their child's name. This can be done during conversations at beginning-of-the-year "Meet the Teacher" events, or you can leverage technology to invite families to make recordings of their child's name. One benefit to recording pronunciations is the ability to listen back and practice the child's name without inconveniencing the family or child.
- When communicating with families, use intentional language. "Family" is more inclusive than "parent/guardian." Even something as seemingly inconsequential as beginning a letter with "Dear Families" instead of "Dear Parents/Guardians" can send a clear message about who is welcome as family in your classroom and beyond.
- Schedule events where other family members are welcome! If you are hosting a celebration of learning, be sure to invite other family members—including younger siblings—and to plan activities to keep family members of all ages engaged and welcome.
- Be aware of limitations on some traditionally framed "family days." "Muffins for Moms," "Donuts for Dads," and even "Grandparents' Day" can be exciting times for young children to share their school experiences with loved ones. However, what happens if a child lives with an extended family member, has two dads, or has grandparents who live far away? Consider reframing "family days" to be more inclusive. In fact, simply calling them "Family Days" would be inclusive of all kinds of families! Furthermore, consider if technology could assist with family engagement for these events. For example, students could use Zoom or other videoconferencing platforms to invite a family member into the classroom who might not have the time or physical resources necessary to be physically present.

Conclusion

Familial capital, the cultural knowledge shaped among **familia** that hold a "sense of community history, memory, and cultural intuition" (Yosso, 2005, p. 79), is built upon relationships. **Familia**, as we saw in the episodes, includes both the family one is born into and the family one creates while going through life. In the opening vignette, two young girls, Justina and Samantha, engaged in a conversation about family. Samantha wondered about Justina's grandmother since she had not seen her lately. Justina shared that although the woman is not her real grandmother, she calls her "**abuela**." They spend a lot of time together and she even takes care of her when her mother is working. Samantha's response, **"Eso no importa. Ella te quiere y te cuida. No tiene que tener tu sangre para ser tu familia. ¿Qué más quieres?"**/ *That does not matter. She loves you and takes care of you. She does not need to have your blood to be your family. What else do you want?*, raises an important issue: blood alone does not make a family. For people living away from family members, it is important and necessary to have relationships with people you trust. The emotional support and love provided by others is necessary to thrive anywhere, and particularly when in unfamiliar surroundings. Schools need to recognize and validate the various family structures students are a part of and view them as sites of support, love, and importance.

Additional Resources

Children's Literature

The following 16 award-winning picturebooks address themes related to familial capital. For a complete list of picturebooks and other areas of community cultural wealth these books may contain, see Appendix A.

Alma and How She Got Her Name (Martinez-Neal, 2018)

Alma Sofia Esperanza José Pura Candela is not a fan of her very long name. When she complains to her father, he explains the long line of family members before her that inspired her very special names. This exploration of familial capital also invites the reader to investigate the origins of their own names (Américas Award, 2019 Commended Title; Caldecott Medal, 2019 Honor Book).

A Gift from Abuela (Ruiz, 2018)

Abuela and Niña love spending time together. Abuela decides to save her **pesos** to buy Niña a special gift, but as the years go by, her plan to save faces many unexpected interruptions. This book addresses familial capital by focusing on the never-ending value of something all the **pesos** in the world could never buy: Abuela's and Niña's love-filled relationship (Américas Award, 2019 Commended Title).

Going Down Home with Daddy (Lyons, 2019)

Lil Alan and his family go "down home" for their family reunion, filled with special events and "love-made dishes," but he is worried that he will not have something special enough to share during the family celebration at the end of the weekend. In time, Lil Alan creates a tribute to the ancestors that came before him. He realizes the power of his familial capital: nothing is more important than family (Caldecott Medal, 2020 Honor Book).

When Aidan Became a Brother (Lukoff, 2019)

When Aidan was born, everyone thought he was a girl, but he knew he was another kind of boy. Then he found out he was going to become a big brother, so Aidan begins preparing to be the best big brother he can be, regardless of who his baby sibling may be. Aidan realizes that loving someone is the most important part of being a brother. This book's familial capital lies in the importance of loving people for who they are, and it incorporates transgender and gender-neutral themes in approachable ways (Stonewall Book Award—Mike Morgan and Larry Romans Children's and Young Adult Literature Award, 2020 Winner).

The Remember Balloons (Oliveros, 2018)

Familial capital involves strong networks of love and support, but sometimes families encounter challenging situations such as aging. This book uses the metaphor of balloons to stand for memories. Grandpa likes to tell his grandson about what's in his balloons, but then his balloons start drifting away. At the end of the story, the grandson realizes that even though Grandpa has lost his own balloons, they aren't gone for good. The aging process—including memory loss—is an unfortunate reality for many families, and this book is a powerful example of the importance of addressing such challenges in honest but child-friendly ways (Schneider Family Book Award, Younger Children Honor Title 2019).

My Grandma and Me (Javaherbin, 2019)

In this beautifully illustrated children's book, the author recalls her own memories of growing up while her grandmother lived with her family in Iran. They did many things together, including sewing, playing, going to the mosque, and celebrating Ramadan. Mina never loved anyone like her grandma and she wanted to be just like her. This book captures the familial capital of learning cultural practices from elders—and, of course, the timeless tradition of love (Middle East Book Award, 2019 Picture Book Honorable Mention).

Along the Tapajós (Vilela, 2019)

On the Tapajós River in Brazil, families live in houses on stilts during the dry season, and they move to the forest to stay dry during the wet season. This book follows a family as they relocate to the forest together, but have to return to their stilted house for an important mission: to save their pet tortoise, who accidentally got left behind when they left. In addition to showing a family's bond, this book shows how people live in the rainforest, which may be a topic few children have read about in other books (Américas Award, 2020 Commended Title).

All Around Us (González, 2017)

A grandfather and his granddaughter work together in the garden and find all kinds of circles around them, including cycles of life and death. They also discuss that what they take from the earth, they return, such as the ashes of ancestors in the backyard. This book demonstrates the familial capital of a grandfather and granddaughter sharing understandings of life together (Tomás Rivera Mexican American Children's Book Award, 2018 Winner).

Double Bass Blues (Loney, 2019)

With examples of onomatopoeia throughout, this book follows Nic as he makes music with his double bass in different spaces, such as in the orchestra at school and on the city street near his home. But his favorite is making music with Granddaddy (Caldecott Medal, 2020 Honor Book).

Julián Is a Mermaid (Love, 2018)

Julián loves mermaids, and he dreams of dressing up as a mermaid after he sees three women dressed up as mermaids on the subway with his abuela. His abuela helps him dress like a mermaid and find other mermaids just like him (Stonewall Book Award—Mike Morgan and Larry Romans Children's and Young Adult Literature Award, 2019 Winner).

May Your Life Be Deliciosa (Genhart, 2021)

Rosie's family has a tradition each Christmas Eve: they gather with Abuela and share stories and make tamales together. As they make tamales, Abuela compares each step of the process with the wishes she has for her family members' well-being throughout their lives (Pura Belpré Children's Youth Illustrator Award, 2022 Honor Title).

Watercress (Wang, 2021)

When a little girl and her family are driving in the car one day and see watercress on the side of the road, everyone stops and gets out to help pick watercress. When it's time to eat the watercress they picked and cooked, though, the little girl is embarrassed that they are eating food they got for free. Her mom talks about how her family ate watercress to survive in China during the famine, and the family makes new memories as they eat watercress together (Caldecott Medal 2022, Honor Title; Newbery Medal 2022, Honor Title).

Grandad's Camper (Woodgate, 2021)

Grandad and Gramps loved to go on adventures together in their camper. Since Gramps died, though, Grandad hasn't wanted to go on adventures. After hearing stories about their adventures, their granddaughter has an idea to help Grandad go on adventures again. This book showcases the power of families to make memories together, even once family members have passed away (Stonewall Book Award—Mike Morgan and Larry Romans Children's and Young Adult Literature Award, 2022 Honor).

I Sang You Down from the Stars (Spillet-Sumner, 2021)

In this beautifully illustrated picturebook, a mother starts to collect gifts to put into her future baby's sacred bundle, gifts that will connect the baby to their Indigenous culture and community. The author identifies as Cree and Trinidadian, and the illustrator identifies as Tlingit and Haida (American Indian Youth Literature Award, 2022 Picture Book Honor Book).

We Wait for the Sun (Roundtree & McCabe, 2021)

Dovey Mae and Grandma Rachel pick blackberries together in the dark woods. Near the end of their time spent picking berries, they get to see the darkness dissipate as they enjoy the sunrise together (Coretta Scott King Book Award, 2022 Illustrator Honor Book).

Soul Food Sunday (Bingham, 2021)

Every Sunday, the whole family gathers at Granny's for soul food. The little boy gets to learn the traditions of cooking soul food alongside his Granny, even adding his own surprise: his own sweet tea recipe (Coretta Scott King Book Award, 2022 Illustrator Honor Book).

Digital Tools

Digital tools that provide a "window" for families to see into their child's learning experience at school are becoming increasingly popular. Whenever possible, leverage digital tools to allow families to share their learning experiences at home too. Knowledge grows in all kinds of environments, not just at school. Digital tools offer unique opportunities to engage many family members in different ways. Table 5.1 offers a few suggestions of digital tools that connect to familial capital.

TABLE 5.1 Digital Tools: Familial Capital

Tool	Description
Digital Surveys (i.e., Google Forms, Microsoft Forms, SurveyMonkey, etc.)	Digital surveys can invite families to share their expertise with classroom teachers—after all, families are our children's first teachers! Consider using a beginning-of-the-year "Family Tips for Success" survey to get to know your students and their families. Using a digital version allows families to complete the survey at their convenience, and having a printed version would support families who prefer a pencil-and-paper modality. Possible questions to include: • What is the best way for me to contact you? (i.e., phone call, text, email, written note, other) • Who is in your family (including pets)? Children often tell us stories about these important people, so knowing how to spell family members' names will help us out! • What holidays do you celebrate or not celebrate? • What motivates your child? Upsets them? • What learning goals do you have for your child? • What does your child love to learn about? • What would you like to teach or share with our class? (i.e., guest speaker, volunteer, guest reader, etc.)
Google Slides	Google Slides can be a free way to make digital books. You can either provide view-only access if you'd like to assemble the books based on family contributions, or you can set the sharing settings so that anyone with the link can edit. That way, families can work together to write their own page for a class book! Teachers will need a Google account to access Google Slides, but families will not need Google accounts to view or edit documents if the sharing settings allow anyone with the link to view or edit. Google Slides can be downloaded or made accessible offline, making them available even without an internet connection. (As a caution, Google Slides does require the app to be downloaded for editing access on mobile devices, which may be a challenge if families have limited storage remaining on phones or tablets.)

References

Cornwall, C. (2022). What's in a name: Pronouncing kids' names correctly matters. Here's how to get it right. *School Library Journal, 68*(9), 28–32.

Cowhey, M. (2022). *Families with power: Centering students by engaging with families and community*. Teachers College Press.

Delgado-Gaitan, C. (2001). *The power of community: Mobilizing for family and schooling*. Rowman & Littlefield Publishers, Inc.

Edwards, P. A. (2016). *New ways to engage parents: Strategies and tools for teachers and leaders, K-12*. Teachers College Press.

Ek, L. D. (2005). Staying on God's path: Socializing Latino immigrant youth to a Christian Pentecostal identity in Southern California. In A. C. Zentella (Ed.), *Building on strengths: Language and literacy in Latino families and communities* (pp. 77–92). Teachers College Press.

González, N., Moll, L. C., & Amanti, C. (Eds.). (2005). *Funds of knowledge: Theorizing practices in households, communities, and classrooms*. Routledge.

López-Robertson, J. (2017). Diciendo cuentos/Telling stories: Learning from and about the community cultural wealth of Latina mamás through Latino children's literature. *Language Arts, 95*(1), 7–16.

López-Robertson, J., & Haney, M. J. (2021). Toward culturally sustaining pedagogy: Engagements with Latina mothers through Latino/Latina children's literature. In K. Nash, C. Glover, & B. Polson (Eds.), *Toward culturally sustaining teaching: Early childhood educators honor children with practices for equity and change* (pp. 61–81). National Council of Teachers of English/Routledge.

Magaña, A. (2022). *If you can pronounce Daenerys Targaryen, then you can learn to say my Latin American Name*. Huffpost. https://www.huffpost.com/entry/pronounce-names-correctly-people-of-color_n_632b679ce4b09d8701bba8cd#

Menjívar, C. (2016). Immigrant criminalization in law and the media: Effects on Latino immigrant workers' identities in Arizona. *American Behavioral Scientist, 60*(5–6), 597–616.

Moll, L., Amanti, C., Neff, D., & González, N. (1992). Funds of knowledge for teaching: Using a qualitative approach to connect homes and classrooms. *Theory into Practice, 31*, 132–141.

Villenas, S., & Deyhle, D. (1999). Critical race theory and ethnographies challenging the stereotypes: Latino families, schooling, resilience and resistance. *Curriculum Inquiry, 29*(4), 413–445.

Yosso, T. J. (2005). Whose culture has capital? A critical race theory discussion of community cultural wealth. *Race Ethnicity and Education, 8*(1), 69–91. doi: http://doi.org/10.1080/1361332052000341006.

Children's Literature

Bingham, W. (2021). *Soul food Sunday* (C. G. Esperanza, Illus.). Abrams Books for Young Readers.

Ewald, W. (2002). *The best part of me: Children talk about their bodies in pictures and words*. Little Brown Books.

Garza, C. L. (1998). *Family pictures/Cuadros de mi familia* (C. L. Garza, Illus.). Lee & Low Books.

Garza, C. L. (2000). *In my family/En mi familia* (C. L. Garza, Illus.). Lee & Low Books.
Genhart, M. (2021). *May your life be deliciosa* (L. Lora, Illus.). Abrams Books for Young Readers.
González, X. (2017). *All around us* (A. M. Garcia, Illus.). Cinco Puntos Press.
Javaherbin, M. (2019). *My grandma and me* (L. Yankey, Illus.). Candlewick.
Loney, A. J. (2019). *Double bass blues* (R. Gutierrez, Illus.). Knopf Books for Young Readers.
Love, J. (2018). *Julián is a mermaid* (J. Love, Illus.). Candlewick.
Lukoff, K. (2019). *When Aidan became a brother* (K. Juanita, Illus.). Lee & Low Books.
Lyons, K. S. (2019). *Going down home with daddy* (D. Minter, Illus.). Peachtree.
Martinez-Neal, J. (2018). *Alma and how she got her name* (J. Martinez-Nea, Illus.). Candlewick.
Oliveros, J. (2018). *The remember balloons* (D. Wulfekotte, Illus.). Simon & Schuster Books for Young Readers.
Roundtree, D. J., & McCabe, K. (2021). *We wait for the sun* (R. Figueroa, Illus.). Roaring Brook Press.
Ruiz, C. (2018). *A gift from abuela* (C. Ruiz, Illus.). Candlewick.
Spillet-Sumner, T. (2021). *I sang you down from the stars* (M. Goade, Illus.). Little, Brown and Company.
Vilela, F. (2019). *Along the Tapajós* (F. Vilela, Illus.). Amazon Crossing Kids.
Wang, A. (2021). *Watercress* (J. Chin, Illus.). Neal Porter Books.
Woodgate, H. (2021). *Grandad's camper* (H. Woodgate, Illus.). Little Bee Books.

6
TOGETHER IN COMUNIDAD
Social Capital

Sitting at Julia's table while waiting for the curriculum night to begin, the mothers talked with Julia about the recent closing of a meat packing plant and the impact it had on some of the community members. Sarai talked about her family's decision to move to a new city within the United States, a decision based on financial benefits (**"era mejor el sueldo"**/*the pay was better*) and on the fact that she had family with already-established ties to the community.

> **Carmelita nos avisó que estaban buscando trabajadores allá en la factoría con Gustavo. Era mejor el sueldo y tenemos familia aquí. Fue una decisión fácil porque aquí están mis primas, hermanos, y unas comadres muy buenas. ¡Como que ellos ya se establecieron, yo solo hice lo que me dijeron, no tuve que preocuparme de lo que no sabía, porque ellos me guiaron en cada paso!** / *Carmelita told us that the factory where Gustavo works was looking for workers. The pay was better, and we had family here. It was an easy decision to make because my cousins, siblings, and good friends were here. Since they had already established themselves [here], I simply did what they told me. I did not have to worry about what I didn't know, because they guided me every step of the way.*

Moving in and of itself is a stressful endeavor; one must contact the utility companies, garbage collection, and figure out transportation to and from work and school. Imagine doing this when you are new to the country and language! This is a daunting experience, and yet immigrant families persevere and engage in these activities, often confronting racism. How do families new to the United States and to the English language steer their way through this sometimes-hostile terrain? It is often done with the help of family and/or community members who have shared similar experiences.

The move was made a little easier because, as Sarai noted, **"no tuve que preocuparme de lo que no sabía"** / *I did not have to worry about what I didn't know*, since her family and **comadres**/*close friends* were already here. Sarai added that she received guidance from her family and friends, her support network, every step of the way in the transition to her new community. As noted by Yosso and García (2007), these peer and other social contacts provided both instrumental and emotional support, which in turn helped residents navigate society's institutions.

In this chapter, we will analyze social capital. How do families build networks that allow them to gain support needed in diverse situations and contexts?

Social Capital

Yosso (2005) explains that social capital consists of "networks of people and community resources" (p. 79) such as those utilized by families to gain access to school and the services provided by the school and community. This networked emotional support helps minoritized communities navigate society and its various structures, many of which are not set up for success for individuals outside of the mainstream cultural norms. People of Color have traditionally used their social capital to gain access to healthcare, employment, justice in the legal system, and education. Furthermore, Yosso (2005) adds that "these Communities of Color give the information and resources they gained through these institutions back to their social networks" (pp. 79–80) to help others move forward. Therefore, social capital is engagement in social networks and entails an ever-evolving, collaboratively built, and an ongoing network of support.

Cuentos from the Field: Social Capital in Action

Monkman et al. (2005) suggest that "social ties are the avenue through which cultural resources and knowledge can (potentially) be transmitted" (p. 25). These social ties are often based on religious affiliation, countries of origin, neighborhoods, children's schooling, work histories, and family. Social capital is closely connected to familial capital, and it may be difficult to distinguish between the two; as many of the families noted, **"aunque no somos sangre, somos familia"** / *Even though we are not blood [related], we are family*. In the opening excerpt, Sarai explained how she and her husband came to the United States; they learned of employment opportunities at Gustavo's place of work through the connection with Carmelita, a close family friend from their country of origin. Identified as intangible resources embedded within communities, relationships, or social institutions, we found social capital evidenced in the episodes that follow through societal norms, information networks, and expectations and responsibilities.

Episode One: Societal Norms

Societal norms are unwritten rules that govern how people act. Everyone follows societal norms; it is important to note, however, that societal norms differ across communities. Simply because someone does not follow *your* societal norm does not mean *they* are wrong. So, in the case of schooling, when we think families are not acting "as they should," this is due to an invisible societal norm; furthermore, they are likely enacting their own societal norms.

A common societal norm is that students must respect their teachers and obediently do as they are told. Angelica shared her confusion about an incident in school involving her daughter, Kayla. Angelica explained that Kayla was told to go to the hallway to work with a group of students. Kayla respectfully asked her teacher if she could work with another group, and was told, "No, do as you are told." Kayla repeated her request and was sent to the principal's office as her teacher became exasperated with Kayla's refusal to "do as she was told." Kayla was assigned detention for the infraction.

Angelica: **Yo no entiendo porque castigaron a mi niña. Los chamacos son muy malos con ella. Yo he hablado con la directora varias veces acerca del modo que tratan a la niña. ¡La maestra sabe que hay problemas y todavía manda a la niña a trabajar con ellos—y en el pasillo donde nadie puede ver lo que está pasando!** / *I do not understand why Kayla was punished. The children do not treat her well. I have spoken with the principal many times about the way they treat her. The teacher knows that there are issues and yet she still sent Kayla to work with them—and in the hallway where no one can see what is going on!*

Marisol: **No, Angelica. Eso no, no se deje. Kayla no es grosera y esos chamacos sí son feos. Yo misma los he visto.** / *No, Angelica. No, do not let them do this. Kayla is not rude, and those children are ugly to her. I have seen it myself.*

Angelica: **Kayla sabe que tiene que obedecer a la maestra y también sabe que se tiene que defender. Yo sé que ella no le falto el respeto a la maestra.** / *Kayla knows that she needs to obey her teacher and she also knows that she needs to defend herself. I know she was not disrespectful to the teacher.*

Angelica's lack of understanding of the situation stems from the fact that both the principal and teacher are keenly aware that the students assigned to work with Kayla have not been kind to her, an issue that Kayla and Angelica have raised repeatedly with the principal and teacher. Marisol, who has a child in the same class, supports Angelica by reminding her that she has witnessed the children's treatment of Kayla. She encourages Angelica to take action and not to let them punish Kayla for standing up for herself. Angelica states that Kayla knows the societal norm of obeying her teacher and adds that she also knows that she must defend herself. Sometimes families do not follow societal norms not because they do not want to but because they do not share those norms and expectations (Monkman et al., 2005); if the norm is to "do as you are told" even when you know something is wrong, Kayla has been taught the societal norm of standing up for yourself.

Episode Two: Information Networks

Information networks are the groups of people who provide instrumental support by making connections to services, agencies, and other people. These networks aid with finding housing, managing school, learning about the community and services that are available, and allaying concerns about safety. Families (people who are blood related and not blood related) may feel a sense of relief once they realize someone has already broken ground in this new community, paving the way for them and making things a bit easier. These networks are particularly helpful because, as noted in the opening, making the move to the United States can be a harrowing experience.

Not all people are as fortunate as Sarai was in the opening vignette in transitioning from one place to another. When people come to the United States (or move within the United States), they may not always make that move as planned. In the excerpt below, Sofia shares how she and her family members were separated during their travels; she was left to survive in a foreign country where she did not know anyone and did not speak English.

> **Vine con mis primos, pero nos separaron. Yo ande sola por unos seis meses. Llegue aquí totalmente sola. Por suerte conocí a Matilde. Ella me llevo a su casa, y me ayudo con todo. Me enseñó donde encontrar recursos. No sé lo que hubiese hecho sin ella. Es mi angelito guardián.** / *I came with my cousins, but they separated us. I was alone for about six months. I arrived completely alone. Luckily, I met Matilde. She took me to her home and helped me with everything. She taught her where to find resources. I don't know what I would have done without her. She is my guardian angel.*

Sofia explains that she was "completely alone" for six months. One can imagine the emotional stress she must have been under; traveling to a foreign country, being separated from family/traveling partners, not knowing anyone, and not knowing the language. After six months of travel, Sofia arrived in the community and through the network was connected to the local church which provided temporary housing (six months, longer in extreme cases) for recent arrivals and helped them settle in the new community. The church held various community events, English classes, and provided other services. It was at an event held by the church that Sofia first met Matilde. They continued to see each other at church events, attended English and sewing classes together, and eventually became friends. Close to the time when Matilde knew that Sofia would need to move out of the church, she asked Sofia to move into her home. Sofia agreed but only if she could "**contribuir**"/*contribute* to the household; "**quiero trabajar**"/*I want to work*.

Matilde solicited help from her network, a group of women from the church and local community, and was able to find Sofia work cleaning homes and sewing. The **comadres**, as Sofia calls her good friends, used their community connections to support her; they "exchanged knowledge, skills, and tools and provided both instrumental and emotional support" (Yosso & García, 2007, p. 162). Pérez Huber's (2009) study examined the way that Latina undergraduates drew from their community cultural wealth to survive higher education. In much the same way, the **comadres** demonstrated that it is "because of the social resources present in their families and communities" (p. 718) that they were able to provide support to Sofia and help survive in a new country.

Episode Three: Expectations and Responsibilities

The research is clear: when families engage in their children's schooling, the children's academics improve (Baquedano-López et al., 2013; Delgado Gaitan, 2001; Edwards, 2016; Mapp et al., 2017). A major consideration when discussing family participation in their child's schooling is that the "knowledge of what and how parents need to negotiate with the school to advocate for their children is often culturally bound" (Delgado Gaitan, 2014, p. 339); some families simply do not know what schools expect of them. Families from working-class backgrounds tend to view the school as the teacher's domain and see the academic development of their children as the teacher's responsibility (González, 2006; Lareau, 2000; Yosso & García, 2022). To complicate things further, most schools are not clear in explaining their expectations to families.

Social capital provides families access to complex networks of support that exist within their community and family and that are critically important for student success. Families who have older children enrolled in school help those with younger children in understanding what is expected in school. Information gained by one family is shared with all families in the network; the information is given back to the community.

An expectation schools have of families, particularly in the early grades, is that they spend time reading with their child every night. There are several reasons why this may not be possible for many families. In the excerpt below, Griselda and Anais, two mothers of first-grade children, discuss this expectation.

Griselda: **La semana pasada fui a la conferencia con la maestra. Me dijo que Betsy estaba atrasada en la lectura. Que se le hace difícil leer.** / *I went to the parent–teacher conference last week. The teacher told me that Betsy was behind in reading. It is difficult for her to read.*

Anais: **A mí me dijo lo mismo de Eduardo. ¿Qué hacemos?** / *She told me the same about Eduardo. What do we do?*

Griselda: **Estaba la maestra de inglés también y me dijeron que le lea a la niña todas las noches.** / *The ESL teacher was there too, and they said that I had to read to Betsy every night.*

Anais: **Pero Grisi, tu inventas unos cuentos fantásticos y a todos los chamacos les encantan. Cada vez que nos juntamos, allí se sientan para oír tus cuentos. Eso vale también.** / *But Grisi, you create the most fantastic stories, and all the children love them. Every time we get together, there they sit to hear your stories. That [storytelling] also counts [as reading].*

Griselda: **Gracias, me encanta inventar los cuentos, así lo hacía mi mamá. ¡Claro que eso vale, para nosotros, pero no para la maestra! Bueno allá sí, pero aquí no [vale].** / *Thank you, I love creating stories, my mom did it too. Of course, it [storytelling] counts, for us, but not for the teacher! Well, it counts there [home country] but not here [the United States].*

Anais: **No entiendo porque no cuenta hacerle un cuento en vez de leer un libro. Además, no sé leer en inglés, y no tengo libros en español. Cuanto no quisiera yo sentarme a leer con Eduardo, pero no tengo tiempo.** / *I don't understand how it does not count to tell a story instead of reading one from a book. Also, I don't know how to read in English, and I don't have any books in Spanish. How I wouldn't love to sit and read with Eduardo, but I don't have the time.*

Griselda: **Yo lo quisiera hacer también, pero, a mí me pasa lo mismo. Como que estaba la maestra de inglés, le pregunte que si me podía mandar libros en español. Le explique que no sé leer en inglés, pero en español sí puedo.** / *I would love to do it too [sit and read] but I have the same issue. Since the ESL teacher was there, I asked if they could send home books in Spanish. I explained that I do not know how to read in English, but I can read in Spanish.*

Anais: **¿Y qué te dijo? Grisi, si tienes libros en español, préstame unos para leer con el niño.** / *And what did she say? Grisi, if you have books in Spanish, share them with me so I can read with Eduardo.*

Griselda: **¿Qué me dijo? Para no enojarme de nuevo, te digo la versión corta. No tenemos libros en español. Solamente tenemos**

	libros en inglés. Los niños necesitan leer en inglés. / *What did she say? So that I don't get angry all over again, I will give you the short version. We don't have Spanish books. We only have English books. The children need to read in English.*
Anais:	**Grisi, pero ¿qué fue eso? Me parece un poco grosera. No me gusta para nada.** / *Grisi, what was that? Seems a little rude to me. I don't like it at all.*
Griselda:	**Me quede bien calladita al oír eso. Voy a hablar con la comadre a ver como se las arregló cuando Estefanía estaba en la clase con esta maestra.** / *I was super quiet once I heard that response. I am going to speak to my comadre to see what she did when Estefania was in this same class.*

At the beginning of the excerpt, Griselda shares with Anais that the teacher told her she needed to read with Betsy for her reading to improve. Both questioned why Griselda's storytelling did not count as reading: they decided that in their home countries oral storytelling counted, but that here in the United States, it was about book reading. Anais then explained some of the issues she had with reading aloud to her son, Eduardo: she did not have books in Spanish, she did not know how to read in English, and that she simply did not have the time to sit and read with her child. These are common reasons why many Spanish-speaking families are unable to read with their children.

Griselda then shared that since the English as a Second Language (ESL) teacher was present (she was acting as the translator), she took advantage of her being there to request that the school send home books written in Spanish. She explained that she would be able to read those with her child. Anais was excited at the prospect of having books to read to her child and asked Griselda to share any books that she obtained from school.

Griselda warned Anais that she did not want to get angry all over again and that she would provide her with the short version of the response. The teacher told Griselda that there were no books available in Spanish, there were books available only in English, and that the children should learn to read in English. Anais was surprised by the response and noted that it was rude. Griselda agreed and then decided that she would speak to her comadre and find out how she dealt with this teacher while her child, Estefania, was in that class a few years ago.

Griselda is using her support network to figure out her next steps in helping her child's reading improvement. Whatever information she gathers, she will share with Anais and any other families dealing with similar situations. Therefore, Griselda is using her social capital to support not only her daughter's literacy development, but also other children's literacy development in her local community through the support networks she has constructed.

When we approach literacy instruction with community cultural wealth in mind, we realize that we must revisit social norms to re-envision asset-based possibilities for *all* our families. In the dialogue above, there were two key assumptions about literacy instruction that prevented families from enacting their community cultural wealth: daily read-alouds as a universal practice and the need for literacy activities to be in English only.

First, the classroom and ESL teachers both assumed that nightly read alouds at home were a universal literacy practice; however, this assumption is culturally biased. Cowhey (2022) shared an interaction from a parent–teacher conference after she (the teacher) had explained the benefits of reading aloud to children every day, when the mother replied:

> I trust you when you say that it will help [my child] if I read aloud to him every day. But you need to listen and hear me when I tell you this "read aloud" is not part of my culture. My parents had fifteen children. No one ever read to me. There were no libraries. I do not have this culture.
> *(Cowhey, 2022, p. 57)*

The mother Cowhey (2022) met with was aware that literacy practices are culturally situated, despite the mistaken assumption of many teachers that certain practices (like reading aloud daily) are common across cultures. As Anais noted, while daily read alouds weren't part of Griselda's family literacy practices, storytelling was. If research has indicated that reading aloud daily supports young children's literacy development, has parallel research looked at other manifestations of shared literacy, including storytelling, that also impact young children's literacy development? How did reading aloud become a common practice in early childhood literacy instruction instead of storytelling, for example?

Second, Griselda recounted the teacher's requirement: "the children need to read in English." If the teacher's goal is to help her students succeed in reading, they should be using all the tools available—that includes accessing books in Spanish, which families like Griselda's *can* read due to their linguistic capital (as discussed in Chapter 4). The teacher's response that reading must be done in English in order to support the child's literacy development is a prime example that "institutional racism is not only characterized by race; it is also based on ethnicity, language, color, gender, sexuality, poverty, and immigration status" (Delgado Bernal & Alemán, 2017, p. 25).

If schools have social norms that expect families will participate actively in their child's learning, then schools need to explain explicitly what is involved in these expectations and social norms and then provide the tools families need to be successful. When intentionally engaging families in their children's education, they become "agents who can intervene and advocate on behalf of their children, and who can make adaptations and resist barriers to education" (Baquedano-López et al. 2013, p. 150). Griselda used her social capital to explore within her own "networks of people and community resources"

(Yosso, 2005, p. 79) how to use her own assets—including storytelling and multilingualism—to support the literacy development of her own child and other children in the community.

> **FEATURED CHILDREN'S LITERATURE WITH SOCIAL CAPITAL**
>
> Khan, H. (2018). *Crescent moons and pointed minarets* (M. Amini, Illus.). Chronicle Books.
>
> With vibrant illustrations, this book highlights common shapes in a space with significant social impact for some students: the mosque. Readers learn not only shapes but also common traditions affiliated with attending a mosque. This book honors the social capital and connections built within shared religious spaces, specifically the mosque.

Applying Social Capital

Social capital depends on building networks of people and community resources. In the strategies below, we offer suggestions for building these networks through classroom instruction and family engagement opportunities.

Classroom Strategies to Honor Social Capital

- Model social networking to support peers and collaboratively solve problems. If a student is struggling with a certain challenge in class, facilitate connections: "I saw Andira trying to do that just yesterday! Let's go ask her how she solved that problem." This response models for students that it is normal to need to ask for support, and often there are other members of our social networks who are positioned to offer that exact support.
- Use problem-based learning in the classroom, highlighting how different students come to different solutions using different resources. For example, use STEM design challenges that ask students to think critically to solve a specific problem. Consider hosting a STEM challenge family night.
- Infuse collaborative learning into the classroom whenever possible. Explicitly name skills you see children practicing during successful collaborative learning ("I see how Zsuzsa asked her partner what they thought before sharing her experience") and teach others. Collaborative learning expands students' worldviews by allowing them to realize the way they perceive situations is just one perspective, not necessarily the only or "right" perspective.

Family Strategies to Honor Social Capital

- Give families formal and informal spaces for building community and supporting each other. Build these spaces *with*, not *for* families. Your families' needs for social networking may differ each year, or even during various parts of the year. In-person opportunities to gather before or after school may be beneficial, or digital groups using tools like WhatsApp may be preferred. If the teacher is invited to be a member of this space, be aware of positionality: teachers should be guests and listeners in such spaces, not just leaders and managers, to create power-sharing, dialectical spaces for social capital to flourish.
- Ask families to suggest classroom visitors from their own social networks. Teachers are expected to plan learning experiences that meet specific learning targets, but families are important partners in planning culturally relevant learning opportunities. Consider using a newsletter, family planning meetings, or preexisting social networking opportunities (explained above) to seek input from families and modify instruction accordingly.
- Explicitly model and teach families literacy practices that are part of traditional American early childhood literacy experiences, but also ask families for their own (like storytelling). When we explicitly teach and model, invisible social norms become visible. While we do not advocate for assimilation—requiring all families to practice literacy in the same way—the reality is that literacy is validated and enacted in very specific ways in many early childhood spaces, and families deserve to be informed of these practices. At the same time, though, we can decolonize expectations by adding additional elements to literacy instruction, like a daily or weekly storytelling time for members of students' social networks.
- One common "social network" for families in schools are Parent–Teacher Organizations (PTO) or Parent–Teacher Associations (PTA). However, these organizations are typically more approachable for White, middle-class families with multiple caregivers at home, due to structural considerations like meeting times and types of activities (Cowhey, 2022). Listen to families to make modifications to PTO/PTA operations to be more inclusive, but also accepting that some families—especially families who do not see themselves and their needs reflected in the PTO/PTA—may choose to build separate social networks to advocate for themselves and their children.

Conclusion

In this chapter, we heard how social networks, with their "**angelitos guardianes**"/*guardian angels*, removed worries and offered opportunities to process hardships because of their constant guidance and presence. Individuals and families learn early on that it is these networks that they form that provide them with the greatest support "because unauthorized immigrants have less access to social services and postsecondary education, their job options are more limited and they may be less able to incorporate successfully into the broader community" (Gándara & Contreras, 2009, p. 3). For this reason, these networks are vital to their survival. While not family in the sense of blood relations, this kinship becomes a lifeline and group they depend on and contribute to. Furthermore, as Yosso and García (2007) note, social networks provide support to navigate societal institutions, which will be discussed in the next chapter.

Additional Resources

Children's Literature

The following 16 award-winning picturebooks address themes related to social capital. For a complete list of picturebooks and other areas of community cultural wealth these books may contain, see Appendix A.

Across the Bay (Aponte, 2019)

Carlitos lives in a charming little town, but his papi lives in the city across the bay. Carlitos takes a ferry across the bay in search of his father, asking varied community members he encounters along his journey if they know his papi. In this story, Carlitos uses networks of people and community resources—his social capital—to search for his papi (Pura Belpré Award, 2020 Illustrator Honor).

Islandborn (Díaz, 2018)

Lola's teacher asks the class to draw the country you're originally from, but Lola left the Dominican Republic when she was a baby and can't remember what it was like. Instead, Lola turns to her family and social networks to construct communal memories of her home country to share with her peers. The book is available in both English and Spanish (Américas Award, 2019 Winner; Pura Belpré Award, 2019 Illustration Honor).

The Cat Man of Aleppo (Latham and Shamsi-Basha, 2020)

In this true story, Mohammad Alaa Aljaleel uses his social networks, such as collaborating with neighbors, to care for the cats left behind by families who fled Aleppo during the war. In addition to establishing a sanctuary for the abandoned cats, he also built a playground for children in the community (Caldecott Medal, 2021 Honor Book).

Thank You, Omu! (Mora, 2018)

Omu is making stew, and the delicious smells make their way to the neighbors. Omu shares the stew with the neighbors, who later return to pay back this kind gesture through their own offerings. This book depicts social capital by showing how the community networks result in sharing resources, including stew (Caldecott Medal, 2019 Honor Book).

Crown: An Ode to the Fresh Cut (Barnes, 2017)

Barbershops have a long history as community resources where social connections are built and fostered, especially in the Black community. This story follows a boy as he gets a fresh cut alongside other members of his community, all of whom leaving feeling "magnificent, flawless, like royalty" (Caldecott Medal, 2018 Honor Book; Newbery Medal, 2018 Honor Book).

A Friend for Henry (Bailey, 2019)

Henry has been looking for a friend in his classroom at school. One day, though, all the activity overwhelms him and his needs as a person with autism, it starts to seem like he will never find a friend—but then his social networks come together (Schneider Family Book Award, Younger Children Honor Title 2020).

Rescue & Jessica: A Life-changing Friendship (Kensky, 2018)

Rescue is in training to be a Seeing Eye dog, but his trainer says being a service dog will be a better fit for him. Jessica is in the hospital, recovering from an injury that caused part of her left leg to be removed. Based on a true story, this book follows both characters as their social networks prepare them for a future where they can support each other (Schneider Family Book Award, Younger Children Winner 2019).

Birdsong (Flett, 2019)

Katherena and her mom have moved to a new place, and they don't know anyone yet. When she meets her next-door neighbor, Agnes, they work on the garden together and discover they share some interests, like nature, crafting, and birds. They support each other as they make salmon stew for neighbors, and then when Agnes becomes too weak to go outside, Katherena comes to hang pictures on Agnes's bedroom walls. This book shows how social networks are built and continue to evolve as individuals' needs change. In addition, the book has a glossary that defines the Cree words used throughout the text. The author/illustrator identifies as Cree-Métis (American Indian Youth Literature Award, 2020 Picture Book Honor Books).

Fry Bread: A Native American Family Story (Maillard, 2019)

Fry bread is many things: food, sound, color, and tradition. This book shares the significance of fry bread in the social and cultural traditions of many Indigenous nations. The author identifies as a member of the Seminole Nation, Mekusukey Band, and the illustrator identifies as Peruvian-American (American Indian Youth Literature Award, 2020 Picture Book Honor Books).

My Two Border Towns (Bowles, 2021)

A boy and his dad travel together between their two border towns on the U.S.–Mexico border. They visit some of their favorite spots in town as they shop for some of their family and friends. They demonstrate their social capital by building networks to help others who cannot acquire their own resources at or across the border (Américas Award, 2022 Winner; Tomás Rivera Mexican American Children's Book Award 2022).

If Dominican Were a Color (Recio, 2020)

If the Dominican Republic were a color, which ones would capture its vibrant culture? This book demonstrates the social capital of groups of people celebrating being Dominican together with vivid visual imagery (Américas Award, 2021 Honorable Mention).

Evelyn Del Rey Is Moving Away (Medina, 2020)

Daniela has a big problem: Evelyn Del Rey, her mejor amiga, is moving away. This book shows the social capital two young girls built together and implies that their connections continue, even when they are no longer neighbors (Américas Award, 2021 Commended Title).

From My Window (Júnior, 2020)

In this book, the narrator marvels at the diversity and connectedness seen outside of their window in a favela. Because favelas are controlled by residents without governmental support, this book is a beautiful depiction of social capital in all its forms (Américas Award, 2021 Commended Title).

Just Ask! Be Different, Be Brave, Be You (Sotomayor, 2019)

As Sonia and her friends plant a garden, they talk about differences: diabetes, asthma, dyslexia, autism, ADHD, allergies, and more. The friends realize a garden with just peas would not be interesting, just as a world without differences would be boring. The book reminds readers to build social networks with an important strategy: "just ask!" (Schneider Family Book Award, Young Children 2020 Winner).

Song of the Old City (Pellicioli, 2020)

As a little girl explores Istanbul, she encounters many people who bestow gifts upon her, such as hot tea, candy, and pomegranate juice. She doesn't just keep the gifts for herself: she helps others in her social network too (Middle East Book Award, 2021 Honorable Mention).

Digital Tools

TABLE 6.1 Digital Tools: Social Capital

Tool	Description
WhatsApp (https://www.whatsapp.com/)	WhatsApp is a free, secure messaging client that can be used on mobile devices and in an internet browser. WhatsApp uses an internet connection and can be used for messaging, voice messaging, voice calls, or video calls, even internationally. Families may choose to create their own groups on WhatsApp to network and solve problems together, thus aligning with social capital.
Class Tag (https://home.classtag.com/)	Class Tag is a free platform that works across platforms and devices and offers a variety of features. Families can choose their preferred method of communication (such as texts, emails, app alerts, or web-based alerts), and correspondence from the teacher will arrive in whichever venue the family prefers. It also offers automatic translation into over 100 languages. Both families and teachers can upload files, photos, and videos, and families can "reply all" to messages from the teacher. Intentional use of this platform's features can allow families to foster social connections with other families in the classroom community.

References

Baquedano-López, P., Alexander, R. A., & Hernández, S. J. (2013). Equity issues in parental and community involvement in schools: What teacher educators need to know. *Review of Research in Education, 37*(1), 149–182.

Cowhey, M. (2022). *Families with power: Centering students by engaging with families and community.* Teachers College Press.

Delgado Bernal, D., & Alemán, E. Jr. (2017). *Transforming educational pathways for Chicana/o students: A critical race feminista praxis.* Teachers College Press.

Delgado Gaitan, C. (2001). *The power of community: Mobilizing for family and schooling.* Rowman and Littlefield.

Delgado Gaitan, C. (2014). Culture, literacy, and power in family-community-school-relationships. In A. Darder & R. D. Torres (Eds.), *Latinos and education: A critical reader* (2nd ed., pp. 339–345). Routledge.

Edwards, P. A. (2016). *New ways to engage parents: Strategies and tools for teachers and leaders, K–12.* Teachers College Press.

Gándara, P., & Contreras, F. (2009). *The Latino education crisis: The consequences of failed social policies.* Harvard University Press.

González, N. (2006). *I am my language: Discourses of women and children in the borderlands.* University of Arizona Press.

Huber, P. (2009). Challenging racist nativist framing: Acknowledging the community cultural wealth of undocumented Chicana college students to reframe the immigration debate. *Harvard Educational Review, 79*(4), 704–730.

Lareau, A. (2000). *Home advantage: Social class and parental intervention in elementary education* (2nd ed.). Rowman & Littlefield Publishers.

Mapp, K., Carver, I., & Lander, J. (2017). *Powerful partnerships: A teacher's guide to engaging families for student success.* Scholastic Publishers.

Monkman, K., Ronald, M., & Théramène, F. D. (2005). Social and cultural capital in an urban Latino school community. *Urban Education, 40*(1), 4–33. doi: https://doi.org/10.1177/0042085904270416.

Yosso, T. J. (2005). Whose culture has capital? A critical race theory discussion of community cultural wealth. *Race Ethnicity and Education, 8*(1), 69–91. doi: http://doi.org/10.1080/1361332052000341006.

Yosso, T., & García, D. (2007). "This is no slum!": A critical race theory analysis of community cultural wealth in Culture Clash's Chavez Ravine. *Aztlan: A Journal of Chicano Studies, 32*(1), 145–179.

Yosso, T. J., & García, D. G. (2022). "Who are these kids, rejects from hell?": Analyzing Hollywood distortions of Latina/o high school students. In E. G. Murillo, Jr., D. Delgado Bernal, S. Morales, L. Urrieta, Jr., E. R. Bybee, J. S. Muñoz, V. Sáenz, D. Villanueva, M. Machado-Casas, & K. Espinoza (Eds.), *Handbook of Latinos and education: Theory, research, and practice* (2nd ed., pp. 309–332). Routledge.

Children's Literature

Aponte, C. (2019). *Across the bay* (C. Aponte, Illus.). Penguin Workshop.

Bailey, J. (2019). *A friend for Henry* (M. Song, Illus.). Chronicle Books.

Barnes, D. (2017). *Crown: An ode to the fresh cut* (G. C. James, Illus.). Agate Bolden.

Bowles, D. (2021). *My two border towns* (E. Meza, Illus.). Kokila.
Díaz, J. (2018). *Islandborn* (L. Espinosa, Illus.). Dial Books.
Flett, J. (2019). *Birdsong* (J. Flett, Illus.). Greystone Kids.
Júnior, O. (2020). *From my window* (V. Starkoff, Illus.). Barefoot Books.
Kensky, J. (2018). *Rescue & Jessica: A life-changing friendship* (P. Downes, Illus.). Candlewick.
Khan, H. (2018). *Crescent moons and pointed minarets* (M. Amini. Illus.). Chronicle Books.
Latham, I., & Shamsi-Basha, K. (2020). *The cat man of Aleppo* (Y. Shimizu, Illus.). G.P. Putnam's Sons.
Maillard, K. N. (2019). *Fry bread: A Native American family story* (J. Martínez-Neal, Illus.). Roaring Press Books.
Medina, M. (2020). *Evelyn Del Rey is moving away* (S. Sanchez, Illus.). Candlewick.
Mora, O. (2018). *Thank you, Omu!* (O. Mora, Illus.). Little, Brown and Company.
Pellicioli, A. (2020). *Song of the old city* (M. Atilgan, Illus.). G.P. Putnam's Sons.
Recio, S. (2020). *If Dominican were a color* (B. McCarthy, Illus.). Simon & Schuster Books for Young Children.
Sotomayor, S. (2019). *Just ask! Be different, be brave, be you* (R. López, Illus.). Philomel Books.

7
MAKING MAPAS
Navigational Capital

While Julia and her teacher-partner were waiting for the families to arrive for the meeting, a few of the mothers were catching up with each other. It had been one month since the group had last gathered and there was excitement in the air. Berta and Sonia called Julia over and asked about getting one of their children to the dentist. Before Julia could answer, Angela, another one of the mothers sitting at a nearby table, offered:

> **Mi hija mayor trabaja en la oficina del dentista allá en la esquina. Ella me dijo que el dentista es parte de un grupo que ofrece sus servicios y un plan de pago. Es el mismo servicio, y es muy bueno, no más que no lo piden todo [el dinero] a la vez.** / *My oldest daughter works at the dentist office there on the corner. She told me that the dentist is part of a group [of dentists] who offer their services and a payment plan. It is the same service, and it is very good, just that you do not need to pay all at once.*

Lucia, Berta's daughter, had to miss school for a couple of days because of a terrible toothache. Berta shared that she had asked the school nurse for help and that the nurse provided her a list of local dentists, but it was unclear who, if any, spoke Spanish or had a Spanish-speaking person in the office. Angela offered that her daughter works part-time as a record keeper at the dentist office while she is in school full-time pursuing a degree in nursing and that the dentist employs several Spanish-speaking people in addition to her daughter. Berta was relieved gaining this information and noted that she would call first thing in the morning to set up an appointment. She offered thanks to Angela: **"Gracias**

Angela, si no fuese por ti, no sé qué hubiera echo" / *Thank you Angela, if it weren't for you, I do not know what I would have done.* Families do not always know where to locate information; moreover, most immigrant families trust that schools are supporting them and providing necessary information and have their children's best interest at heart (Nieto, 2009; Reyes, 2011).

In this chapter, we will examine how to support minoritized families as they actively push against the barriers they are confronted with on a regular basis. How do families obtain necessary information? How do they navigate through social institutions not made for them?

Navigational Capital

Navigational capital describes the "skills of maneuvering through social institutions" (Yosso, 2005, p. 80) such as schools, jobs, and healthcare. Most social institutions are designed around mainstream culture and values, which situates minoritized communities as outsiders (Alim & Paris, 2017; Kinloch, 2017; Villenas et al., 2006). Take, for instance, families immigrating from Mexico, the country representing the highest immigrant population in the United States (Krogstad et al., 2022). Although they are hardworking and contribute significantly to the U.S. economy (New American Economy Research Fund, 2021), they are often viewed through a deficit lens due to their perceived immigration status and inability to communicate effectively in English. Attitudes toward them impact the way information is shared—if it is shared at all.

The excerpt above provided a glimpse into one immigrant family's struggle with navigating healthcare for their young child. The school nurse provided a list of local dentists, as she is required to do, but she did not inquire about additional needs the family may have had—specifically someone who could communicate with them in Spanish. Because the school nurse was an English-speaking member of the mainstream culture, she may never have encountered a situation where a medical provider did not speak her language, and therefore did not consider the experience of her multilingual families. Instead, multilingual families were left to fend for themselves. In this case, the immigrant community worked together to provide the information that the family needed that the school nurse did not provide.

Gaining navigational skills is essential for success in the American public schools and the United States in general, but how do families gain access to necessary information when schools do not provide it? How do schools shift their deficit view of families as passive recipients of information to one that recognizes their strengths in using their assets to navigate through systems that are not necessarily created for them?

Cuentos from the Field: Navigational Capital in Action

The American educational system is set up for the success of a certain group and is built upon the assumption that everyone has the tools required to maneuver through it (Davila & de Bradley, 2010; Valdez et al., 2022). Particular ways of doing things are valued and seen as the norm, while any deviation is viewed as deficient (García-Sánchez & Orellana, 2019). Minoritized families, both newcomers and those who are more established, often do not possess the tools needed to navigate these complex systems and are often negatively impacted by "educational policies that have systematically disadvantaged and oppressed Chica@ and Latin@ students, parents, and communities" (Delgado Bernal & Alemán, 2017, p. 4). These families depend on their social networks and other families to maneuver their way through schooling and other services in their new communities.

In the episodes that follow, we share several instances where families provided support to each other for issues surrounding healthcare (as we saw in the opening vignette), the libraries' community services, and navigating schooling through course offerings and communication opportunities.

Episode One: Navigational Capital for Healthcare

Healthcare is a major issue of concern for many families and can be particularly stressful and full of unknowns. As noted in the opening vignette, Berta's daughter Lucia was suffering from a painful toothache, and it was not until she raised a concern in our meeting that Angela, another mother, provided useful information to help Lucia. Angela's daughter, Maribel, provided families with much needed support in terms of healthcare; in addition to her job at the dentist office, Maribel's role as a nursing student at the local university gave her access to faculty and medical professionals who offered their support whenever possible.

While talking about *Mi Papi tiene una moto/My Papi Has a Motorcycle* (Quintero, 2019), a story about a young girl named Daisy who enjoys riding on the back of her father's motorcycle, Berta recalled how Maribel was able to obtain bicycle helmets for the children in the neighborhood to keep them safe: **"Pues yo no usaba casco cuando era niña. No reconocí el peligro hasta que el chamaco, Luis, se cayó y golpeo su cabecita"** / *I did not use a helmet when I was a child. I did not realize the danger [of not wearing a helmet] until the little boy, Luis, fell and hurt his head.*

Angela explained that Maribel was at the hospital during a nursing practicum and saw firsthand the result of not wearing a helmet: **"¡Nos contó que una chamaca se tropezó en su bici y cayó firme en el andén y se golpeó la cabeza!"** / *She told us about a little girl who fell off her bike and fell to* *the ground and bumped her head!* Angela added that Maribel did not want that to happen to her siblings or any other children in the neighborhood, so she applied for a community grant and was able to provide 20 bicycle helmets to the children in the neighborhood.

Similar to the role of language broker who has language as a commodity, Maribel's access to medical professionals and information positioned her as a "liaison between the home linguistic/cultural environment and the larger dominant society" (Pérez et al., 2016, p. 262). Maribel actively used her resources as a nursing student to provide her family and community with information and materials that they may not have received otherwise. Angela shared with the group that Maribel was adamant about not simply giving the information.

Angela: **Ella nos enseña como encontrar la información y con quien hay que hablar.** / *She teaches us how to search for the information and who to speak with.*

Berta: **Ella tiene razón cuando dice que no estará aquí con nosotros siempre. Ella quiere que aprendamos para poder hacerlo todo solas.** / *She [Maribel] is right when she says that she may not always be here with us. She wants us to learn so that we can do this all by ourselves.*

Angela: **Me dice siempre, 'mami, tenemos derechos. Hay que saber cuáles son, cómo cuidarse y en donde buscar ayuda. No se puede esperar que nos ayuden.'** / *She [Maribel] always tells me, mami, we have rights. We must know what they are, how to take care of ourselves and where to look for help. We cannot wait for others help us.*

Berta: **Maribel tiene razón. ¿Pues, si no nos cuidamos, quien lo hará? Nos temenos que ayudar y cuidar.** / *Maribel is right. Well, if we do not take care of ourselves, who will? We must help and take care of each other.*

Families use all available resources to navigate their way through these systems that were not created with them in mind. Those resources include people: sons and daughters, other families, and community members. Families need to be taught how to seek out the information because they are capable and know how to maneuver through obstacles. They will not—and cannot—wait for others to help them.

Episode Two: Navigational Capital for Libraries' Community Services

Julia and her teacher-partner usually set out a selection of picturebooks on a table for the mothers to browse as everyone waited to begin the meeting. Sara, who was new to the community and had a child in kindergarten, was flipping through one book and commented on the bright and beautiful illustrations and lamented the fact that she could not afford to purchase such books for her little boy: **"Los he visto en la tienda, pero son tan caros"** / *I have seen them in the store, but they are so expensive.* Matilde, who had one child in fourth grade and one in first grade, offered that the children are allowed to take books home: **"Ellos van a la biblioteca y buscan libros y los traen a la casa cada semana"**/ *They go to the library and look for books and bring them home every week.* On hearing this, Sara was overjoyed and a little surprised: **"¿No hay que pagar nada?"** / *We do not have to pay for anything.* Matilde responded, **"Por eso pagamos impuestos"** / *That is why we pay taxes.* Matilde's claim is supported by the New American Economy Research Fund (2019), who found that in 2019 alone, immigrants from Mexico "earned almost $92 billion in household income and contributed almost $9.8 billion in federal, state, and local taxes" (para. 5). While some may claim that undocumented immigrants do not pay their fair share and do not have rights, this is not the case.

While Sara was new to the community and school, the other mothers, Matilde, Barbara, and Susana, had been in the community for a few years and saw their roles as helping newer families get off to a good start in the school and community. Barbara had a child in middle school and had been in the community since he was in Pre-K. Susana had been in the community the longest; she had a child in high school and another in middle school. Matilde shared that **"cuando yo llegué aquí, Barbara y Susana me ayudaron con todo"** / *When I got here, Barbara and Susana helped me with everything.* As noted above by Maribel, "we must know how to take care of ourselves." The notion of networks of support is not new. There are several strong networks that have been in place for over 50 years; Mexican immigrants have been supporting each other in Chicago since the bracero program of the 1960s (Farr & Barajas, 2005), while Cuban immigrants have assumed responsibility for newcomers in Miami since the first wave of immigration in 1959 (Ferrer, 2021; Library of Congress, n.d.).

As they continued browsing books, Matilde stressed that while the school library had many books, the public library had many more books in Spanish, and there were materials beyond books for families to borrow: **"Tienen revistas, hasta tienen videos. No hay que ir a rentar la película, se la prestan para la semana"** / *[The public library] has magazines, they even have videos. You do not need to go rent movies; the library lends them for the week.* Barbara then explained other materials and resources available at the library.

Barbara: **La biblioteca pública tiene mucha información sobre servicios como para los niños. Y la biblioteca en el centro hasta tiene máquinas de coser—uno no se las lleva a la casa, pero dan clases o también permiten que uno las use. Yo he ido unas cuantas veces. Ahora el único problema es que necesito**

	un carro porque mi esposo se lo lleva al trabajo./ *The library also has information on services like for the children. And the library downtown even has sewing machines—you cannot take them home, but they have classes, and you are able to use the machines. I have been a few times. Now, the only problem is that I need a car because my husband takes it to work.*
Matilde:	**Tienen muchos recursos, solo hay que tomar el tiempo para aprender sobre ellos.**/ *They have so many resources, you just have to take time to learn about them.*
Susana:	**Pedir que alguien quien habla español te ayude.** / *Ask for someone who speaks Spanish to help you.*

Matilde added that they were also able to use the library to borrow materials and that they needed to obtain library cards. The mothers continued to share navigational capital about the library with one another.

Sara:	**Pero cómo le hacemos, yo no tengo dinero para hacer eso. ¿Cuánto cuesta la carta?** / *But how do we do it, I do not have money to do that. How much does the card cost?*
Matilde:	**No, Sara, no se paga. Nosotros pagamos impuestos y el gobierno también paga para estos servicios. Uno llena la aplicación. Tienes que llevar prueba de residencia del condado de Lakeside—una cuenta de luz o agua sirve. Llenas el papel, y ese día puedes llevar solo 5 materiales, pero cuando te llega la carta en la casa puedes hacer mucho más.** / *No, Sara, you do not pay for it. We pay taxes and the government also pays for the services. You fill out an application. You need to take proof of residency in Lakeside County—an electricity or water bill will do. Fill out the form that day and you can take home 5 materials, but when you get the card at home you can do much more.*
Sara:	**¿De veras? ¿Cómo? ¿Cuándo vamos?** / *Really? How? When are we going?*
Susana:	**Bueno comadres, yo tengo carro. ¿Qué les parece si nos reunimos y vamos juntas? Yo no tengo carta tampoco. Matilde nos puede hacer un paseo como hacen las maestras—no es cierto Julia?** / *Well, good friends, I have a car. What do you think about our going together? I do not have a card. Matilde can take us on a field trip like the teachers, right Julia?*

As Maribel noted when speaking to the mothers above, you cannot wait for others to do things for you; you must learn to do them for yourselves. We had taken the mothers on a field trip to the public library the year before Sara joined our group. During our tour, they learned about all the services available to them: the books, videos, sewing machines, and information on city and county services were also discussed. Teaching the families how to locate resources is more impactful than simply giving them the resources. Families support each other; once someone learns new information or how to locate something, they share with the others.

Episode Three: Navigating Schooling—Advanced Courses

At the beginning of the meetings, Julia and her co-teacher, Ms. Jones, set aside time where everyone present was invited to share something. The time was theirs to tell a story, ask questions, or read some of the books laying on the tables. One day, Matilde walked in with a paper in hand that the school district sent home. Her child had scored high on the standardized tests and was eligible for taking advanced math classes; however, the information was sent in English, and although Matilde was learning English, she did not understand it. Julia read the letter and passed it to her co-teacher, who was the reading coach in the school. We explained the letter and Matilde understood. Susana shared that the same thing happened to her a few years ago.

Susana: **Eso le pasó a mi niña hace años. Yo tampoco sabía lo que significaba porque estaba en inglés. Hable con Ms. Jones y me explico todo. Si tienen calificaciones altas los ponen en clases avanzadas.** / *That happened to my daughter a few years ago. I did not know what it meant since it was written in English. I spoke with Ms. Jones, and she explained everything. If the students have high scores, they place them in advanced classes.*

Matilde: **¿Por qué no mandan la información en español para que uno lo entienda?** / *Why is the information not sent in Spanish so that we can understand it?*

Matilde knew that the school expected her to read important information sent home; however, she did not have access to the information due to it being written only in English. Instead of ignoring the paper, she turned to her navigational capital. She knew that her group of mothers and the school employees supporting them would be able to help her navigate the system and advocate for her child's needs.

In response to Matilde's wondering, "**¿Por qué no mandan la información en español?**" / *Why is the information not sent in Spanish?*: federal law requires that parents receive information in a language that they understand. The Equal Educational Opportunities Act of 1974 (U.S. Department of Justice, n.d.) requires that school districts take action to overcome language barriers that impede students from participating equally in state and district educational programs. Denying families the ability to understand academic information "distorts the ability to see working class minority-language communities in the United States as worthy of full educational rights" (Darder & Uriarte, 2014, p. 147). Families have rights, and it is our responsibility to ensure that they know what they are and to assure that they are met.

Episode Four: Navigating Schooling—Communicating in School

Within the school setting, there are many elements families need to learn to navigate, including translation, communication, school visits, and at-home learning support. For multilingual families navigating schools where English is the primary language of communication, navigational capital allows families to seek resources to help translate materials into the languages they speak. Some families work around this barrier by asking family members, such as other children, to assist with translation responsibilities, utilizing linguistic capital (see Chapter 4). Many schools also have resources in-house that can assist with translation, and it is important to make families aware of these resources. For example, when Kadence asked one mother about the opportunities for communication they had had during the year, one mother explained a challenge she faced navigating Class Dojo: **"Por ejemplo en Class Dojo, yo no sé escribir mucho inglés. Y por eso, yo no escribo tanto"**/*For example in Class Dojo, I didn't know how to write much English. For this reason, I didn't write much.* Kadence was surprised to learn about this challenge and explained, "*You can always send me stuff in Spanish, and I can get it translated for you if need be.*" The mother was surprised to discover she could have been sending notes to school in Spanish all year and they would have been translated at school.

Schools often have specific protocols for communication that families are expected to use. Sometimes these communication venues rely on technology, like apps on a smartphone, to work. Kadence used Class Dojo to communicate with her families using both the behavioral points system and the messaging platform. Families commented on how convenient it was to send and receive quick correspondence. At the end of the year, however, the mother of one of Kadence's students admitted she did not know about the messaging feature on Class Dojo, saying she would have used it if she had known it existed.

In addition, families must navigate expectations of at-home support of their child's learning. For example, some families must navigate homework that is given with directions only in English. Kadence acknowledged that, as a monolingual teacher, she sent home homework primarily in English. Families use navigational capital to find varying venues of support for tasks like homework—other children in the household or extended family members, community members, or school-based programs before or after the regular school day with built-in homework support. In one afterschool homework club, a leader noticed that some families experienced unspoken expectations of ways they should be supporting their child's learning at home—such as reading—but no specific ways to do so. Some families may not be familiar with specific aspects of curriculum in their child's school, especially if they themselves did not attend school in the United States. In the "Applying Navigational Capital" section, we will offer some suggestions for working around these kinds of assumptions and allowing families to leverage and augment their navigational capital as they learn to navigate the complex U.S. school system.

> **FEATURED CHILDREN'S LITERATURE WITH NAVIGATIONAL CAPITAL**
>
> Quintero, I. (2019). *My papi has a motorcycle* (Z. Peña, Illus.). Kokila.
>
> Daisy Ramona loves riding around town on the back of her papi's motorcycle. As they ride together, Daisy reflects on the things in her community that are familiar, but also things in her community that are beginning to change. One thing will never change: the bond she shares with her papi.

Applying Navigational Capital

Families are implementing and building their navigational skills every day, and early childhood educators can build these strengths into their classrooms. The strategies in the following section highlight ways to apply navigational classroom in the classroom and when working with families.

Classroom Strategies to Honor Navigational Capital

- Navigating technology, especially the many and varied technology platforms used on a daily basis at school, can be complicated for students and families alike. Explicitly teach and model digital systems for students, from both their end and their families' user interfaces when possible. This also allows young children to strategically utilize their digital literacy to teach their families at home. Of course, the opposite applies: young children may have navigational capital and understand more than the teacher does about innovative technologies, and the students can be invited to teach so that the teacher can learn.
- Invite community members to be expert speakers. Ask families to help connect you with community experts from different social institutions (healthcare workers, educators, public libraries, and other community service agencies) as well. Write a summary of the visit, including what students

learned and key contact information for the individual or agency, to share with families in a weekly newsletter.
- Consider discussing important paperwork or communications that will be coming home during morning or closing meetings, or during small group meetings. For example, if a group of students receive an invitation to participate in a specific educational opportunity (like intervention or accelerated learning), explain to students what the opportunity will involve and invite them to ask questions. They could then be able to help answer questions at home for families (but families also need opportunities to gain information about these opportunities, as will be explained below).
- Engage in an inquiry-based community mapping project. Community mapping involves inquiring into a specific geographic area to analyze resources available that relate to cultural and linguistic practices within that area (Ordoñez-Jasis & Jasis, 2011). The focus of the mapping can be aligned with units of study: for example, options for public transportation and their "hubs" could be mapped during a unit on transportation, or mapping and counting signs in different languages can align with language and math learning objectives. What do these resources say about our community? What resources seem to be missing? Students can also work with families and community members to conduct interviews and learn more about ways different individuals navigate their unique community spaces. They can be assigned specific roles like photographer, notetaker, collector, or interviewer (adapted from Tindle et al., 2005). Community mapping can interrupt stereotypes, reposition schools as *not* being the center of all community activity, and discover relationships between community resources and school-based learning (Dunsmore et al., 2013).

Family Strategies to Honor Navigational Capital

- Build a resource center that families can access in the front office or designated family room. Within this resource center, include brochures and contact information for local community agencies from various sectors (healthcare, employment agencies, translation support, and more). Include a place where families can suggest agencies that should be included in the resource center, or where they can comment on needs they have that current resources do not meet.
- Offer support connecting families with local resources, such as the local library, and listen to families' challenges with accessing these resources to brainstorm ways to solve problems together.
- School systems have their own invisible cultures, and sometimes we assume families know how to navigate these spaces. Instead, make these systems and norms transparent. For example, visiting their children at school can involve

navigating some complicated procedures that may be unknown to some families. Explicitly communicate how to check into the front office, what documentation may be involved (for example, does it have to be a driver's license, or are there other accepted forms of identification?), and other procedures that can be daunting for first-time visitors. Similarly, Julia's families expressed confusion about advanced courses. When inviting students to participate in opportunities like extracurricular clubs, intervention groups, or accelerated learning classes, make sure to also explain to families what these opportunities involve.

- Families also may not know their rights when navigating U.S. educational spaces. For example, remind families of their rights for a translator to be present during Individualized Education Plan (IEP) meetings if the family speaks a language other than English.
- As noted above, navigating the many and varied technology platforms used on a daily basis at school can be complicated, especially for families who may not have had access to these kinds of tools in their own schooling. Explicitly teach and model digital systems families can use through digital tool workshop nights, flipped videos explaining how to navigate tools, or gathering tools into one easy-to-navigate location like a Wakelet.
- Include information about community agencies in family newsletters. The week that a guest from a community agency has come to do a talk about their job or to read a story to the class, take pictures and include a quick blurb about the visitor, what they did in the classroom that week, and what their community connection is.
- Use newsletters to support families navigating the classroom curriculum, especially when they are expected to have a working knowledge of the curriculum in order to assist with tasks such as homework. Classroom newsletters can be used to share videos about content learned in class or ideas for ways to practice certain skills at home. Instead of assuming families know how to support a child's learning, provide specific tips. If you expect families to read together at home, explain your expectations: are families reading aloud to their children, are children reading aloud to others in the family, are they talking about reading after it is finished, or are there other kinds of expectations?
- Plan and implement family field trips. These field trips can help familiarize families with the community resources available to them, and allow families to highlight resources they are already connected to that others might not be aware of. When Julia did this with her group of mothers, some of the locations they visited included the Art Museum, Botanical Gardens and Zoo, and the main branch of the Public Library.
- Listen to families and follow their lead—and their needs. For example, if a group of Latina mothers start networking and realizing that their

shared experiences and resources position them to support each other in a unique way, consider working with your administration to start an affinity group.
- Challenge deficit narratives about minoritized students and families. Sometimes these narratives are enacted in seemingly supportive initiatives, such as a local community agency donating shoes to every student in a high-poverty school. While the local community agency may mean well, did they ask if all students wanted or needed shoes, or did they assume they were filling a need? Families use their navigational capital to provide for themselves, and such "handouts" that assume all families from high-poverty or minoritized backgrounds need the same things actually support deficit narratives. Instead, encourage community agencies to network with local families and community members to listen to their goals and needs and plan targeted support initiatives that build off families' navigational capital.

Conclusion

Navigational capital describes the "skills of maneuvering through social institutions" (Yosso, 2005, p. 80) such as schools, jobs, and healthcare. In this chapter, we saw examples of families navigating through the system to attain access to healthcare, community resources, and schooling. As new families joined the community, more established families shared information; as Berta noted, "**que nos ayuda entender cómo hacer cosas necesarias**"/*that helps us understand how to do necessary things.*

Families depend on their community networks for support and information on how to navigate through social institutions, which is vital particularly because schools do not always provide this support. The mothers in these episodes took the responsibility to help new community members navigate their new situations and surroundings. As educators, we need to view families through an asset-based lens "examining the breadth of knowledge across contexts [that] can only open up new opportunities for navigating across life spaces" (Lee, 2019, p. 252). Through networks made up of family members and friends, the families navigate their way through systems that are not made for them and do so successfully.

Additional Resources

Children's Literature

The following 12 award-winning picturebooks address themes related to navigational capital. For a complete list of picturebooks and other areas of community cultural wealth these books may contain, see Appendix A.

Planting Stories: The Life of Librarian and Storyteller Pura Belpré (Denise, 2019)

After growing up in Puerto Rico, Pura Belpré moved to New York City in 1921. After taking a job in a garment factory, she then began working for the New York Public Library as one of their first bilingual librarians. When Pura couldn't find the Puerto Rican stories her grandmother used to tell her, she began planning her own stories through puppets and storytimes before writing a story and sending it to a publisher. This story demonstrates navigational capital because Pura knew how to reach out to publishers and community agencies to plant her stories honoring the folkloric traditions of Puerto Rico (Américas Award, 2020 Commended Title; Pura Belpré Award, 2020 Honor).

When Angels Sing: The Story of Rock Legend Carlos Santana (Mahin, 2018)

Before Carlos Santana became a famous musician, he had to build his navigational capital. When he moved, he had to learn new systems: how to ride the bus, how the schools worked, how to make new friends in a new place. He also had to learn how to leverage his talents to make an income. He searched for how to make a mark in the world of music, often feeling like he was an outsider, despite the tremendous impact he ultimately made (Américas Award, 2019 Commended; Pura Belpré Award, 2019 Illustration Honor).

A Different Pond (Phi, 2017)

This story follows Bao and his father as they go on a fishing trip on a small pond. As they wait for fish to bite, Bao's father tells stories of another pond he used to fish in when he lived in Vietnam. Navigational capital appears throughout the book, such as the father working two jobs because everything in America is more expensive and knowing where to get bait and go fishing to obtain affordable food (Caldecott Medal, 2018 Honor Book).

All the Way to the Top: How One Girl's Fight for Americans with Disabilities Changed Everything (Pimentel, 2020)

As a person with disabilities, Jennifer Keelan-Chaffins had to learn how to use her navigational capital to make a difference for other people like herself. Based on her true story, this book shows how Jennifer used her navigational capital to protest, demonstrate, and go to meetings. When she realized news channels weren't covering the Americans with Disabilities Act (ADA), she had to find another way to get the word out: she and other individuals with disabilities went to Washington, DC, themselves, where they participated in the Capitol

Crawl: they crawled up the steps to the Capitol to demonstrate how the building was inaccessible to individuals with mobility challenges, which ultimately led to the signing of the ADA (Schneider Family Book Award, Younger Children Honor Title 2021).

Itzhak: A Boy Who Loved the Violin (Newman, 2020)

In this picturebook biography, Itzhak Perlman wants to play the violin, and his family has to navigate through numerous obstacles to allow this dream to become reality. Finances were tight for his immigrant family, and Itzhak also got polio at the age of 4. Due to mobility challenges caused by polio, the family had to move so that Itzhak could live in an apartment without stairs and go to school. Itzhak and his family had to learn how to create opportunities for him to demonstrate his talent, ultimately leading to his status as a world-renowned violinist (Schneider Family Book Award, Younger Children Honor Title 2021).

RESPECT: Aretha Franklin, the Queen of Soul (Weatherford, 2020)

This picturebook biography follows the life of Aretha Franklin, "the Queen of Soul." As the daughter of a gospel singer and a pastor, Aretha and her family had many opportunities to draw upon their navigational capital as Aretha rose to fame. After becoming known for her talent while singing in her father's church, Aretha had to learn how to navigate the music industry as a Black female artist, all while continuing to advocate for civil rights and against injustice (Coretta Scott King, 2021 Illustrator Winner).

Coquí in the City (Perez, 2021)

Miguel and his pet frog, Coquí, love navigating through San Juan, but then Miguel has to move to New York City and leave his beloved Coquí behind. He has to learn how to navigate in an unfamiliar place until one day, he finds a familiar one: a park with frogs. Through his development of navigational capital, Miguel learns to find the familiar in the unfamiliar (Américas Award, 2022 Commended Title; Pura Belpré Children's Author Award, 2022 Honor Title; Pura Belpré Children's Youth Illustrator Award, 2022 Honor Title).

Digging for Words: José Alberto Gutiérrez and the Library He Built (Kunkel, 2020)

In Bogotá, Colombia, there are two Josés: Señor José, who is a garbage collector, and Little José, who is a boy who loves visiting the Paradise Library on Saturdays. Representing the real-life José Alberto Gutiérrez, Señor José implements his navigational capital by using his daily garbage route to collect discarded books and starting a library for kids in their local neighborhood: Paradise Library (Américas Award, 2021 Winner).

Bright Star (Morales, 2021)

In this beautifully illustrated book, a young fawn learns how to navigate her world after being separated from her mother. At the end of the book, the animals the fawn encounters during her journeys are shown to be humans, revealing how this book represents the migrant experience through allegory (Pura Belpré Children's Youth Illustrator Award, 2022 Honor Title; Tomás Rivera Mexican American Children's Book Award 2022).

My City Speaks (Lebeuf, 2021)

Using her multisensory navigational capital, a young girl who cannot see explores her city through sound, touch, and smell. This book is a powerful story about the assets of individuals with disabilities (Schneider Family Book Award, Young Children 2022 Winner).

The Library Bus (Rahman, 2020)

In Kabul, Afghanistan, access to education—especially for girls—is not guaranteed. Pari and Mama use their navigational capital to bring books and literacy to villages and refugee camps without access to schools via their Library Bus. In addition, when Pari shares her dreams of being able to read one day, Mama shares how her family used navigational capital to allow her to learn to read during a time when girls were not allowed to go to school: her grandpa taught her at home (Middle East Book Award, 2021 Winner).

Exquisite: The Poetry and Life of Gwendolyn Brooks (Slade, 2020)

Before she became an award-winning poet, Gwendolyn Brooks had to learn how to navigate publishing systems that were not built to include people like her. She first published poems in a neighborhood newspaper before later finding an opportunity to publish in a nationwide magazine. While she dreamed of sharing her poetry with others, she also had to use her navigational capital to find other ways to earn an income when her poems were not accepted for publication. She also knew she needed to learn more about writing poetry, so she used her navigational capital to take a poetry class at night after she had a child. Amidst many rejections, Gwendolyn kept writing poems and ultimately became the first Black person awarded the Pulitzer Prize for poetry in 1950 (Coretta Scott King Book Award: 2022 Illustrator Honor Book).

Digital Tools

TABLE 7.1 Digital Tools: Navigational Capital

Tool	Description
Video conferencing (Zoom, Skype, etc.)	Video conferencing platforms can be used to connect families, local community agencies, and classrooms, even when physically navigating to a location may be limited. For example, a family might not be able to attend a family–teacher conference or a special event at school due to childcare or work responsibilities, but they may be able to use a videoconferencing platform from their current location to join virtually during a work break or child's naptime. Work with your administration to re-envision possibilities for families to navigate certain school events or community resources in ways that are accessible to families.
Seesaw (https://web.seesaw.me/)	Seesaw is a multimodal digital platform where students can submit a variety of learning artifacts, such as videos and artwork, to document their learning. Each student's journal can be shared with up to ten of their family members, who can "like" and comment on their child's work. Teachers can also share multimodal artifacts (such as photos, videos, files, and links) via whole-class correspondence or announcements. Seesaw also offers embedded translation services in 100+ languages. Seesaw functions in a web-based client or in apps for Android or Apple. This platform has the ability to make classroom practice more transparent, offering families more explicit opportunities to exercise navigational capital as they engage with their child's classroom-based learning. Intentional opportunities can be extended for students and families to document learning beyond the classroom setting as well.
Wakelet (https://wakelet.com/)	Wakelet is a digital curation tool that can gather a variety of multimodal sources (including videos, links, images, and social media content) into one place called a "collection." Similar to Padlet, these collections can be configured in different ways, such as grids, columns, or mood boards. It can be used in a variety of ways to engage families. For classroom instruction, teachers can use Wakelet to collect resources to teach a unit of study, soliciting input from families about what kinds of resources they find helpful or interesting relating to the topic. For navigational capital, gather the never-ending stream of educational resources in one place for families to access and navigate with ease. Families can be added as collaborators to a Wakelet by sharing a unique link or QR code.

(Continued)

TABLE 7.1 (Continued)

Tool	Description
Screen Recording (i.e., ScreenPal, Zoom recording)	Flipped videos can give students and families ownership over their needs and learning by providing a library of on-demand resources. For example, teachers can screen record videos that walk through navigating digital platforms used for educational purposes, or the teacher could invite families to record these videos. Families could also provide narration for screencasts in multiple languages, which increases accessibility to these videos and online tools.
Google My Maps (https://mymaps.google.com/)	Students, families, and teachers can work together to create maps of local community resources or agencies by dropping different location pins on a specially created Google Map. The creator of the map will need a Google account. In their Google Drive, they can click "New," then "More," and then "Google My Maps." The sharing options currently only allow other users to view, not to edit, but Google makes frequent changes to sharing permissions, and this could change in the future.

References

Alim, H. S., & Paris, D. (2017). What is culturally sustaining pedagogy and why does it matter? In D. Paris & H. S. Alim (Eds.), *Culturally sustaining pedagogies: Teaching and learning for justice in a changing world* (pp. 1–21). Teachers College Press.

Darder, A., & Uriarte, M. (2014). The politics of restrictive language policies: A postcolonial analysis of language and schooling. In A. Darder & R. D. Torres (Eds.), *Latinos and education: A critical reader* (pp. 141–163). Routledge.

Davila, E. R., & de Bradley, A. A. (2010). Examining education for Latinas/os in Chicago: A CRT/LatCrit approach. *Educational Foundations, 24*, 39–58.

Delgado Bernal, D., & Alemán, E., Jr. (2017). *Transforming educational pathways for Chicana/o students: A critical race feminista praxis.* Teachers College Press.

Dunsmore, K., Ordoñez-Jasis, R., & Herrera, G. (2013). Welcoming their worlds: Rethinking literacy instruction through community mapping. *Language Arts, 90*(5), 327–338.

Farr, M., & Barajas, E. D. (2005). Mexicanos in Chicago: Language ideology and identity. In A. C. Zentella (Ed.), *Building on strengths: Language and literacy in Latino families and communities* (pp. 46–59). Teachers College Press.

Ferrer, A. (2021). *Cuba: An American history.* Scribner.

García-Sánchez, I. M., & Orellana, M. F. (2019). Introduction. Everyday learning: Centering in schools the language and cultural practices of young people from non-dominant groups. In I. M. García-Sánchez & M. F. Orellana (Eds.), *Language and cultural practices in communities and schools: Bridging learning for students from non-dominant groups* (pp. 1–23). Routledge.

Kinloch, V. (2017). You ain't making me write": Culturally sustaining pedagogies and Black youths' performance of resistance. In D. Paris, & H. S. Alim (Eds.), *Culturally sustaining pedagogies: Teaching and learning for justice in a changing world* (pp. 25–41). Teachers College Press.

Krogstad J. M., Passel, J.S., & Noe-Bustamante (2022). *Key facts about U.S. Latinos for National Hispanic Heritage Month*. Pew Research Center. https://www.pewresearch.org/fact-tank/2021/09/09/key-facts-about-u-s-latinos-for-national-hispanic-heritage-month/

Lee, C. D. (2019). Don't believe the hype: Reality rules. In I. M. García-Sánchez & M. F. Orellana (Eds.), *Language and cultural practices in communities and schools: Bridging learning for students from non-dominant groups* (pp. 248–255). Routledge.

Library of Congress (n.d.). *Transforming a city.* https://www.loc.gov/classroom-materials/immigration/puerto-rican-cuban/transforming-a-city/

New American Economy Research Fund (2021, March 8). *Examining the economic contributions of undocumented immigrants by country of origin.* https://research.newamericaneconomy.org/report/contributions-of-undocumented-immigrants-by-country/

Nieto, S. (2009). *The light in their eyes: Creating multicultural learning communities* (2nd ed.). Teachers College Press.

Ordoñez-Jasis, R., & Jasis, P. (2011). Mapping literacy, mapping lives: Teachers exploring the sociopolitical context of literacy and learning. *Multicultural Perspectives, 13,* 189–196.

Pérez, W., Vásquez, R., & Buriel, R. (2016). Zapotec, Mixtec, and Purepecha youth: Multilingualism and the marginalization of indigenous immigrants in the United States. In H. S. Alim, J. R. Rickford, & A. F. Ball (Eds.), *Raciolinguistics: How language shapes our ideas about race* (pp. 255–271). Oxford University Press.

Reyes, M. D. (2011). Overcoming the odds: Lessons across generations. In M. Reyes (Ed.), *Words were all we had: Becoming biliterate against the odds* (pp. 143–157). Teachers' College Press.

Tindle, K., Leconte, R., Buchanan, L., & Taymans, J. (2005). Transition planning: Community mapping as a tool for teachers and students. *National Center on Secondary Education and Transition (NCSE), Research to Practice Brief, 4*(1). http://www.ncset.org/publications/researchtopractice/ncsetresearchbrief_4.1.pdf

U.S. Department of Justice (n.d.). *Educational Opportunities Section.* Civil Rights Division. https://www.justice.gov/crt/educational-opportunities-section

Valdez, V. E., Fránquiz, M. E., & Turner, L. D. (2022). Young Latinx learners in early childhood education: Shifting trends and future directions. In E. G. Murillo, Jr., D. Delgado Bernal, S. Morales, L. Urrieta, Jr., E. R. Bybee, J. S. Muñoz, V. Sáenz, D. Villanueva, M. Machado-Casas, & K. Espinoza (Eds.), *Handbook of Latinos and education: Theory, research, and practice* (2nd ed., pp. 343–354). Routledge.

Villenas, S., Godinez, E., Delgado Bernal, D., & Elenes, C. A. (2006). Chicanas/Latinas building bridges: An introduction. In D. D. Bernal, C. A. Elenes, F. E. Godinez, & S. Villenas (Eds.), *Chicana/Latina education in everyday life: Feminista perspectives on pedagogy and epistemology* (pp. 1–9). SUNY Press.

Yosso, T. J. (2005). Whose culture has capital? A critical race theory discussion of community cultural wealth. *Race Ethnicity and Education, 8*(1), 69–91.

Children's Literature

Denise, A. A. (2019). *Planting stories: The life of librarian and storyteller Pura Belpré* (P. E. Harper, Illus.). HarperCollins.

Kunkel, A. B. (2020). *Digging for words: José Alberto Gutiérrez and the library he built* (P. Escobar, Illus.). Schwartz & Wade.

Lebeuf, D. (2021). *My city speaks* (A. Barron, Illus.). Kids Can Press.

Mahin, M. (2018). *When angels sing: The story of rock legend Carlos Santana* (J. Ramirez, Illus.). Atheneum Books for Young Readers.

Morales, Y. (2021). *Bright star* (Y. Morales, Illus.). Neal Porter Books.

Newman, T. (2020). *Itzhak: A boy who loved the violin* (A. Halpin, Illus.). Abrams Books for Young Readers.

Perez, N. (2021). *Coquí in the city* (N. Perez, Illus.). Dial Books.

Phi, B. (2017). *A different pond* (T. Bui, Illus.). Capstone Young Readers.

Pimentel, A. B. (2020). *All the way to the top: How one girl's fight for Americans with disabilities changed everything* (N. H. Ali, Illus.). Sourcebooks Explore.

Quintero, I. (2019). *Mi papi tiene una moto* (Z. Peña, Illus.). Kokila.

Rahman, B. (2020). *The library bus* (G. Grimard, Illus.). Pajama Press.

Slade, S. (2020). *Exquisite: The poetry and life of Gwendolyn Brooks* C. A. Cabrera, Illus.). Abrams Books for Young Readers.

Weatherford, C. B. (2020). *RESPECT: Aretha Franklin, the queen of soul* (F. Morrison, Illus.). Atheneum Books for Young Readers.

8
SÍ SE PUEDE
Resistant Capital

In the excerpt below, a group of Latina mothers from Honduras, El Salvador, and Mexico discuss the importance of resisting the temptation to abandon their language and culture regardless of what they and their children are being told in school.

> **Claro que sería más fácil dejar que los niños hablen en inglés, pero tenemos que resistir la tentación de abandonar nuestro idioma. Si no nos cuidamos, aquí nos quitan todo.** / *Of course, it would be easier to let the children speak English, but we have to resist the temptation to abandon our language. If we are not careful, they [the United States] will take everything away from us.*
>
> **Tiene razón, la maestra le dijo a la niña que el Día de los Muertos es una cosa que es de allá y que aquí se celebra el Halloween. Le dijo que no es importante lo que hacíamos en nuestros países porque ahora estamos aquí.** / *She is correct, the teacher told my daughter that the Day of the Dead is something from over there and that here we celebrate Halloween. She [teacher] told her [my daughter] that what we used to do in our countries isn't important because we are here [the United States] now.*
>
> **No, no, no. Eso no está bien. Este es mi país adoptado y lo quiero, pero no me voy a olvidar de donde vine ni quien soy. Voy a resistir la tentación y no voy a abandonar mis costumbres. Les voy a enseñar a mis niños todo lo de su herencia.** / *No, no, no. That is not right. This is my adopted country and I love it, but I am not going to forget where I came from or who I am. I am going to resist the temptation and I will not abandon my customs. I am going to teach my children everything about their heritage.*

Schools are more than places of learning: they are critical sites "through which issues of national identity and linguistic diversity are continually contested and reproduced" (García-Sánchez, 2016, p. 291). Schools socialize children and families and serve to "maintain privilege by taking dominant-culture knowledge forms and content and defining it as legitimate knowledge to be preserved and transmitted" (Darder, 2017, p. 20); as such, it is not uncommon for teachers to encourage families to stop speaking their home language as they erroneously believe that this will positively impact students' academic progress.

Considering that "identities are complex because of the experiences and relationships created with others" (Irizarry, 2007, p. 22), a lack of support from teachers may lead students to question their identity, which may negatively impact their sense of belonging (García-Sánchez, 2013). Rather than give into these notions, the mothers actively resist the majoritarian story of assimilation and explain that while they love their "adopted country" (the United States), they will not forget where they came from and will resist the temptation to abandon their language and customs.

In this chapter, we will explore the final form of capital in Yosso's (2005) theory of community cultural wealth, resistant capital. How do families challenge inequality? How do we reframe resistance as the act of love that it is?

Resistant Capital

Resistant capital recognizes "those knowledges and skills fostered through oppositional behavior that challenges inequality" (Yosso, 2005, p. 80). Minoritized communities have long histories of resisting racism and inequity to transform oppressive realities for the future, and as Lee (2019) notes, "there are no periods in human history in which persons from disenfranchised communities have not engaged in active resistance" (p. 249). Resistance is not a bad thing. Resistance is a form of strength. Minoritized and/or immigrant families often struggle to hold onto their traditions, cultural ways of being, and ways of communicating. They must actively resist, which takes strength and stamina. In the excerpt above, one of the mothers noted that although it would be easier to let the children speak in English, she recognized the importance of resisting the temptation of the easier route and instead keeping their language and customs. She warned the others that if we are not careful, "they [the United States] will take everything away from us." It takes strength, courage, and conviction to resist.

Cuentos from the Field: Resistant Capital in Action

Children and families confront attempts at assimilation daily; they face pressure to conform to the majoritarian culture, language, and ways of making meaning. In order to maintain their familial and cultural ways of being, families must actively resist the push to conform. In the episodes that follow, we will explore how families enacted their resistant capital in educational spaces.

Episode One: Resistance to Cultural Assimilation through Día de los Muertos

In the opening excerpt, the group of mothers were speaking about the importance of maintaining their language and culture. One mother noted a specific instance where her child's teacher communicated to her that Día de los Muertos does not belong in the United States; it is "from over there."

> **Tiene razón, la maestra le dijo a la niña que el Día de los Muertos es una cosa que es de allá y que aquí se celebra el Halloween. Le dijo que no es importante lo que hacíamos en nuestros países porque ahora estamos aquí.** / *She is correct, the teacher told my daughter that the Day of the Dead is something from over there and that here we celebrate Halloween. She [teacher] told her [my daughter] that what we used to do in our countries isn't important because we are here [the United States] now.*

The teacher added that what the families did in their countries of origin does not matter because they are now in the United States. How are children supposed to succeed in school when their language, cultures, and families are not being accepted and are instead being actively devalued? Delgado Bernal and Alemán (2017) remind us that "an education that is disconnected from one's lived experiences and history further excludes and marginalizes the lives and knowledge of Chican@ Latin@ students in particular" (p. 39). By marginalizing the child's lived experiences and cultural way of being, this teacher missed a wonderful opportunity to engage the child and their family in learning about Día de los Muertos. Sadly, situations like these are common in U.S. classrooms. In response to these attacks, families form networks of support consisting of family and community members, and together they actively resist cultural assimilation, linguistic assimilation, and outside deficit views.

Episode Two: Resistance to Cultural Assimilation: "Porque Así Ya Conocemos"

At Melissa's school, one network of support that a mother noted was the classroom's digital learning community. When asked if families being able to post media for other families to view was significant, the mother replied:

> **[Y]o pienso que sí, es importante porque así ya conocemos de otras culturas de las personas que tal vez nostros no lo hacemos, como méxicanos es diferente? Yo pienso que sí. Es importante.** / *I think that yes, it is important because we already know about other cultures of people that maybe don't do it like us, like how Mexicans are different? I think so. It is important.*

In this exchange, the mother practiced resistant capital by interrupting deficit narratives. The mother advocated for what she already knew—"**porque así ya conocemos**"/*because we already know*—clearly addressing that spaces for families to share their existing knowledge with other families and with the teacher were necessary. When Melissa asked the mother if there was something from her culture that she wished the school knew, the mother explained:

> **Hay muchas cosas que son diferentes. Por ejemplo en México, es diferente. Se celebra el Día del Niño? Es el 30 de abril. Y aquí ya no lo hacemos. Allá lo más importante es el 6 de enero. Es cuando los niños se les regala jugetes y todo. Y aquí ya no se hace. Del los Reyes Mago. Y allá casi no el 24 de deciembre? No es. Se son muchas culturas diferentes.** / *There are many things that are different. For example in Mexico, it's different. They celebrate the Day of the Child? It's April 30. And here we don't do it. There the most important thing is January 6. It's when the children are given toys and everything. And here it's not done. Of the Magi Kings. And there almost none of December 24? It's not. There are many different cultures.*

This mother was practicing resistant capital by calling out the holidays the school chose to celebrate with its students—for example, activities near winter break that reflected Christmas traditions—and how they did not reflect all students' cultures and beliefs. This exchange caused Melissa to consider how additional celebrations from students' lives and cultures—such as el Día del Niño/Day of the Child—could be woven into classroom and school events, and how families could be involved in sharing these celebrations with other students and families.

Episode Three: Resistance to Cultural Assimilation through El Ratón Pérez

During a read aloud of *The Tooth Fairy Meets El Ratón Pérez* (Colato Laínez, 2010), a story about a daring mouse who collects teeth from children in Latin America and Spain, the first-grade children were asked to turn to a partner and share their thoughts about the story so far.

Sarah and Steven:	*I have never heard of the mouse. We have a tooth fairy.*
Michael:	*Yeah, that is gross to have a mouse coming into your house.*
Mira and Tomás:	*It is not gross. It is different. Just because you don't like it doesn't mean it is gross.*

Another pair of students:	*We can do things differently. Different doesn't mean bad, it means another way.*
Steven:	**"¡En mi casa, el ratón y la fairy vienen!"**
Jessica:	*You're so lucky, you get the mouse and the fairy! Do they each bring something?*
Mira:	**"Mi mamá dice que debo tener orgullo y lo tengo. Yo soy de Venezuela y El Ratón Pérez es importante para mí y mi familia."** / *My mom says that I need to be proud and I am. I am from Venezuela and El Ratón Pérez is important to me and my family.*
Tomás:	**"Yo también soy fuerte y soy de Honduras y el Ratón es mi amigo."** / *I am also strong and I am from Honduras. [continuing in English] Don't be mean, it is not gross. We can do what makes our family happy.*

The lively discussion continued throughout the read aloud as the children happily and eagerly shared their opinions on El Ratón and the tooth fairy. The children had very strong opinions; the Spanish-speaking children were very clear in stating that El Ratón Pérez was important to them and their families, and they defended their cultural way of being by stating that being different does not mean "gross." This sentiment was shared by the pair of children who added that "different means another way." Toward the end of the excerpt, Mira added that her mother tells her to have **orgullo**/*pride* in who she is; Mira shared her pride in being from Venezuela and was adamant about the importance of El Ratón in her family. Tomás noted that he is from Honduras, and that he too is strong (supporting Mira's feeling of pride). Mira's initial statement of showing **orgullo**/*pride* demonstrates that families are having conversations about cultural pride with their children. Families "play critical roles in shaping their children's cultural environment through language and literacy in their home and community" (Delgado Gaitan, 2014, p. 341) and this begins before they are even born!

Throughout the discussion, children shared what their lost teeth brought them: "I got two dollars and a toy car," "I got a book," and "I got a movie ticket." One child excitedly wondered if both El Ratón and the tooth fairy visited their homes and if each brought them something in exchange for their tooth! Repeatedly, the children shared the sentiment that being different did not equate being wrong and that "we do things to make our families happy." The Latinx children were insistent on explaining the important role El Ratón played in their families: it is keeping their culture alive. This discussion among young children provides an example of active resistance: the children stood their ground by sharing their cultural traditions and not accepting the normalized tooth fairy.

Episode Four: Resistance to Linguistic Assimilation

A very real concern for our families is language loss due in part to policies reflecting the current "xenophobic English-only movement" (Bartolomé, 2014, p. 136); therefore, keeping their languages is an active form of resistance. Families and children are bombarded daily with messages indicating that speaking a language other than English is "un-American," or that it is harmful to children to speak to them in languages other than English. Families receive these messages indirectly, and sometimes directly, from their children's teachers, especially if those teachers and individuals are not aware of the power of the families' existing linguistic capital (see Chapter 4). Hilda shared an instance where she attempted to communicate with her child's teacher in Spanish, the only language she knew, and was met with disrespect and aggression.

> **Yo le escribí una nota a la maestra porque no entendía la tarea y no le pude ayudar a Maribel. La maestra escribió en mi nota, "English please, you are not helping her by writing in Spanish," así encima de mis palabras.** / *I wrote a note to the teacher because I did not understand the homework and could not help Maribel. The teacher wrote back on my note, "English please, you are not helping her by writing in Spanish," directly on top of my words.*

As Hilda talked, the others gasped and had looks of shock and disbelief on their faces. When she finished sharing, the others provided support by consoling her, providing strategies on how to communicate with the school (i.e., Google Translate), and telling her who to talk to about this incident (they provided support by accompanying her to school). A message that continued to be communicated among the group throughout the discussion was **"no vamos a dejar nuestra idioma"**/*we are not going to leave our language*. Families provide each other support in keeping their languages and cultural ways of knowing and in actively resisting schools' attempts at erasing their language.

For Hilda, like many others, abandoning one's language is akin to giving up a part of their culture and a part of their identity (Anzaldúa, 2007; González, 2006):

> **Si dejo de hablar español, siento que me voy a partir en dos, la Hilda de Honduras y la Hilda de aquí. No puedo hacer eso, yo soy hondureña, hablo español, y ahora pertenezco a este gran país que nos aceptó y nos dio refugio.** / *If I stop speaking Spanish, I feel like I am going to split in two, the Hilda from Honduras and the Hilda from here [the United States]. I cannot do that, I am Hondureña, I speak Spanish, and now I belong here in this great country [the United States] that accepted us and gave us refuge.*

Hilda explained how she would feel "split in two" if she had to abandon speaking Spanish, supporting Anzaldúa's (2007) notion that "ethnic identity is twin skin to linguistic identity" (p. 81). A few other mothers agreed:

Lisandra: **No hay razón tener que escoger idioma o país. Estamos aquí pero todavía podemos hablar español.** / *There is no reason why we must choose between language or country. We are here [the United States] but we can still speak Spanish.*

Maria: **Estar aquí no es abandonar nuestras raíces o idioma. Podemos hacer los dos; hablar español y vivir aquí.** / *Being here [the United States] is not abandoning our roots or language. We can do both; speak Spanish and live here.*

While families like those above are clear in understanding that it is not necessary to choose between speaking Spanish and living in the United States, there are some who are fed misinformation and live in fear for their children. Families who have suffered discrimination, humiliation, and intimidation do not want their children to suffer as they did and end up abandoning their home language. Rosalia shared that her sister-in-law, Marisol, was threatened when she was at the grocery store: **"le dijeron que iban a llamar la policía si ella seguía hablando en español"**/*they told her if she did not stop speaking Spanish, they would call the police.* Rosalia explained that Marisol was with her two young children and was scared for their lives. That was the last day Marisol spoke Spanish outside of her community.

Johana offered that she did not want her children to speak English with an accent because **"la gente los mal tratan"** / *people mistreat them.* She added that her desire was for her children to be **"americanos verdaderos para que no los desprecien"** / *real Americans so that they would not be looked down upon.* For this reason, she was doing what the teacher told her: she would not speak Spanish to her children.

Perez et al. (2016) note that "language choices available to children and their parents, as well as the discursive practices that are encouraged and supported in school, have an important impact on children's identity and their possibilities of developing agency or resisting" (p. 265). Schools must adapt to the languages and cultures present in their communities and must learn to view these through an asset-based lens and understand that there is value in being bilingual and bicultural. Schools are integral parts of the communities in which they reside, and as such should represent the communities and view them as partners in education.

For immigrant families risking everything to come to the United States, it is frightening to go against the grain, and yet families support each other by providing encouragement to **"resistir la tentación"**/*resist the temptation* to abandon their heritage language and actively resist linguistic assimilation.

Episode Five: Resistance to Outside Deficit Voices

Families encounter negative voices when out in the community. Above, Rosalia mentioned an incident that involved her sister-in-law, Marisol. Marisol explained that she was grocery shopping with her two children and was pointing out the names of various pieces of produce [in Spanish] when she noticed two women watching her and whispering. **"Me pareció extraño que nos seguían mirando"**/*It seemed strange that they [the women] kept looking at us.* She noted that the women followed her in the store and told her that she was not allowed to speak Spanish. Marisol felt afraid as these two women followed her and her children and left the grocery store without her items. A mother should not feel afraid to go to the grocery store with her children. Rosalia was angry at what happened to Marisol.

Rosalia: **No hay razón que nos miren así y que hablen de nosotros. Aquí llegamos a trabajar y compartir una vida con nuestra familia y comunidad.** / *There is no reason for them to look at us like that and talk about us. We come to this country to work and share our lives with our family and community.*

Hilda: **Algo muy parecido me pasó a mi, el otro día andaba allá en la tienda hablando español y note como me estaba mirando esta mujer. Ella estaba diciendo algo. Tenía unas ganas decirle algo. Aunque no sé realmente lo que decía, porque apenas entiendo inglés, la mirada me lo dijo todo. Yo trabajo duro y nadie me va a despreciar.** / *Something very similar happened to me, the other day I was in the store speaking Spanish and I noticed how this woman was looking at me. She was saying something. I wanted to say something to her. Although I do not really know what she was saying, because I only understand a little bit of English, her look said it all. I work hard and no one is going to devalue me.*

The climate in the nation (Bartolomé, 2014; Early, 2017) has made mundane events like grocery shopping stress-inducing and intimidating, leading some families to fear for their lives. Rosalia and Hilda noted that they came to this country to work hard, and to share their lives with their families and communities; they should not be subjected to this treatment. As Hilda noted above, it is not necessary to completely understand English in order to communicate and understand, such as interpreting the meaning behind someone's facial expression. It was clear from the looks the strangers gave both Marisol and Hilda that speaking Spanish was not okay. Although they do not know English (yet!), the mothers are acutely aware of their surroundings. As a result of the incidents involving Marisol and Hilda, the mothers decided that they would not go out of their immediate community unaccompanied. **"Cuando hay que hacer** compras, vamos juntas"/*when we need to go shopping, we will go together*. It takes courage to stand up for oneself, particularly when immersed in a hostile environment that does not respect the vulnerable and views difference as a threat.

Some families have literally risked their lives and made countless other sacrifices to come to the United States. They want to belong, and they also want to keep their dignity; the mothers often say, **"nadie me va despreciar"**/*no one is going to devalue me*. They plead that **"necesitan dar tiempo que uno se acostumbre estar aquí"**/*they need to give us time to get used to being here*. Hilda added, **"pues ellos también deben acostumbrarse a nosotros"**/*that they also need to get used to us*.

Episode Six: Not Giving into the "American" Way

An important component of dignity is respecting names (see Chapter 5). During one meeting, the families were actively engaged in talking about the book, *René has Two Last Names/René tiene dos apellidos* by René Colato Laínez (2010). The book tells the author's story of moving to the United States and his struggle to keep his last name. In many Spanish-speaking countries, the tradition is to use both last names, the paternal and maternal. Many families actively voiced their frustration that schools like to Americanize their children's names and often insist on one last name. Lisandra explained,

> **Yo insisto que reconozcan el nombre entero de la niña, María Isabel Cantos Rodríguez. Los nombres son nombres de familia, por eso lo tienen. Cada que vengo a la escuela, le recuerdo a la maestra del nombre. Ella no entiende, pero tiene que aprender.** / *I insist that [the school] recognize her whole name, María Isabel Cantos Rodríguez. They are family names, that is why she has them. Every time I come to school, I remind the teacher of my daughter's name. She [the teacher] does not understand but will need to learn.*

Rather than assimilating to the "American" way of using only one last name, usually the paternal last name, Lisandra, like the other families, is asking for their cultural tradition of using both last names to be respected in schools. Lisandra notes that every time she visits the school, she reminds the teacher of María Isabel's full name. It takes courage to continually raise the issue and demand respect for a cultural tradition in a place where it is not the way and where difference is seen as a threat and/or wrong. Lisandra demonstrates her resistant capital as she advocates for her daughter. Rosalia joins in:

Rosalia: **Les digo siempre a las niñas que tengan orgullo en quienes son y parte de eso el nombre**. / *I always tell my girls to have pride in who they are and a part of that is their name.*

Lisandra: **La maestra le dijo "Mary" a la niña. Aunque le dijo muchas veces que su nombre era María Isabel, le dijo "Mary" hasta que fui a hablar con ella. No sé inglés, pero la hice entender. Bueno, como dije hay que seguir diciéndole, pero yo no me voy a dejar.**/ *The teacher called her [my daughter] Mary. Even though she [daughter] told her many times that her name is María Isabel, the teacher called her "Mary" until I spoke with her. I do not speak English, but I made her understand. Well, like I said, I must continue telling her, but I am not going to give in.*

Living in the United States does not mean assimilating and giving up one's language, culture, or ways of being. Lisandra continues to demonstrate resistant capital but not only actively resisting assimilation, but simultaneously continuing to actively teach her children about their culture:

No, no, no. Eso no está bien. Este es mi país adoptado y lo quiero, pero no me voy a olvidar de donde vine ni quien soy. Voy a resistir la tentación y no voy a abandonar mis costumbres. Les voy a enseñar a mis niños todo lo de su herencia. / *No, no, no. That is not right. This is my adopted country and I love it, but I am not going to forget where I came from or who I am. I am going to resist the temptation and I will not abandon my customs. I am going to teach my children everything about their heritage.*

As seen in the excerpt, families love their "adopted country" and recognize that being in the United States does not mean forgetting one's roots or giving up traditions. Families support each other in a variety of ways to resist the temptation to assimilate. Children have the right to know about their heritage, hold onto their traditions, and speak their community's language; it does not make them any less "American."

FEATURED CHILDREN'S LITERATURE WITH RESISTANT CAPITAL

Colato Laínez, R. (2010). *The Tooth Fairy meets El Ratón Pérez* (T. Lintern, Illus.). Tricycle Press.

When a Mexican-American boy loses a tooth, an issue arises: who should get to collect the tooth, the Tooth Fairy or El Ratón Pérez, who collects children's lost teeth in Latin America and Spain? This book aligns with resistant capital with its playful interruption of assumed shared norms about what happens when young children lose teeth in early childhood classrooms—not every culture has the same Tooth Fairy!

Applying Resistant Capital

Early childhood settings are often explicitly or implicitly expected to enculturate young children into the expectations of school. Sometimes these expectations include elements like following rules or demonstrating other behaviors aligned with compliance. While a safe, trusting classroom environment is vital to a young child's social, emotional, and intellectual health, interrogate how those environments are crafted and maintained. If the expectation is that the teacher establishes norms and the children and families must follow them, this environment does not align with a child- and family-centered approach. The following sections provide some strategies for honoring resistant capital in the classroom and when working with families.

Classroom Strategies to Honor Resistant Capital

- When establishing classroom norms and procedures, engage in open discussions about why rules exist, who tends to make rules, and who tends to follow rules. Build norms together as a class whenever possible, and establish what to do if a child feels like a norm is resulting in harmful outcomes so that norms can be revisited as a group when necessary.
- Listen to behavior, and recognize behavior is not necessarily a personal affront. Behavior is a form of communication, and if a child seems to be going against some established norms, they may be trying to communicate and advocate for themselves in a situation they perceive as unjust.
- Incorporate social/emotional learning into the classroom by talking about feelings and building vocabulary. Young children sometimes need help processing big feelings by putting names to those feelings and realizing that it is OK to be angry, frustrated, or disappointed, and to provide strategies for self-regulation.
- Explicitly teach strategies for practicing resistant capital through scaffolds such as sentence stems or role-playing. Remember to address both sides: speaking up to advocate for self in an unjust situation, and responding to resistance received.
- Read and write counternarratives. A counternarrative is an approach frequently used in critical race theory to recast an existing narrative (see Chapter 1). Brainstorm times when students felt like other people jumped to conclusions about them. Maybe they assumed that a student who speaks another language is an undocumented immigrant, or a girl would want a pink toy, or all students who speak a certain language like a certain type of food. Encourage students to tell their own stories about who they are and what they want other people to know about them.

- Model interrupting deficit assumptions encountered in classroom discussions, books, media, or other sources. Some of the strategies referenced above can come into play here as well. The bottom line is that early childhood educators need to support and practice resistant capital with their students and families as well.

Family Strategies to Honor Resistant Capital

- Adapt existing structures to facilitate multidirectional feedback. During family conferences, reserve time for families to provide feedback or suggestions in addition to reporting on the child's experience and outcomes. Make notes of families' comments so that you can revisit them and act upon them.
- Establish trusting forms of communication where families can offer suggestions or critiques. Consider options that align with various communication strategies. For example, some families may feel comfortable advocating for their children in a conference with the teacher, whereas others may feel more comfortable advocating anonymously through a Google Form. Be aware that there are benefits and drawbacks to any method of communication; for example, anonymous feedback, especially when provided online behind the safety of a screen, can be more caustic.
- When you receive resistance from families, follow up. Let them know how you have taken their feedback or concerns and made changes, or if you cannot change certain elements, explain why not and offer other possible solutions.
- Constructive criticism can be hard to process for adults and children alike. Be prepared to accept and respond to constructive criticism in empathetic ways. Recognize families are a child's first advocates, and more often than not, resistance arises from a place of love and hope for their child's future.
- Finally, be willing to grow and commit to equity work. Families may bring to your attention a certain practice, book, or activity that may inadvertently be perpetuating inequity and injustices. Be willing to engage in critical self-reflection and to take action. On the other hand, you may be intentionally selecting activities to interrupt inequity that some families perceive as going against their beliefs or norms, especially when those beliefs or norms align with mainstream, power-holding groups. Be ready to explain why or how you approach certain topics while also advocating for your students and families.

Conclusion

Children and their families are creators and holders of knowledge (Delgado Bernal, 2002), and schools must acknowledge this. To start, schools must realize that resistance is not a bad thing. Resistance is a form of strength.

Schools must also recognize that, as Marisol noted, "**Tenemos sueños para nosotros y también para nuestros niños**"/*We have dreams for ourselves and our children.* Therefore, resistance is a sign of love. Our families love their children and want the best for them, and sometimes the best way to show their love is to resist inequitable structures and systems—even those we might not realize are presenting themselves within our early childhood classrooms.

While resistance is often portrayed as negative and contrarian, in reality, resistant capital comes from a place of love. Families draw upon capital in all kinds of areas—linguistic, aspirational, familial, social, and navigational—and in doing so, they often encounter many barriers. Refusing to accept barriers that may limit their child's potential or their own potential is at the root of resistant capital. Instead of perceiving resistance as problematic or threatening, educators need to listen from a place of love. What is this resistance communicating? What changes can we make or facilitate to be more inclusive and welcoming of all children and families? We can walk alongside our families as we reimagine possibilities in early childhood instead of simply following the status quo that may not allow all children and families to be their fullest selves.

Additional Resources

Children's Literature

The following 14 award-winning picturebooks address themes related to resistant capital. For a complete list of picturebooks and other areas of community cultural wealth these books may contain, see Appendix A.

Between Us and Abuela: A Family Story from the Border
(Perkins, 2019)

María and Juan are excited to celebrate La Posada Sin Fronteras with their abuela, but they live in the United States and she lives in Mexico: the fence at the border stands between them. This story demonstrates resistant capital as the children find creative ways to transcend the barriers separating them from their abuela and to celebrate together as a family (Américas Award, 2020 winner).

Freedom Soup (Charles, 2021)

Belle is ready to learn how to make Freedom Soup from Ti Gran. As Ti Gran prepares ingredients and makes the soup with Belle, she sprinkles in information about her Haitian history and culture. She shares stories of enslaved ancestors and how they fought for freedom as the duo builds new memories making Freedom Soup together (Américas Award, 2020 Commended Title).

Auntie Luce's Talking Paintings (Latour, 2018)

Auntie Luce paints "to remember": to remember the present and past of her Haitian people. Her niece, who was not born in Haiti, comes to visit, and gets to hear all about the stories and memories preserved in her aunt's paintings. This book aligns with resistant capital by choosing to see the good *and* bad in Haiti's complicated history, and also in the young niece's resistance to define herself as either Haitian or American: she realizes *both* are parts of who she is (Américas Award, 2019 Honorable Mention).

Sharuko: El Arqueólogo Peruano/Peruvian Archaeologist Julio C. Tello (Brown, 2020)

This bilingual biography (Spanish and English) introduces readers to Julio C. Tello, who became an archeologist in the late 1800s and advocated for celebrating Peru's Indigenous history. He earned his nickname, Sharuko, for his bravery. The book addresses resistant capital by highlighting how families passed on culture and traditions despite the unfair treatment of Indigenous people in Peru, which dated back to the Spanish invasion of Peru in the 1500s. In addition, Tello's work proved the gifts of the Indigenous Peruvian culture, some of which had been misattributed to other cultures over the years (Pura Belpré Award, 2021 Youth Illustrator Honor).

We Are Water Protectors (Lindstrom, 2020)

In this beautifully written and illustrated book, the main character resists the negative implications of the Dakota Access Pipeline. Additionally, lines such as "We are still here" and "We fight for those who cannot fight for themselves" align with resistant capital. Both the author and illustrator are Indigenous, and Michaela Goade was the first Indigenous recipient of the Caldecott Medal (Caldecott Medal, 2021 Winner).

The Undefeated (Alexander, 2019)

Through poetry, this book serves as a historical survey of Black resistance in the United States. The text balances hardships, achievements, survival, and perseverance as a clear portrayal of how Black Americans have implemented resistant capital. The end of the book also includes detailed accounts of some of the historical events or individuals alluded to through the poetry and illustrations to build readers' background knowledge (Caldecott Medal, 2020 Winner; Newbery Medal, 2020 Honor Book).

I Talk Like a River (Scott, 2020)

When a young boy feels frustrated because his words get "stuck" because he stutters, his dad takes him to a river to show him the parallels between his voice and the river's. Jordan Scott writes from his own experience to represent resistant capital by recasting what is beautiful in language and expression (Schneider Family Book Award, Younger Children Winner 2021).

At the Mountain's Base (Sorell, 2019)

This lyrical text follows a Cherokee family, waiting in their cabin for their family member, a female fighter pilot, to come home from war. This book exemplifies resistant capital by representing the American Indian women who have served in the U.S. armed forces, even though their stories are rarely told or honored in mainstream sources. The author identifies as Cherokee and the illustrator identifies as Tongva/Scots-Gaelic (American Indian Youth Literature Award, 2020 Picture Book Honor Book).

The Life of/La Vida de Dolores (Rodriguez & Stein, 2021)

This bilingual biography follows the life of Dolores Huerta, who became famous for co-founding the United Farm Workers of America. When she was a young adult, she saw students with empty stomachs and bare feet and wanted to make change, so she became a teacher. In addition to creating a labor union organization to fight for farm workers' rights, she also organized a five-year boycott on grapes that resulted in improved conditions for farm workers. Throughout her life, Dolores Huerta demonstrated resistant capital as she found ways to make changes and improvements in her community and beyond (Américas Award, 2022 Commended Title).

Boogie Boogie, Y'all (Esperanza, 2021)

In this brightly illustrated picturebook, the children in a community marvel at something the adults sometimes don't notice: the magical art of graffiti. This book aligns with resistant capital by acknowledging graffiti as its own distinct art form (Pura Belpré Children's Youth Illustrator Award, 2022 Honor Title).

The Spirit of Chicano Park/El Espíritu del Parque Chicano (Zamora, 2020)

This book tells the true story of a community coming together to create Chicano Park, located under a bridge in Barrio Logan in San Diego, California. The community members came together to meet a need in their local community that wasn't being met by other entities, demonstrating their resistant capital (Tomás Rivera Mexican American Children's Book Award, 2021 Winner).

We Are Still Here! Native American Truths Everyone Should Know (Sorell, 2021)

Told through a series of "presentations," each two-page spread in this book addresses a specific aspect of Native American history rarely taught in traditional history curricula. The structure of this book makes it easy for readers to pick out a few specific topics to focus on, as the entire book and some topics may be a bit complex for young readers. This book provides an important counternarrative by highlighting truths, even unpleasant ones, about how Native Americans have been persecuted throughout the history of the United States, and how they have resisted and overcome many different challenges. The author identifies as Cherokee (American Indian Youth Literature Award, 2022 Picture Book Honor Book).

The People Remember (Zoboi, 2021)

This picturebook is an artful counternarrative of Black achievements throughout history. Through the seven principles of Kwanzaa, the narrative retells the history of African descendants in America—what their languages and traditions were in Africa, how they resisted and survived centuries of oppression and prejudice in the United States, and how they thrived. This book demonstrates resistant capital by presenting a celebratory, asset-based history of these African ancestors and how they have continued to shape and influence American culture and history (Coretta Scott King Book Award, 2022 Author Honor Book).

Nina: A Story of Nina Simone (Todd, 2021)

Nina Simone, who grew up in North Carolina as Eunice Kathleen Waymon, lived a life shaped by music. She started her musical development playing classical pieces on the piano, but as she got older, she learned how to use her musical talents—including her voice—to resist the injustices in the world around her, especially during the Civil Rights Movement (Coretta Scott King Book Award, 2022 Illustrator Honor Book).

Digital Tools

TABLE 8.1 Digital Tools: Resistant Capital

Tool	Description
Flip (https://info.flip.com/en-us.html)	Formerly known as Flipgrid, Flip is a video and voice discussion platform. Teachers post a "topic" that community members are prompted to respond to by recording videos or voice memos. It is accessible across devices both as a web-based and as an app-based client. Users can re-record videos or voice memos as many times as needed before submitting the recording, and teachers can limit the length of the submissions. The teacher will need to create a Flip account, and then additional users can be added via emails or usernames. Guest Mode allows guests, including families, to contribute to topics. Flip aligns with resistant capital by positioning families as experts and creators who can share their own knowledge instead of merely receiving knowledge from other individuals or institutions.
Social media (Facebook, Instagram, TikTok, Twitter, etc.)	One of the most revolutionary aspects of the emergence of social media was the voice and agency it situated with individual users who wished to connect with other users. When organizing to oppose inequity, this kind of agency is vital. Families can network using the social media of their choice, and can use these spaces to initiate change, such as fostering connections with local community agencies. Clear community values and norms of use can be established among the families each year, and families could be tasked with helping to moderate posts. This repositions the teacher as the "owner" of the space while also holding users accountable for their activities in the digital space.

References

Anzaldúa, G. (2007). *Borderlands la frontera: The new mestiza* (3rd ed.). Aunt Lute.

Bartolomé, L. (2014). The struggle for language rights: Naming and interrogating the colonial legacy of "English Only." In A. Darder & R. D. Torres (Eds.), *Latinos and education: A critical reader* (2nd ed., pp. 133–140). Routledge.

Darder, A. (2017). *Reinventing Paulo Freire: A pedagogy of love* (2nd ed.). Routledge.

Delgado Bernal, D. (2002). Critical race theory, Latino critical theory, and critical raced-gendered epistemologies: Recognizing students of color as holders and creators of knowledge. *Qualitative Inquiry, 8*(1), 105–126.

Delgado Bernal, D., & Alemán, E., Jr. (2017). *Transforming educational pathways for Chicana/o students: A critical race feminista praxis.* Teachers College Press.

Delgado Gaitan, C. (2014). Culture, literacy, and power in family-community-school relationships. In A. Darder & R. D. Torres (Eds.). *Latinos and education: A critical reader* (2nd ed., pp. 339–345). Routledge.

Early, J. S. (2017). Escribiendo juntos: Toward a collaborative model of multiliterate family literacy in English only and anti-immigrant contexts. *Research in the Teaching of English, 52*(2), 156–180.

García-Sánchez, I. M. (2013). The everyday politics of "cultural citizenship" among North African immigrant school children in Spain. *Language and Communication, 33*(4), 481–499.

García-Sánchez, I. M. (2016). Multilingualism and its discontents: Essentializing ethnic Moroccan and Roma identities in classroom discourse in Spain. In H. S. Alim, J. R. Rickford, & A. F. Ball (Eds.), *Raciolinguistics: How language shapes our ideas about race* (pp. 291–308). Oxford.

González, N. (2006). *I am my language: Discourses of women and children in the borderlands.* University of Arizona Press.

Irizarry, J. G. (2007). Ethnic and urban intersections in the classroom: Latino students, hybrid identities, and culturally responsive pedagogy. *Multicultural Perspectives, 9*(3), 21–28. doi: https://doi.org/10.1080/15210960701443599.

Lee, C. (2019). Don't believe the hype: Reality rules. In I. M. García-Sánchez & M. F. Orellana (Eds.), *Language and cultural practices in communities and schools: Bridging learning for students from non-dominant groups* (pp. 248–255). Routledge.

Perez, W., Vasquez, R., & Buriel, R. (2016). Zapotec, mixtec, and purepecha youth: Multilingualism and the marginalization of Indigenous immigrants in the United States. In H. S. Alim, J. R. Rickford, & A. F. Ball (Eds.), *Raciolinguistics: How language shapes our ideas about race* (pp. 255–271). Oxford University Press.

Yosso, T. J. (2005). Whose culture has capital? A critical race theory discussion of community cultural wealth. *Race Ethnicity and Education, 8*(1), 69–91.

Children's Literature

Alexander, K. (2019). *The undefeated* (K. Nelson, Illus.). Versify.

Brown, M. (2020). *Sharuko: El arqueólogo peruano/Peruvian archaeologist Julio C. Tello* (E. Chavarri, Illus.). Lee & Low Books.

Charles, T. (2021). *Freedom soup* (J. Alcántara, Illus.). Candlewick.

Colato Laínez, R. (2009). *René has two last names/René tiene dos apellidos* (F. Graullera Ramirez, Illus.). Arte Público Press.

Colato Laínez, R. (2010). *The Tooth Fairy meets El Ratón Pérez* (T. Lintern, Illus.). Tricycle Press.

Esperanza, C. G. (2021). *Boogie Boogie, y'all* (C. G. Esperanza, Illus.). Katherine Tegen Books.

Latour, F. (2018). *Auntie Luce's talking paintings* (K. Daley, Illus.). Groundwood Books.

Lindstrom, C. (2020). *We are water protectors* (M. Goade, Illus.). Roaring Brook Press.

Perkins, M. (2019). *Between us and abuela: A family story from the border* (S. Palacios, Illus.). Farrar, Straus and Giroux.

Rodriguez, P., & Stein, A. (2021). *The life of/La vida de Dolores* (C. Reyes, Illus). Lil' Libros.

Scott, J. (2020). *I talk like a river* (S. Smith, Illus.). Neal Porter Books.

Sorell, T. (2019). *At the mountain's base* (W. Alvitre, Illus.). Kokila.

Sorell, T. (2021). *We are still here! Native American truths everyone should know* (F. Lessac, Illus.). Charlesbridge.

Todd, T. N. (2021). *Nina: A story of Nina Simone* (C. Robinson, Illus.). G.P. Putnam's Sons.

Zamora, B. (2020). *The spirit of Chicano Park/El espíritu del parque Chicano* (M. Meza, Illus.). Tolteca Press.

Zoboi, I. (2021). *The people remember* (L. Wise, Illus.). Balzer + Bray.

9
CONCLUSION: VOCES IN ACTION
Using Community Cultural Wealth to Engage in Action

At the beginning of the school year, three teachers met after school to discuss an upcoming required parent training event. The discussion began with the teachers sharing their displeasure at a few aspects: the title ("parent training"), the fact that attendance by the "parents" was required by their program director, and that there was a set curriculum. The three teachers engage in translanguaging frequently; the language noted is the language they spoke, followed by a translation, if necessary.

Jasmine: How are they going to require "parents" to come? Some of my kids live with their grandparents, this is not okay. And how do we know what the families need? Did anyone bother to ask them?

Paulina: **Sí, Jasmine estoy de acuerdo. Para trabajar con las familias hay que saber lo que necesitan. Claro, que uno se puede imaginar lo que les hace falta, pero verdad que hay que hablar con ellos.** / Yes, Jasmine, I agree. To work with the families, we need to know what they need. Of course, we can imagine what that might be, but really we have to talk with them.

Rose: **Y hay que escuchar lo que dicen. No les ayuda a nadie hacer lo que nosotras pensamos, ellos saben y nos dicen.** / And we have to listen to what they say. It does not help anyone if we do what we think [they need], they know and will tell us.

Paulina: **Si, pero acuérdense que ellos están desilusionados. No hemos trabajado por el bien de ellos, se han hecho cosas porque nos han dicho [a nosotras] que tenemos que hacerlo.** / Yes, but remember that they are disillusioned. We have not done right by them, we have done things that we were told we had to do.

DOI: 10.4324/9781003344377-9

Rose: **No podemos seguir así, nosotras sabemos como trabajar con las familias. Vamos a hacer lo que nosotras sabemos, no lo que nos mandan hacer.** / *We cannot continue like this, we know how to work with families. Let's do what we know, and not what they tell us.*

Paulina: **Sí entiendo, estoy de acuerdo, eso se acabó. Hay que escuchar y no presumir que todo se hace de tal manera.** / *Yes, I understand and agree, this is over. We need to listen and not presume that things are done in only one manner.*

Jasmine: *I am tired. I have been teaching for a very long time and one thing I know is that we have to stop thinking we have all the answers. We have to sit there and be quiet [and listen to the families]. We are never going to get anything done if we always come off like we have the answers.*

Rose: *Yes, Jasmine! We need to be quiet!*

Paulina: *We know our families are good people. They work hard and we have to work with them. Together with them. Well, let's go!*

In the excerpt, the teachers used their **voces** to advocate for their families' community cultural wealth (CCW). They expressed concerns with many of the mandates they have been given by their director: they questioned the required attendance of "parents," raised the issue that some of the children are being raised by grandparents, and had concerns with the fact that they were given a curriculum to follow for the event without asking the families about their needs. Paulina reminded the group that **"que ellos están desilusionados"**/*the families are disillusioned* because we had not done right by them; she was referring to last school year, when the school continued hosting events even though the times were inconvenient, no translation was offered, the families were treated poorly, and no childcare was available.

After some discussion, the teachers agreed that they have had enough, **"eso se acabó"**/*that is over* and that it was time to do what they [the teachers] know; they needed to "sit there and be quiet." Paulina, Jasmine, and Rose agreed that they need to sit and listen to the families *tell them* [the school] what they need rather than the teachers telling the families. As Paulina stated, "We have to work with them, together." They reviewed the curriculum and found it incongruent with the needs of their families. They began to brainstorm ideas and decided that this first required event would be for families, not only parents, and that their main goal was to openly speak with the families about their needs for the school year. They recognized that after last year, it would take some time to "win" the families' trust back, but they were willing to put in the time and work together with the families.

Moving from discussion to action, the teachers used their **voces** to advocate for families at their monthly meeting with the director the following week. While met with some resistance at first, they were able to convince the director that after careful consideration and reflection on the last few years of work they have done with families, it was best to let the families guide them—at least for the first meeting, and that it was important to work together.

The teachers demonstrated what Darder (2017) meant by "self-reflection is important and necessary, but lacks the dialogical reflection that provides different ways of thinking about our practice in relationship to our students, communities, and the world and from which transformative action can emerge" (p. 85). The teachers considered their actions and impact of the mandates over the past few family events, and shifted their practice. Rather than dictate to families what their needs are, they are asking and listening—they [the teachers] are going beyond the single story (Adichie, 2009) of minoritized families' needs and are engaging with the families in the work of teaching and learning.

In this final chapter, we will take one more look at CCW, especially how the various forms of capital intersect. We will also address some "frequently asked questions" that may arise as educators and other stakeholders approach family engagement through an asset-based lens. Finally, we will consider where we go from here, combining talk and action to move toward "transformative action" (Darder, 2017 p. 85).

Putting It All Together: One More Look at Community Cultural Wealth

As microcosms of society, schools mirror the attitudes, ideologies, and beliefs held by those in power, sometimes positive and other times negative—particularly about minoritized populations. We view schools as "potential sites for the contestation of hegemonic ideologies and practices" (Martínez et al., 2022, p. 110) and believe in the "potential of community cultural wealth to transform the process of schooling" (Yosso, 2005, p. 70). We recognize that any attempt at transforming schooling must be done in partnership with families.

Re-envisioning schooling means working *with* families: viewing them from an asset-based lens that values their ways of making meaning, recognizes that they contribute positively to their children's learning, and respects their myriad ways of knowing. It involves deeply listening to families, engaging in conversations, and then taking action to transform teaching and learning. As Darder (2017) reminds us, it is not enough to talk: "revolutionary praxis is rooted in our capacity to take action" (p. 85). We seek to disrupt a deficit narrative of children and families of color by viewing them through an asset-based lens and believe that the CCW framework allows schools to do this.

The forms of capital included in Yosso's (2005) conceptualization of CCW—aspirational, linguistic, familial, social, navigational, and resistant—are not the only forms of capital our families possess. As we shift toward an asset-based lens, we become more able to identify and validate *all* kinds of capital, even those beyond the original conceptualization of CCW. For example, spiritual capital includes "religious, indigenous, and ancestral beliefs and practices learned from one's family, community, and inner self" (Pérez Huber, 2009, p. 721) and connects an "individual and/or a community to a bigger sense of the divine, supernatural, and/or transcendent" (Park et al., 2020, p. 128). Spirituality may be practiced collectively or independently, and, as we saw in Chapter 5, has no age restrictions.

In Chapter 5 (focused on familial capital), Samantha and Justina made connections with an image found in one of the illustrations of the book, *Family Pictures* (Lomas Garza, 1998): a picture of **La Virgen de Guadalupe**. Pointing to the page, they talked about the many ways they and their families enact their faith: saying their nightly prayers, going to church to pray to the Virgin, reading the Bible and the book of Bible stories/prayers for children. Later while at school, the girls' mothers made connections to the same page in the book and stressed the importance of having the Bible stories available in Spanish because it helped "**enseñarles a leer y también compartir nuestra religión y fé con ellos en un modo divertido**"/*to teach them how to read and to share our religion and faith with them in a fun way.*

The mothers noted the importance of having books available in Spanish to help their children learn to read *and* learn about their religion and faith, extending Park et al.'s (2020) notion that "through music, stories, testimonies, teaching, and other forms of communication, religion and spirituality are taught, expressed, practiced, and reinvented over the generations" (p. 144). Pérez Huber (2009) suggests that while spiritual capital interconnects with the other forms of CCW, it is itself a distinctive source and form of CCW. Spiritual capital represents another opportunity for teachers to begin to "create a common culture with families, a culture based on conditions that allow all to participate and express themselves in meaningful ways" (Delgado Gaitan, 2014, p. 342).

Community Cultural Wealth: A Kaleidoscope of Capitals

In Chapters 3–8, we delved into each of the forms of capital Yosso (2005) named in her theorization of CCW: aspirational, linguistic, familial, social, navigational, and resistant. In reality, though, these forms of CCW often intertwine and are not present in isolation. As Pérez Huber (2009) noted, "similar to the view through a kaleidoscope lens, these forms of capital are interrelated and shift and overlap depending on the focus of analysis" (p. 712).

For a more holistic perspective, we will revisit one episode from Chapter 6 to analyze the multiple forms of capital that occurred. In Episode Three ("Expectations and Responsibilities"), we heard Griselda and Anais, two mothers of first-grade children, discussing the teacher's expectation that they read aloud to their children every night. In Table 9.1, we revisit that interchange to analyze where they enacted multiple forms of CCW throughout their discussion.

TABLE 9.1 Intersectional Analysis of "Expectations and Responsibilities" Episode (Chapter 6) for Community Cultural Wealth

Turn	Dialogue	CCW Analysis
1	Griselda: **La semana pasada fui a la conferencia con la maestra. Me dijo que Betsy estaba atrasada en la lectura. Que se le hace difícil leer.** / *I went to the parent–teacher conference last week. The teacher told me that Betsy was behind in reading. It is difficult for her to read.*	Navigational
2	Anais: **A mí me dijo lo mismo de Eduardo. ¿Qué hacemos?** / *She told me the same about Eduardo. What do we do?*	Social
3	Griselda: **Estaba la maestra de inglés también y me dijeron que le lea a la niña todas las noches.** / *The ESL teacher was there too, and they said that I had to read to Betsy every night.*	
4	Anais: **Pero Grisi, tu inventas unos cuentos fantásticos y a todos los chamacos les encantan. Cada vez que nos juntamos, allí se sientan para oír tus cuentos. Eso vale también.** / *But Grisi, you create the most fantastic stories, and all the children love them. Every time we get together, there they sit to hear your stories. That [storytelling] also counts [as reading].*	Linguistic Social Resistant
5	Griselda: **Gracias, me encanta inventar los cuentos, así lo hacía mi mamá. ¡Claro que eso vale, para nosotros, pero no para la maestra! Bueno allá sí, pero aquí no [vale].** / *Thank you, I love creating stories, my mom did it too. Of course, it [storytelling] counts, for us, but not for the teacher! Well, it counts there [home country] but not here [the United States].*	Familial Navigational
6	Anais: **No entiendo porque no cuenta hacerle un cuento en vez de leer un libro. Además, no sé leer en inglés, y no tengo libros en español. Cuanto no quisiera yo sentarme a leer con Eduardo, pero no tengo tiempo.** / *I don't understand how it does not count to tell a story instead of reading one from a book. Also, I don't know how to read in English, and I don't have any books in Spanish. How I wouldn't love to sit and read with Eduardo, but I don't have the time.*	Resistant
7	Griselda: **Yo lo quisiera hacer también, pero, a mí me pasa lo mismo. Como que estaba la maestra de inglés, le pregunte que si me podía mandar libros en español. Le explique que no sé leer en inglés, pero en español sí puedo.** / *I would love to do it too [sit and read] but I have the same issue. Since the ESL teacher was there, I asked if they could send home books in Spanish. I explained that I do not know how to read in English, but I can read in Spanish.*	Linguistic Navigational
8	Anais: **¿Y qué te dijo? Grisi, si tienes libros en español, préstame unos para leer con el niño.** / *And what did she say? Grisi, if you have books in Spanish, share them with me so I can read with Eduardo.*	Social

(Continued)

TABLE 9.1 (Continued)

Turn	Dialogue	CCW Analysis
9	Griselda: **¿Qué me dijo? Para no enojarme de nuevo, te digo la versión corta. No tenemos libros en español. Solamente tenemos libros en inglés. Los niños necesitan leer en inglés.** / *What did she say? So that I don't get angry all over again, I will give you the short version. We don't have Spanish books. We only have English books. The children need to read in English.*	Resistant
10	Anais: **Grisi, pero ¿qué fue eso? Me parece un poco grosera. No me gusta para nada.** / *Grisi, what was that? Seems a little rude to me. I don't like it at all.*	Resistant
11	Griselda: **Me quede bien calladita al oír eso. Voy a hablar con la comadre a ver como se las arregló cuando Estefanía estaba en la clase con esta maestra.** / *I was super quiet once I heard that response. I am going to speak to my comadre to see what she did when Estefanía was in this same class.*	Social Resistant

When we consider the intersection of various forms of capital within CCW, we gain a deeper understanding of the assets Griselda and Anais demonstrate in their dialogue. Throughout this episode, the mothers demonstrate their navigational capital. They know the importance of attending parent–teacher conferences to support their child's learning (Turn 1), and they also know that the school is a resource they can turn to for obtaining what they need to support their child's learning (Turn 7, when Griselda shares her request for books in Spanish). They also are acutely aware of the difference between what counts as literacy in U.S. schools and schools in their home countries (Turn 5). These mothers know how to navigate U.S. schools, but they also know that there are other ways to "do school"—the U.S. approach is just one way, not the only way.

Multiple exchanges align with linguistic and familial capital. In Turn 4, Anais recognizes Griselda's storytelling as linguistic capital, and in Turn 5, Griselda acknowledges that she learned this skill from her mother. In Turn 7, Griselda explains how she told the teacher that she can read in Spanish. Therefore, the mothers know that they have gifts—their Spanish and their storytelling, which they learned from their first teachers, their families—that they can leverage to support their children's literacy development.

Social capital also appears several times in this episode. In Turn 4, Anais references spending time together listening to Griselda's stories. In Turn 2, Anais realizes she has received the same feedback from her son's teacher, and she wonders, "¿Qué hacemos?"/*What do we do?* She does not wonder what *"I"* as an individual needs to do, but rather what *"we"* as a social network need to do to support their children collectively. This same social approach to supporting their children's learning emerges in Turn 8, when Anais asks Griselda to share any books she has in Spanish. In Turn 11, Griselda decides to use her social network to ask another mother how she responded when she also received the same feedback about her child's reading. Throughout these exchanges, the mothers know that they have a strong social network that will come together to find and implement the support needed.

Most significantly, though, the mothers enact resistant capital as they draw upon their linguistic, familial, social, and navigational capital. Nowhere in this exchange do the mothers submit to the demands of the teacher to read aloud to their children nightly in English. Instead, they fight for the legitimacy of their own forms of literacy, such as storytelling (Turns 4 and 6), and their rights to maintain their own language (Turn 9). In Turns 10 and 11, Anais and Griselda advocate for their right to be recognized for their assets instead of being rudely dismissed for what the teacher perceived as deficits (not reading aloud nightly in English). Even Griselda's self-reported silence is a form of resistance: "in dialogue, one has the right to be silent" (Shor & Freire, 1987, p. 102).

Zooming out, we also see an overarching theme related to aspirational capital. Anais and Griselda want their children to have opportunities to succeed in school and in life. However, they see all the capitals their children do have access to, and know the barriers they will have to navigate in order to see their children succeed. When our families are given spaces to bring their full selves to our classroom spaces and our larger communities, when they are recognized for all the capitals they *do* possess, that is the space where we can re-envision opportunities for family engagement and literacy that is empowering for all stakeholders—families, students, educators, and more.

Children's Literature Analysis

Throughout this book, we have analyzed award-winning children's literature that aligns with specific capitals within CCW. Now, we will revisit a few titles that are powerful examples of multiple capitals intertwining in one picture book.

Planting Stories: The Life of Librarian and Storyteller Pura Belpré (Denise, 2019)

This story demonstrates Pura Belpré's many forms of CCW as she forever changed the approach to stories in U.S. public libraries. She learned the art of storytelling from her grandmother (linguistic and familial capital). Her bilingual talents gained her employment as one of the first bilingual assistants in the

New York Public Library (linguistic capital). Weaving together her Spanish language and *cuentos folklóricos* from her home country of Puerto Rico (linguistic capital, familial capital, and social capital), Pura dreamed of a different storytelling approach to engaging families in the public library (aspirational capital). She knew how to reach out to schools, community agencies, publishers, and other stakeholders to plant stories (navigational capital). All of these forms of capital intertwine with resistant capital: Pura found a way to plant her grandmother's stories in her local community and beyond, reshaping how libraries are centers for stories (Américas Award, 2020 Commended Title; Pura Belpré Award, 2020 Honor).

Soldier for Equality: José de la Luz Sáenz and the Great War (Tonatiuh, 2019)

During his life, José de la Luz Sáenz enacted multiple forms of CCW. He experienced prejudice as a young American citizen with familial roots in Mexico (familial capital), and he later became a teacher to use knowledge as a weapon, teaching kids during the day at a Mexican school and adults at night (navigational and resistant capital). When he joined the U.S. army, he witnessed the discrimination against Native American and Mexican American soldiers, and he dreamed of the United States recognizing that these individuals loved their country and being willing to fight for it (aspirational capital). While in Europe, he was able to use his Spanish background to quickly learn French (linguistic capital), which allowed him to be assigned to the Intelligence Office. He also taught English to Mexican American soldiers (linguistic and resistant capital). To make his dream of Mexican Americans being treated fairly in the army a reality (aspirational capital), after the war he worked with other Mexican American veterans to form the League of United Latin American Citizens (LULAC), the largest and oldest organization focused on Latinx civil rights (resistant capital) (Américas Award, 2020 Commended Title; Pura Belpré Award, 2020 Honor).

Dreamers (Morales, 2018)

As a mother and infant son journey together to the United States (familial capital), they dream of one day becoming something they haven't yet imagined (aspirational capital). The book is filled with examples of navigational capital: how they learned the "rules" they were expected to follow in U.S. society and culture, the mistakes they made (like learning that public fountains are mostly for decoration, not actual use), learning to trust, and learning the magic of the library. The library was where they enacted their multilingual linguistic capital and leveraged books and writing as a form of resistant capital.

Morales advocates, "We are stories. We are two languages. We are lucha. We are resilience. We are hope. We are dreamers, soñadores of the world" (Américas Award, 2019 Commended; Pura Belpré Award, 2019 Illustration Award; Tomás Rivera Mexican American Children's Book Award, 2019 Winner).

Child of the Flower-Song People: Luz Jiménez, Daughter of the Nahua (Amescua, 2021)

Luz learned the traditions of her Indigenous Nahua people by growing up alongside them (social capital). However, she and her family had to leave her village behind during the Mexican Revolution, when they were forced to relocate to Mexico City. The government attempts to "modernize" the Nahua people, attempting to force them to speak Spanish and dress "appropriately." Luz resists, however, preserving her culture and maintaining her Nahuatl language (linguistic, social, and resistant capital). She first makes a living in Mexico City through practicing the traditional Indigenous artforms she learned as a child (social and navigational capital). This allowed her to be connected with famous artists who wished to portray an authentic, non-Europeanized representation of Mexico in their art and used her as a model (navigational and resistant capital). She had always dreamed of becoming a teacher (aspirational capital), and her dreams came true: she taught others about her Indigenous culture through the artists' portrayals of her, became a guide on tours, and worked with scholars and anthropologists to preserve her Nahua language and culture as a living link to the past (linguistic, social, navigational, and resistant capital) (Américas Award, 2022 Winner; Pura Belpré Children's Author Award, 2022 Honor Title).

My Two Border Towns (Bowles, 2021)

As a boy and his dad cross between their two border towns, they demonstrate various forms of capital. The book follows the pair as they visit their favorite spots in both towns (social and navigational capital), including the jewelry shop that belongs to the boy's aunt and uncle, where he gets to play with his primos (familial capital). While in Mexico, they visit various shops to acquire goods for families and friends (social and navigational). Their dialogue also reminds readers about the original Indigenous people who lived in the border town in Mexico, the Coahuiltecans (resistant capital). As they head back to their U.S. border town, the little boy and his dad stop to help some children waiting at the border (navigational and resistant capital), as they dream of a day when other friends can travel back and forth between the two border towns, just as they do (aspirational capital) (Américas Award, 2022 Winner; Tomás Rivera Mexican American Children's Book Award 2022).

Bright Star (Morales, 2021)

This story follows the journey of a young fawn who is separated from her mother, an allegory for the migrant experience. The book uses tranlanguaging between English and Spanish throughout (linguistic capital) as the young fawn learns how to navigate a world with her mother's influence by her side (familial and navigational capital). In one particularly powerful spread, the fawn yells "No!" at the border wall (resistant capital). The fawn is reminded, "You are a bright star inside our hearts" (aspirational capital) (Pura Belpré Children's Youth Illustrator Award, 2022 Honor Title; Tomás Rivera Mexican American Children's Book Award, 2022 Winner).

The Library Bus (Rahman, 2020)

On the "Library Bus," Pari and her mother are bringing books to villages near Kabul, Afghanistan. Pari dreams of learning to read and write in English and Farsi (aspirational and linguistic capital). Her mother recalls how she had to learn to read and write from her grandpa because girls were not allowed to attend school in Afghanistan when she was little (familial and resistant capital). The library bus brings books and literacy to people in the villages and refugee camps they visit, where there is limited access to schools (navigational and resistant capital) (Middle East Book Award, 2021 Winner).

Family Engagement through Community Cultural Wealth: Frequently Asked Questions

Even with the best intentions to pursue family engagement through an asset-based approach, challenges still arise. In this section, we approach some common issues framed as "Frequently Asked Questions" with some possibilities to consider.

I've tried everything, and I still can't get families to engage. Why? Now what?

With asset-based family engagement approaches, the importance of a "grass-roots" approach (Cowhey, 2022) cannot be overlooked. An important starting place is simply listening to families and then designing opportunities *with* families, not *for* them (Freire, 1970). If you are getting stuck, consider these opportunities to reflect.

- What spaces currently exist for family engagement in your educational setting? What is their origin story? Who created them and why? What do they

look like? When and where do they meet? Who tends to be involved, and why? Who seems to be absent, and why? How can you lean into spaces to hear the voices that are traditionally absent to learn more about *why* and *how* you might create a space that is more responsive to their needs?
- Has something worked in the past that isn't working now? What about your context has changed? How could you use families' input to adapt your approaches to be more responsive to your current context?
- What are some ways you can leverage families' existing CCW to co-design opportunities for engagement?

It is important to realize that grassroots, asset-based family engagement naturally changes over time. What worked last year may or may not be successful the next year. As Cowhey (2022) noted in her own work with family engagement, "authentic interest, volunteer energy, and commitment powered these programs and naturally shifted in response to issues in the school or community and the life challenges of students and adults" (p. 14). Each of the interactions we've described in this book are the products of a very specific context—an intersection of time, place, people, and needs—that may or may not apply to your situation. Especially now, as we navigate the shifting landscape of education in a post(continuing?)-pandemic context with education facing increasing regulation from outside forces, opportunities for family engagement may look very different from what has been successful in the past.

What if I don't live in the same community as my students and families?

Even if you live in a different community, you can still be proactive about finding opportunities to be active in the community where your students and families reside. Allow students and families to be your guides. When possible, accept invitations to participate in community events that are important to your students and families, positioning yourself as a guest and learner.

In addition, be cautious of space racism (Kendi, 2019). Sometimes, our schools and communities with larger populations of People of Color are labeled through deficit perspectives as "not safe." In fact, you may have even been told that you cannot conduct home visits to get to know your students' families because it's "not safe." When Melissa's administration told her she could not do home visits because it was "not safe," she got around it by inviting an administrator to come with her. You could also invite a co-teacher, paraprofessional, or community member, or you could offer to meet in a community-based venue, like a public library or laundromat. While safety for students, families, and educators does need to be prioritized, sometimes "safety" is used as a stereotypical manifestation of space racism.

All of this sounds amazing, but it also sounds like a substantial investment of time. I'm already not compensated for all the time and effort I put into designing high-quality instruction.

We agree, educators deserve compensation that correlates to the investment they make on a daily basis. We also acknowledge that listening to families and designing personalized opportunities that leverage their CCW takes time, and teachers need to set reasonable boundaries for their own mental health. However, a grassroots effort should not rely on just one person. We again echo Freire's call to do liberation work *with, not for* (Freire, 1970). One single teacher should not be trying to do all this work in isolation. Indeed, Freire cautioned individual teachers against thinking they were one of the few fighting for justice, as this can lead to non-productive self-righteousness (Darder, 2017). Families can use their social and familial networks to scale opportunities for engagement.

We also believe, though, that this work rehumanizes education for students, families, and educators alike. Freire believed "a humanizing education is the path through which men and women can become conscious about their presence in the world" (Darder, 2017, p. 34), and that it is "impossible to teach without educators' knowing what took place in their students' world" (Darder, 2017, p. 46). Therefore, while family engagement may feel like one more thing in the laundry list of educators' responsibilities, we firmly believe we cannot teach effectively without it.

What about other content areas? Can family engagement relate to those?

Absolutely! Cowhey (2022) talks about ways she listened to her families' strengths and needs to create math clubs with her families. While most opportunities for family engagement seem to center on literacy, they do not have to. For example, during and after the COVID-19 pandemic shut down schools, schools often assumed that families knew how to use technology, both the computers and the apps. Many students have school-issued Chromebooks and while (most) students know how to use them, their families do not necessarily have that knowledge. Additionally, schools used apps and other school-issued technology that families were not familiar with. Hosting technology nights where families can learn how to use the computers, technology, and/or apps would prove helpful for all families.

Where Do We Go from Here?

Through the **voices** of families, students, and educators, we have begun to fill the gap between theory and practice related to CCW that Acevedo and Solorzano (2021) named:

> We see the need for scholars to collaborate with practitioners and showcase the importance of using CCW as an approach to facilitate learning

in various PK-20 contexts. CCW represents a tool to implement research, praxis, and policies that challenge ongoing overt and covert institutional and individual attempts to marginalize Communities of Color.

(Acevedo and Solorzano 2021, p. 12)

We hope our work in this space is only the beginning. We need more educators, scholars, and communities to continue exploring spaces where CCW can be enacted in K-20. In the sections that follow, we offer four invitations for where to go from here: actively pursuing asset-based perceptions; creating spaces to listen and learn; redefining literacy; and critically consuming digital tools for family engagement.

Actively Pursuing Asset-based Perceptions

First and foremost, systems of educational stakeholders need to actively pursue asset-based perceptions of families and students, especially those from populations that have been historically marginalized and stigmatized. Larrotta and Yamamura (2011) assert, "Schools will also need to attend to their often shallow perceptions of parents and shift to assets-based perceptions in which parents are viewed as cultural experts and capable adults who can play an active role in their children's education" (p. 82). Almost daily, families who come from non-mainstream backgrounds encounter some form of negative talk connected to their language, culture, or way of being. Using their various forms of CCW, families can choose to actively resist the majoritarian notion of assimilation and accompanying messages (either overt or covert); some families even *choose* assimilation due to many factors, including fear and intimidation. Educators can take initiative to change assumptions and center assets so that families do not have to choose to resist or to assimilate; they can simply flourish.

Actively pursuing asset-based perceptions also involves interruption of deficit-based ones. Learning for Justice's "Speak Up at School" guide provides four tools for disrupting deficit-based language and situations (Willoughby, 2018).

- *Interrupt*: Stop deficit-oriented language and assumptions when they arise.
- *Question*: When deficit-based comments are made, ask the speaker questions to learn more about why they said, what they did, and how to respond constructively.
- *Educate*: Teach the speaker why a term or belief is hurtful.
- *Echo*: When someone else speaks up to interrupt a deficit-based comment, thank and echo this individual's interruption.

When we remain silent, we allow harmful deficit narratives to continue. Speaking up is an important place to start as we re-center the assets our families *do* possess.

Creating Spaces to Listen and Learn

Truly responsive, asset-centered approaches to family engagement start from spaces where educators and families can listen and learn with and from each other. Traditionally, families are positioned as the ones who need to listen and learn from the schools. We challenge you to flip that narrative. As educators, we have much to gain from listening and learning. We "need to continually educate ourselves about the nuances within Latinx communities that we may not understand, because they are not reflected in our own personal experiences, but nonetheless shape the realities of Latinx peoples" (Socorro & Delgado Bernal, 2022, p. 4). While this specific charge comes from a focus on Latinx people, this same charge clearly applies to our work with *all* families.

The onus of change lies with educational systems. As we have demonstrated throughout this book, families do have the assets necessary to initiate and sustain change; however, this burden should not fall on them. If the current systemic approach to education does not allow *all* students and families to be viewed in their full humanity, the system must change. Educators positioning themselves as listeners and learners is an important place to start.

Most importantly, the framework we present in this book is not a recipe of prescriptive elements and steps to take. It is a framework for knowing students and families deeply, for crafting strength-based counternarratives, and for taking critically informed action that designs equitable spaces for families to serve as experts and meaningful contributors to their children's learning experiences, both in and out of school. We have shown what it looked like in our own experiences and given you some ideas to show you what it could look like in your own educational spaces. If you do not start with listening to families, their strengths, and their needs, whatever you plan is likely to fail.

Asset-based family engagement is an ongoing, evolving journey, not a final destination. There is no "magic bullet" to family engagement other than centering assets, listening, and being responsive. The partnerships that result from this approach will look different in each unique context, but these principles must be at the center of any family–school partnerships.

Redefining Literacy

Traditionalized views of literacy place students' success with standardized testing at a premium, focusing on their ability to read and write using Standardized English. While literacy is an amalgamation of many different skills and mental processes, standardized tests reward student abilities in a very defined format. This limited view of literacy needs to shift to one rooted in the belief that children and families possess diverse repertoires of knowledge and that children are engaged in their communities' ways of knowing, communicating, and making sense of the world on a daily basis.

As we aim to incorporate minoritized families as resources in the learning process, a CCW framework provides teachers a lens through which to view the myriad forms of wealth that minoritized families possess and draw from daily. A CCW framework focuses teachers to:

- Recognize the role of language and culture in teaching;
- Understand that literacy is context-specific and socially situated;
- Value children's and families' repertoires of knowledge; and
- Recognize that students are more successful in school when their language, culture, and lived experiences are valued by using the language and cultural practices in their families and communities as foundations upon which to build.

Critically examine current framing of recognized literacy practices in educational contexts surrounding you. Consider moving toward culturally sustaining pedagogies in literacy, which allow educators to "create reading processes and practices that are life-affirming and build on their capacities, interests, and values" (Nash et al., 2022). Intentionally select materials to engage with, being cautious to "resist the temptation to choose for read-alouds and teaching writer's craft those books that only resonate with us [the educators]; we must instead choose books that will resonate with the children we teach" (Gangi, 2008, p. 34). Actively include manifestations of literacy that may be left out of some traditional spaces, like storytelling. NCTE's "Teaching Storytelling Position Statement" (NCTE, 2022) includes helpful information about the benefits of including storytelling in classroom spaces. In addition, incorporating multimodal literacies allows children varied opportunities to understand and be understood. If "young children practice multimodal literacies naturally and spontaneously" (NCTE, 2005, para. 2), we owe it to our students to adjust our literacy instruction to leverage these literacy skills that they already utilize. When we redefine what counts as literacy, we open new worlds of possibilities for expression and identity for our students and families.

Critically Consuming Digital Tools for Family Engagement

There are many tools and approaches to maximize family engagement; however, it is important to critically consume these products and ideas. As a specific example, we have shared ideas for using digital tools to align with families' CCW throughout this book. New digital tools marketed for family engagement are released frequently, but not all of them are designed with the asset-based approach to family engagement and CCW that we use as the framework of this book.

When analyzing new tools, consider the following areas for analysis. These questions should be used to critically analyze and select digital platforms that facilitate family engagement, both to screen in and to screen out tools.

- Whose interests seem to be at the center of the tool? Is advertising and support more targeted toward families or schools and teachers?
- What kinds of activities are supported in the platform? Not supported?
- What data is collected or provided to define "engagement"?

As an example, on the ClassTag website (https://home.classtag.com/), we can gain some valuable insights by using these types of critical questions. On the home page, the top right corner bears links "For Teachers" and "For Districts and Schools." There is no link "For Families." Therefore, viewers gain the impression that the primary audience for this website—and possibly the marketing of this platform—seems to be school-based, not family-based. This impression is further solidified in other places within the website, such as one that states, "ClassTag Connect is an all-in-one community engagement platform for district administrators, principals, and teachers. We create a humanized experience that improves two-way engagement and family communication through a single, easy-to-use unified platform with a focus on full control and visibility across the entire district" (M., 2021, "ClassTag Connect vs Blackboard: How Our Main Focus Differs," para. 1). This quote explicitly names who this platform is for—all of whom are school-based stakeholders, not families.

As for activities, ClassTag allows families to see upcoming and past activities, sign up for conferences, access a directory of contact information for all families in the class who opted into this service, add co-parents and guardians to access the app, initiate group or one-on-one conversations, and access a library "where you can find class and event photos and videos, class files, and even upload your own files, photos, and videos to share with other members of the class" (Karl, n.d., "Library," para. 1). These activities provide families with agency to initiate engagement not only with the teacher or school, but also with other families in the class. When combined with the platform's ability to translate to and from over 100 languages, we can see opportunities for using ClassTag in ways that align with families' linguistic, familial, social, and navigational capitals.

A critical analysis of the communication metrics built into ClassTag is also insightful. There is a "Family Engagement Dashboard," which reports if families have been active within the past 7, 14, or 21 days, or whether they are labeled as unreachable, no contacts, awaiting confirmation, or unresponsive.

Additionally, the "Students at Risk Dashboard shows which families are responsive, unresponsive, unreachable, and have no contact information" (M., 2021, "Students at Risk Report," para. 1). Framing this report with a deficit narrative—that students are at risk if their families are not active on the app—does not align with asset-based approaches to family engagement. Therefore, while ClassTag does have some unique features that can be used to engage families in humanizing dialogic ways, it also has some deficit-based, school-centric beliefs about what constitutes family engagement.

With intentionality, though, even some tools that seem to be more teacher- or school-centered can be leveraged in ways that provide families with agency. For example, if a platform only allows for the teacher to share messages with the entire community, this positions the teacher as the one with the most power and owner of information that needs to be shared. Such a limitation can be worked around if the teacher shares messages that other family members wish to be shared with the entire community, signing the names of the message creators. Similarly, some platforms now allow families to "reply all" to a message the teacher sends instead of limiting responses to private messages directly to the teacher, which allows for two-way communication between teachers and individual families but does not leverage social capital. Teachers could push out a message with an invitation to "reply all" whenever families need a space to communicate with each other, thus giving families agency to build social networks as needed. As these examples show, we can "hack" platforms to meet our purposes for asset-based family engagement, but this often needs to be done very intentionally.

In summary, family engagement is a common interest, and many new tools and apps will be developed and released. Whenever considering which tools to use and how, critically analyze them to see how families and schools are positioned. Use the tool's features to interrupt deficit-based views of families, and work with families to build asset-based digital spaces for engagement instead.

Conclusion

In this book, we have responded to the call of García-Sánchez and Orellana (2019) to "[focus] our efforts on identifying similarities and generative points of continuity between everyday and school practices in order to develop a responsive approach to classroom practices that centers linguistic and cultural diversity as the bedrock of educational achievement and expands possibilities for all" (p. 9). We hope that the **voces** you have heard throughout this book—from families, students, and educators—have inspired you to take action toward these efforts in your own educational spaces as well.

When we re-envision family engagement and literacy in early childhood classrooms, we see centering families' strengths as the norm. We see classrooms that celebrate all the forms of CCW—aspirational, linguistic, familial, social, navigational, resistant capital, *and more*. We see classrooms that start to question what has always been done in the realms of family engagement and literacy to re-envision practices that are asset-based instead of traditions-based. We see spaces where families' voices, gifts, and needs are at the center of all family engagement opportunities. Instead of asking our families to assimilate to a system of American education that may not acknowledge their varied ways of knowing, what if we restructured that educational system to value what our students and families *do* bring to our educational spaces, communities, and society every single day?

As **one** mother so beautifully said: **porque así ya conocemos**—*because we already know.*

References

Acevedo, N., & Solorzano, D. G. (2021). *An overview of community cultural wealth: Toward a protective factor against racism*. Urban Education. https://doi.org/10.1177/00420859211016531

Adichie, C. (2009, July). *Chimamanda Adichie: The danger of a single story* (Video). TED. https://www.ted.com/talks/chimamanda_ngozi_adichie_the_danger_of_a_single_story

Carly, M. (2021, April 26). *ClassTag connect vs. blackboard: Which is best for family engagement and communication?* ClassTag Blog. https://home.classtag.com/blog/classtag-connect-vs-blackboard-for-family-engagement/

Cowhey, M. (2022). *Families with power: Centering students by engaging with families and community*. Teachers College Press.

Darder, A. (2017). *Reinventing Paulo Freire: A pedagogy of love* (2nd ed.). Routledge.

Delgado Gaitan, C. (2014). Culture, literacy, and power in family-community-school relationships. In A. Darder & R. D. Torres (Eds.), *Latinos and education: A critical reader* (2nd ed., pp. 339–345). Routledge.

Freire, P. (1970). *Pedagogy of the oppressed*. Continuum.

Gangi, J. M. (2008). The unbearable whiteness of literacy instruction: Realizing the implications of the proficient reader research. *Multicultural Review*, 17(1), 30–35.

García-Sánchez, I. M., & Orellana, M. F. (2019). Introduction: Everyday learning: Centering in schools the language and cultural practices of young people from non-dominant groups. In I. M. García-Sánchez, & M. F. Orellana (Eds.), *Language and cultural practices in communities and schools: Bridging learning for students from non-dominant groups* (pp. 1–23). Routledge.

Karl, A. (n.d.). *What can parents see and do on ClassTag?* ClassTag Blog. https://help.classtag.com/en/articles/2547185-what-can-parents-see-and-do-on-classtag

Kendi, I. X. (2019). *How to be an antiracist*. Random House.

Larrotta, C., & Yamamura, E. K. (2011). A community cultural wealth approach to Latina/Latino parent involvement: The promise of family literacy. *Adult Basic Education and Literacy Journal*, 5(2), 74–83.

Martínez, R. A., Vieyra, V. M., Ahmad, N. B., & Stovall, J. L. (2022). Prefiguring translingual possibilities: The transformative potential of translanguaging for dual language bilingual education. In M. T. Sánchez, & O. García (Eds.), *Transformative translanguaging espacios: Latinx students and their teachers rompiendo fronteras sin miedo* (pp. 95–112). Multilingual Matters.

NCTE (2005, November 17). *Multimodal literacies position statement.* National Council of Teachers of English. https://ncte.org/statement/multimodalliteracies/

NCTE (2022, December 1). *Teaching storytelling position statement.* National Council of Teachers of English. https://ncte.org/statement/teaching-storytelling-position-statements/

Nash, K. T., Arce-Boardman, A., Peele, R., & Elson, K. (2022). *Culturally sustaining language and literacy practices for pre-K-3 classrooms.* Teachers College Press.

Park, J. J., Dizon, J. P. M., & Malcolm, M. (2020). Spiritual capital in communities of color: Religion and spirituality as sources of community cultural wealth. *The Urban Review, 52*(1), 127–150.

Pérez Huber, L. (2009). Challenging racist nativist framing: Acknowledging the community cultural wealth of undocumented Chicana college students to reframe the immigration debate. *Harvard Educational Review, 79*(4), 704–730.

Shor, I., & Freire, P. (1987). What is the "dialogical method" of teaching? *Journal of Education, 169*(3), 11–31. doi: https://doi.org/10.1177/002205748716900303.

Socorro, M., & Delgado Bernal, D. (2022). History, theory, and methodology: An introduction. In E.G. Murillo, Jr., D. Delgado Bernal, S. Morales, L. Urrieta, Jr., E. R. Bybee, J. S. Muñoz, V. Sáenz, D. Villanueva, M. Machado-Casas, & K. Espinoza (Eds.), *Handbook of Latinos and education: Theory, research, and practice* (2nd ed., pp. 3–7). Routledge.

Willoughby, A. (2018). *Speak up at school: How to respond to everyday prejudice, bias, and stereotypes.* Learning for Justice/Southern Poverty Law Center. https://www.learningforjustice.org/sites/default/files/2019-04/TT-Speak-Up-Guide_0.pdf

Yosso, T. J. (2005). Whose culture has capital? A critical race theory discussion of community cultural wealth. *Race Ethnicity and Education, 8*(1), 69–91.

Children's Literature

Amescua, G. (2021). *Child of the flower-song people: Luz Jiménez, daughter of the Nahua* (D. Tonatiuh, Illus.). Abrams Books for Young Readers.

Bowles, D. (2021). *My two border towns* (E. Meza, Illus.). Kokila.

Denise, A. A. (2019). *Planting stories: The life of librarian and storyteller Pura Belpré* (P. E. Harper, Illus.). HarperCollins.

Garza, C. L. (1998). *Family pictures/Cuadros de mi familia* (C. L. Garza, Illus.). Lee & Low Books.

Morales, Y. (2018). *Dreamers* (Y. Morales, Illus.). Neal Porter Books.

Morales, Y. (2021). *Bright star* (Y. Morales, Illus.). Neal Porter Books.

Rahman, B. (2020). *The library bus* (G. Grimard, Illus.). Pajama Press.

Tonatiuh, D. (2019). *Soldier for equality: José de la Luz Sáenz and the Great War* (D. Tonatiuh, Illus.) Abrams Books for Young Readers.

APPENDIX A

Analysis of CCW Themes in Selected Children's Literature

Appendix A **159**

Children's Literature Information		CCW Analysis					
Title of the Book	Award (Year)	Aspirational	Linguistic	Familial	Social	Navigational	Resistant
A Different Pond (Bao Phi, author; Thi Bui, illustrator)	Caldecott Medal, 2018 Honor Book	(x)	x			x*	
A Drop of the Sea (Ingrid Chabbert, author; Raúl Nieto Guridi, illustrator)	Middle East Book Award, 2019 Picture Book Winner	x*	x				
A Friend for Henry (Jenn Bailey, author; Mika Song, illustrator)	Schneider Family Book Award, 2020 Younger Children Honor Title			x	x*		
A Gift from Abuela (Cecilia Ruiz, author and illustrator)	Américas Award, 2019 Commended Title			x*			(x)
ABC El Salvador (Holly Ayala, author; Elizabeth Gómez, illustrator)	Américas Award, 2022 Commended Title		x*				
Across the Bay (Carlos Aponte, author and illustrator)	Pura Belpré Award, 2020 Illustrator Honor			(x)	x*		
All Around Us (Xelena González, author; Adriana M. Garcia, illustrator)	Tomás Rivera Mexican American Children's Book Award, 2018 Winner			x*			

(Continued)

Appendix A

Children's Literature Information		CCW Analysis					
Title of the Book	Award (Year)	Aspirational	Linguistic	Familial	Social	Navigational	Resistant
All the Way to the Top: How One Girl's Fight for Americans with Disabilities Changed Everything (Annette Bay Pimentel, author; Nabi H. Ali, illustrator)	Schneider Family Book Award, 2021 Younger Children Honor Title	x					x
Alma and How She Got Her Name (Juana Martinez-Neal, author and illustrator)	Américas Award, 2019 Commended Title; Caldecott Medal, 2019 Honor Book	(x)	(x)	x*		x*	(x)
Along the Tapajós (Fernando Vilela, author and illustrator)	Américas Award, 2020 Commended Title			x*	(x)	(x)	
At the Mountain's Base (Traci Sorell, author [Cherokee]; Weshoyot Alvitre, illustrator [Tongva/Scots-Gaelic])	American Indian Youth Literature Award, 2020 Picture Book Honor Book			x			x*
Auntie Luce's Talking Paintings (Francie Latour, author; Ken Daley, illustrator)	Américas Award, 2019 Honorable Mention		(x)	x	(x)		x*

(Continued)

Appendix A **161**

Children's Literature Information		CCW Analysis					
Title of the Book	Award (Year)	Aspirational	Linguistic	Familial	Social	Navigational	Resistant
Between Us and Abuela: A Family Story from the Border (Mitali Perkins, author; Sara Palacios, illustrator)	Américas Award, 2020 Winner	(x)	(x)				x*
Birdsong (Julie Flett, author and illustrator [Cree-Métis])	American Indian Youth Literature Award, 2020 Picture Book Honor Book				x*		
Boogie, Y'all (C. G. Esperanza, author and illustrator)	Pura Belpré Children's Youth Illustrator Award, 2022 Honor Title					(x)	x*
Bowwow Powwow: Bagosenjige-niimi'idim (Brenda J. Child, author [Red Lake Ojibwe]; Gordon Jourdain, translator [Lac La Croix First Nation]; Jonathan Thunder, illustrator [Red Lake Ojibwe])	American Indian Youth Literature Award, 2020 Picture Book Winner	x*		x			
Brick by Brick (Heidi Woodward Sheffield, author and illustrator)	Américas Award, 2021 Commended Title	x*		x		x	x

(Continued)

162 Appendix A

Children's Literature Information		CCW Analysis					
Title of the Book	Award (Year)	Aspirational	Linguistic	Familial	Social	Navigational	Resistant
Bright Star (Yuyi Morales, author and illustrator)	Pura Belpré Children's Youth Illustrator Award, 2022 Honor Title; Tomás Rivera Mexican American Children's Book Award, 2022 Winner	x	(x)	x	x	x*	x
Carmela Full of Wishes (Matt de la Peña, author; Christian Robinson, illustrator)	Américas Award, 2019 Commended Title	x*	(x)	(x)	(x)	(x)	
Child of the Flower-Song People: Luz Jiménez, Daughter of the Nahua (Gloria Amescua; author; Duncan Tonatiuh, illustrator)	Américas Award, 2022 Winner; Pura Belpré Children's Author Award, 2022 Honor Title	(x)	x*		(x)	x	x
Classified: The Secret Career of Mary Golda Ross, Cherokee Aerospace Engineer (Traci Sorell, author [Cherokee]; Natasha Donovan, illustrator [Métis])	American Indian Youth Literature Award, 2022 Picture Book Honor Book	x*				x	x

(Continued)

Appendix A **163**

Children's Literature Information		CCW Analysis					
Title of the Book	Award (Year)	Aspirational	Linguistic	Familial	Social	Navigational	Resistant
Coquí in the City (Nomar Perez, author and illustrator)	Américas Award, 2022 Commended Title; Pura Belpré Children's Author Award, 2022 Honor Title; Pura Belpré Children's Youth Illustrator Award, 2022 Honor Title		x	x		x★	
Crescent Moons and Pointed Minarets (Hena Khan, author; Mehrdokht Amini, illustrator)	Middle East Book Award, 2018 Picture Book Honorable Mention				x★		
Crown: An Ode to the Fresh Cut (Derrick Barnes, author; Gordon C. James, illustrator)	Caldecott Medal, 2018 Honor Book; Newbery Medal, 2018 Honor Book	x			x★		
Dancing Hands: How Teresa Carreño Played the Piano for President Lincoln (Margarita Engle, author; Rafael López, illustrator)	Pura Belpré Award, 2020 Illustration Award Winner	x★		x		(x)	(x)

(Continued)

Children's Literature Information

Title of the Book	Award (Year)	CCW Analysis					
		Aspirational	Linguistic	Familial	Social	Navigational	Resistant
Digging for Words, José Alberto Gutiérrez and the Library He Built (Angela Burke Kunkel, author; Paola Escobar, illustrator)	Américas Award, 2021 Winner	(x)				x★	x
Double Bass Blues (Andrea J. Loney, author; Rudy Gutierrez, illustrator)	Caldecott Medal, 2020 Honor Book			x★	(x)		
Dreamers (Yuyi Morales, author and illustrator)	Américas Award, 2019 Commended Title Pura Belpré Award, 2019 Illustration Award Tomás Rivera Mexican American Children's Book Award, 2019 Winner	x★	(x)	(x)	(x)	(x)	x
Evelyn Del Rey Is Moving Away (Meg Medina, author; Sonia Sanchez, illustrator)	Américas Award, 2021 Commended Title			x	x★	(x)	

(Continued)

Appendix A **165**

Children's Literature Information		CCW Analysis					
Title of the Book	Award (Year)	Aspirational	Linguistic	Familial	Social	Navigational	Resistant
Exquisite: The Poetry and Life of Gwendolyn Brooks (Suzanne Slade, author; Cozbi A. Cabrera, illustrator)	Coretta Scott King Book Award, 2022 Illustrator Honor Book	x				x*	x
Freedom Soup (Tami Charles, author; Jacqueline Alcántara, illustrator)	Américas Award, 2020 Commended Title			x	(x)		
From My Window (Otávio Júnior, author; Beatriz C. Dias, translator; Vanina Starkoff, illustrator)	Américas Award, 2021 Commended Title			x	x*	(x)	(x)
Fry Bread: A Native American Family Story (Kevin Noble Maillard, author [Seminole Nation, Mekusukey Band]; Juana Martinez-Neal, illustrator [Peruvian-American])	American Indian Youth Literature Award, 2020 Picture Book Honor Book			x	x*	(x)	(x)

(Continued)

Appendix A

Children's Literature Information		CCW Analysis					
Title of the Book	Award (Year)	Aspirational	Linguistic	Familial	Social	Navigational	Resistant
Fuego Fueguito/Fire, Little Fire/Tit, Titchin (Jorge Tetl Argueta, author; Felipe Ugalde Alcántara, illustrator)	Américas Award, 2020 Commended Title		x★				
Going Down Home with Daddy (Kelly Starling Lyons, author; Daniel Minter, illustrator)	Caldecott Medal, 2020 Honor Book	x		x★			(x)
Grandad's Camper (Harry Woodgate, author and illustrator)	Stonewall Book Award—Mike Morgan and Larry Romans Children's and Young Adult Literature Award, 2022 Honor Book			x★			
I Sang You Down from the Stars (Tasha Spillett-Summer, author [Cree and Trinidadian]; Michaela Goade, illustrator [Tlingit & Haida])	American Indian Youth Literature Award, 2022 Picture Book Honor Book			x★			
I Talk Like a River (Jordan Scott, author; Sydney Smith, illustrator)	Schneider Family Book Award, 2021 Younger Children Winner			x			x★

(Continued)

Children's Literature Information		CCW Analysis					
Title of the Book	Award (Year)	Aspirational	Linguistic	Familial	Social	Navigational	Resistant
If Dominican Were a Color (Sili Recio, author; Brianna McCarthy, illustrator)	Américas Award, 2021 Honorable Mention				x*		
Isabel and Her Colores Go to School (Alexandra Alessandri, author; Courtney Dawson, illustrator)	Américas Award, 2022 Commended Title					x	
Islandborn (Junot Díaz, author; Leo Espinosa, illustrator)	Américas Award, 2019 Winner Pura Belpré Award, 2019 Illustration Honor	(x)	x*	x	x*		
Itzhak: A Boy Who Loved the Violin (Tracy Newman, author; Abigail Halpin, illustrator)	Schneider Family Book Award, 2021 Younger Children Honor Title	x		(x)	(x)		x
Julián Is a Mermaid (Jessica Love, author and illustrator)	Stonewall Book Award—Mike Morgan and Larry Romans Children's and Young Adult Literature Award, 2019 Winner			x*		x*	x

(Continued)

Appendix A

Children's Literature Information		CCW Analysis					
Title of the Book	Award (Year)	Aspirational	Linguistic	Familial	Social	Navigational	Resistant
Just Ask! Be Different, Be Brave, Be You (Sonia Sotomayor, author; Rafael López, illustrator)	Schneider Family Book Award, 2020 Younger Children Winner				x*	x	x
Magnificent Homespun Brown: A Celebration (Samara Cole Doyon, author; Kaylani Juanita, illustrator)	Coretta Scott King Book Award, 2021 Illustrator Honor Book			x			x
Maryam's Magic (Megan Reid, author; Aaliya Jaleel, illustrator)	Middle East Book Award, 2021 Honorable Mention						x
May Your Life Be Deliciosa (Michael Genhart, author; Loris Lora, illustrator)	Pura Belpré Children's Youth Illustrator Award, 2022 Honor Title	x*		x*			
Maybe Something Beautiful: How Art Transformed a Neighborhood (Isabel Campoy and Theresa Howell, authors; Rafael López, illustrator)	Tomás Rivera Mexican American Children's Book Award, 2017 Winner	x*		(x)	x		(x)
My City Speaks (Darren Lebeuf, author; Ashley Barron, illustrator)	Schneider Family Book Award, 2022 Younger Children Winner					x*	

(Continued)

Appendix A **169**

Children's Literature Information		CCW Analysis					
Title of the Book	Award (Year)	Aspirational	Linguistic	Familial	Social	Navigational	Resistant
My Grandma and Me (Mina Javahertin, author; Lindsey Yankey, illustrator)	Middle East Book Award, 2019 Picture Book Honorable Mention			x★	x		
My Papi Has a Motorcycle (Isabel Quintero, author; Zeke Peña, illustrator)	Américas Award, 2020 Honorable Mention Pura Belpré Award, 2020 Illustration Honor Pura Belpré Award, 2020 Illustration Honor Tomás Rivera Mexican American Children's Book Award, 2020 Winner		(x)	x	(x)	x★	(x)
My Two Border Towns (David Bowles, author; Erika Meza, illustrator)	Américas Award, 2022 Winner Tomás Rivera Mexican American Children's Book Award, 2022	x		(x)	x★	x	x★
Nina: A Story of Nina Simone (Traci N. Todd, author; Christian Robinson, illustrator)	Coretta Scott King Book Award, 2022 Illustrator Honor Book			(x)		x	
Planting Stories: The Life of Librarian and Storyteller Pura Belpré (Anika Aldamuy Denise, author; Paola Escobar Harper, illustrator)	Américas Award, 2020 Commended Title Pura Belpré Award, 2020 Honor	(x)	(x)	(x)	(x)	x★	x

(Continued)

Appendix A

Children's Literature Information		CCW Analysis					
Title of the Book	Award (Year)	Aspirational	Linguistic	Familial	Social	Navigational	Resistant
Rescue & Jessica: A Life-changing Friendship (Jessica Kensky, author; Patrick Downes, illustrator)	Schneider Family Book Award, 2019 Younger Children Winner				x★		
RESPECT: Aretha Franklin, the Queen of Soul (Carole Boston Weatherford, author; Frank Morrison, illustrator)	Coretta Scott King, 2021 Illustrator Winner	x		(x)		x★	x
Salma the Syrian Chef (Danny Ramadan, author; Anna Bron, illustrator)	Middle East Book Award, 2020 Picture Book Winner	(x)	x★	x		x	
Seven Special Somethings (Adib Khorram, author; Zainab Faidhi, illustrator)	Middle East Book Award, 2021 Honorable Mention	x★		x			
Sharuko: El Arqueólogo Peruano/Peruvian Archaeologist (Julio C. Tello, Monica Brown, author; Elisa Chavarri, illustrator)	Pura Belpré Award, 2021 Youth Illustrator Honor	x	(x)	(x)			x★
Soldier for Equality: José de la Luz Sáenz and the Great War (Duncan Tonatiuh, author and illustrator)	Américas Award, 2020 Commended Title						
	Pura Belpré Award, 2020 Honor	x	x★	(x)	(x)	(x)	x

(Continued)

Appendix A **171**

Children's Literature Information		CCW Analysis					
Title of the Book	Award (Year)	Aspirational	Linguistic	Familial	Social	Navigational	Resistant
Song of the Old City (Anna Pellicioli, author; Merve Atilgan, illustrator)	Middle East Book Award, 2021 Honorable Mention				x★		
Soul Food Sunday (Winsome Bingham, author; C. G. Esperanza, illustrator)	Coretta Scott King Book Award, 2022 Illustrator Honor Book			x★			
Thank You, Omu! (Oge Mora, author and illustrator)	Caldecott Medal, 2019 Honor Book				x★		
The Cat Man of Aleppo (Irene Latham and Karim Shamsi-Basha, authors; Yuko Shimizu, illustrator)	Caldecott Medal, 2021 Honor Book	(x)			x★		x
The Library Bus (Bahram Rahman, author; Gabrielle Grimard, illustrator)	Middle East Book Award, 2021 Winner	(x)	(x)	x		x★	x
The Life of/La Vida de Dolores (Patty Rodriguez and Ariana Stein, authors; Citlali Reyes, illustrator)	Américas Award, 2022 Commended Title	x			x	x	x★

(Continued)

Children's Literature Information		CCW Analysis					
Title of the Book	Award (Year)	Aspirational	Linguistic	Familial	Social	Navigational	Resistant
The Me I Choose to Be (Natasha Anastasia Tarpley, author; Regis and Kahran Bethencourt, illustrators)	Coretta Scott King Book Award, 2022 John Steptoe Award for New Talent (Illustrator)	x★					x
The People Remember (Ibi Zoboi, author; Loveis Wise, illustrator)	Coretta Scott King Book Award, 2022 Author Honor Book	x					x★
The Remember Balloons (Jessie Oliveros, author; Dana Wulfekotte, illustrator)	Schneider Family Book Award, 2019 Younger Children Honor Title			x★			
The Spirit of Chicano Park/ El Espíritu del Parque Chicano (Beatrice Zamora, author; Maira Meza, illustrator)	Tomás Rivera Mexican American Children's Book Award, 2021 Winner				(x)	(x)	x★
The Undefeated (Kwame Alexander, author; Kadir Nelson, illustrator)	Caldecott Medal, 2020 Winner Newbery Medal, 2020 Honor Book	(x)			(x)	x	x★
Tomorrow (Nadine Kaadan, author and illustrator)	Middle East Book Award, 2019 Picture Book Honorable Mention	x★		x			x

(Continued)

Appendix A **173**

Children's Literature Information		CCW Analysis					
Title of the Book	Award (Year)	Aspirational	Linguistic	Familial	Social	Navigational	Resistant
Watercress (Andrea Wang, author; Jason Chin, illustrator)	Caldecott Medal, 2022 Honor Title; Newbery Medal, 2022 Honor Title						(x)
We Are Grateful: Otsaliheliga (Traci Sorell [Cherokee], author; Frané Lessac, illustrator)	American Indian Youth Literature Award, 2020 Picture Book Honor Books		x*	x	x		(x)
We Are Still Here! Native American Truths Everyone Should Know (Traci Sorell [Cherokee], author; Frané Lessac, illustrator)	American Indian Youth Literature Award, 2022 Picture Book Honor Book					x	x*
We Are Water Protectors (Carole Lindstrom, author; Michaela Goade, illustrator)	Caldecott Medal, 2021 Winner	(x)		(x)	(x)	(x)	x*
We Wait for the Sun (Dovey Johnson Roundtree and Katie McCabe, authors; Raissa Figueroa, illustrator)	Coretta Scott King Book Award, 2022 Illustrator Honor Book			x*	x		

(Continued)

Appendix A

Children's Literature Information

Title of the Book	Award (Year)	CCW Analysis					
		Aspirational	*Linguistic*	*Familial*	*Social*	*Navigational*	*Resistant*
When Aidan Became a Brother (Kyle Lukoff, author; Kaylani Juanita, illustrator)	Stonewall Book Award—Mike Morgan and Larry Romans Children's and Young Adult Literature Award, 2020 Winner			x★			x
When Angels Sing: The Story of Rock Legend Carlos Santana (Michael Mahin, author; Jose Ramirez, illustrator)	Américas Award, 2019 Commended Pura Belpré Award, 2019 Illustration Honor		(x)	(x)	(x)	x★	x

Notes
x★ Signifies focus/feature theme
x Signifies primary theme
(x) Signifies secondary theme.

INDEX

Note: Page numbers in **Bold** refer to tables; and page numbers in *italics* refer to figures

ABC El Salvador (Ayala, 2021) 63–64, **159**
Acevedo, N. 30, 150, 151
Across the Bay (Aponte, 2019) 96, **159**
Ada, A. F. 54
Adichie, C. 141
Alcántara, F. U. **165**
Alcántara, J. **164**
Alemán, E. 36, 39, 93, 104, 123
Alessandri, A. 64, **166**
Alexander, K. 134–135, **172**
Alim, H. S. 26, 30
Ali, N. H. **159**
All Around Us (González, 2017) 81, **159**
Allen, J. 23, 24
All the Way to the Top: How One Girl's Fight for Americans with Disabilities Changed Everything (Pimentel, 2020) 114–115, **159**
Alma and How She Got Her Name (Martinez-Neal, 2018) 79, **159**, **160**
Along the Tapajós (Vilela, 2019) 81, **160**
Alvitre, W. **160**
American education 26
Americans with Disabilities Act (ADA) 114
Amescua, G. 63, 147
Anzaldúa, G. 126, 127

Aponte, C. 96, **159**
Argueta, J. T. 62, **165**
aspirational capital: in action 36–37; as advocacy 39–40; children's literature 40; classroom strategies 41–42; digital tools **47**; dreams for our children 37–39; family strategies 42–43
Atilgan, M. **170**
At the Mountain's Base (Sorell, 2019) 135, **160**
Auntie Luce's Talking Paintings (Latour, 2018) 134, **160**
Ayala, H. 63–64, **159**

Bailey, J. 97, **158**
Bakhtin, M. 13, 21, 22
Baquedano-López, P. 26, 90, 93
Barajas, E. D. 106
Barnes, D. 97
Barron, A. **168**
Bartolomé, L. 126
Bear, D. R. **29**
Beaver, J. **29**
Bell, D. 27
Bernal, D. D. 10
The Best Part of Me: Children Talk about Their Bodies in Pictures and Words (Ewald, 2002) 74

Bethencourt, K. **171**
Bethencourt, R. **171**
Between Us and Abuela: A Family Story from the Border (Perkins, 2019) 133, **160**
Bialystok, E. 61
Bingham, W. 82, **170**
Birdsong (Flett, 2019) 97–98, **160**
Bishop, R. S. 2, 13, 28
Boogie Boogie, Y'all (Esperanza, 2021) 135, **160**
Bourdieu, P. 29, 30
Boutte, G. S. 12, 58, 59
Bowles, D. 98, 147, **169**
Bowwow Powwow: Bagosenjige-niimi'idim (Child, 2018) 45, **161**
Brick by Brick (Sheffield, 2020) 46, **161**
Bright Star (Morales, 2021) 116, **161**
Bron, A. **170**
Brooks, G. 116
Brown, M. 134, **170**
Bui, T. **158**
Burns, P. C. **29**
Butler, D. 28

Cabrera, C. A. **164**
Campano, G. 19
Campoy, I. 45, **168**
Carmela Full of Wishes (de la Peña, 2018) 44, **161**
The Cat Man of Aleppo (Latham and Shamsi-Basha, 2020) 96–97, **171**
Cazden, C. B. 58
Chabbert, I. 45, **158**
Charles, T. 133–134, **164**
Chavarri, E. **170**
Child, B. J. 45
Child of the Flower-Song People: Luz Jiménez, Daughter of the Nahua (Amescua, 2021) 63, **162**
children's literature 11–12
Chin, J. **172**
Class Dojo **65**
Classified: The Secret Career of Mary Golda Ross, Cherokee Aerospace Engineer (Sorell, 2021) 46, **162**
classroom strategies: aspirational capital 41–42; familial capital 77–78; linguistic capital 59–60; navigational capital 110–111; resistant capital 131–132; social capital 94

Class Tag **99**
Colato Laínez, R. 124, 129, 130
comadres 86, 87, 90
community cultural wealth (CCW): children's literature analysis **146–148, 158–174**; conceptualization of 141, 142; context of classroom practice 12; create spaces to listen and learn 152; different forms 9; digital tools for family engagement 153–155; expectations and responsibilities **143–144**; family engagement in early childhood settings 13; kaleidoscope of capitals 142, 144–145; pursuing asset-based perceptions 151; redefining literacy 152–153; re-envisioning schooling 141; theoretical framework 28–30; through the lens of family engagement 30; voces 140, 150
Compton-Lilly, C. 20
confianza 22, 36, 42–44
Contreras, F. 96
Coquí in the City (Perez, 2021) 115, **162**
Cornwall, C. 76, 77
COVID-19 8, 150
Cowhey, M. 19, 23, 24, 77, 93, 148–150
Crescent Moons and Pointed Minarets (Khan, 2018) 94, **163**
critical race theory (CRT) 13, 27
Crown: An Ode to the Fresh Cut (Barnes, 2017) 97, **163**
Cummins, J. 61

Daley, K. **160**
Dancing Hands: How Teresa Carreño Played the Piano for President Lincoln (Engle, 2019) 44–45, **163**
Darder, A. 109, 122, 141, 150
Davila, E. R. 26, 104
Dawson, C. **166**
de Bradley, A. A. 26, 104
deficit thinking 27
Delange, A. P. 57
de la Peña, M. 44
Delgado Bernal, D. 28, 36, 39, 93, 104, 123, 132, 152
Delgado-Gaitan, C. 36, 90
Delgado, R. 27, 90
Delpit, L. 26, 55, 58, 59

Denise, A. A. 114, 145–146, **169**
Deyhle, D. 19, 30, 36, 70
Dias, B. C. **164**
Díaz, J. 96, **166**
A Different Pond (Phi, 2017) 114, **158**
Digging for Words: José Alberto Gutiérrez and the Library He Built (Kunkel, 2020) 115–116, **163**
digital surveys **83**
Dixon, L. Q. 51, 53
Doake, D. 28
Double Bass Blues (Loney, 2019) 81, **163**
Downes, P. **169**
Doyon, S. C. 47, **167**
Dreamers (Morales, 2018) 40, 146–147, **164**
A Drop of the Sea (Chabbert, 2018) 45, **158**
Dunsmore, K. 111

early childhood classrooms: engaging families with technology 24–25; family involvement *vs.* family engagement 18–19; family–school communication 20–22; home–school knowledge exchanges 23–24
Early, J. S. 8, 53
Edwards, P. 19, 70, 90
Engle, M. 44–45, **163**
episodes and counternarratives 10–11
Equal Educational Opportunities Act 108
Esperanza, C. G. 135, **170**
Espinosa, L. **166**
Evelyn Del Rey Is Moving Away (Medina, 2020) 98, **164**
Exquisite: The Poetry and Life of Gwendolyn Brooks (Slade, 2020) 116, **164**

Faidhi, Z. **170**
Fain, J. G. 23
familial capital: children and families with their cultural knowledge 71–73; children's literature 76; classroom strategies 77–78; digital tools 83, **83**; family strategies 78; gift of names 75–76; networks to help and support each other 73–74; overview 70; sewing as 74–75
family engagement: classroom teaching 6–7; consuming digital tools 153–155; *vs.* family involvement 18–19; focused affinity groups 8–9; lens of CWW 30; NAFSCE 19; recommendations 19; special events 7–8; through CWW 148–150
Family pictures/Cuadros de familia (Garza, 1998) 71–73, 76
Family, School, and Community Engagement (NAFSCE) 19
family–school communication: multidirectional flow 21, *21*, 22; unidirectional flow 20, *20*
family strategies: aspirational capital 42–43; familial capital 78; linguistic capital 60–61; navigational capital 111–113; resistant capital 132; social capital 95
Farr, M. 106
Ferlazzo, L. 18
Ferrer, A. 106
Figueroa, R. **173**
Flett, J. 97–98
Flint, A. S. 23
Flip **137**
Fountas, I. C. **29**
Franklin, A. 115
Freedom Soup (Charles, 2021) 133–134, **164**
Freire, P. 20, 25, 26, 148, 150
A Friend for Henry (Bailey, 2019) 97, **158**
From My Window (Júnior, 2020) 98–99, **164**
Fry Bread: A Native American Family Story (Maillard, 2019) 98, **165**
Fuego Fueguito/Fire, Little Fire/Tit, Titchin (Argueta, 2019) 62, **165**

Gaitan, D. 19, 71, 90, 125, 142
Gándara, P. 96
Gangi, J. M. 28, 153
Garcia, A. M. **159**
García, D. 87, 90, 96
García, O. 51, 55
García-Sánchez, I. M. 10, 54, 104, 122, 155
García, S. B. 27
Garza, C. L. 69, 71, 76
Gay, G. 26, 27
Genhart, M. 81, **168**
A Gift from Abuela (Ruiz, 2018) 79, **159**
Goade, M. **166**, **173**

Going Down Home with Daddy (Lyons, 2019) 80, **165**
Goldthorpe, J. H. 29
Gomez, C. 4
Gómez, E. **159**
González, N. 9, 26, 36, 39, 56, 70, 75, 81, 90, 126
González, X. **159**
Google Slides **83**
Google Translate **64**
Goudvis, A. 29
graduate students 14
Grandad's Camper (Woodgate, 2021) 82, **165**
Greenberg, J. B. 22
Gregory, E. 20
Grimard, G. **171**
Guerra, P. L. 27
Guridi, R. N. **158**
Gutiérrez, K. D. 25
Gutierrez, R. **163**

Halpin, A. **167**
Haney, M. J. 8, 9, 74
Harper, P. E. **163**, **169**
Harro, B. 27
Harvey, S. 29
Heath, S. B. 58
Henderson, A. T. 24
Holdaway, D. 28
Holloway, E. L. 10
home–school knowledge exchanges: co-developed family events 23–24; community visits 23; family engagement opportunities 24; family journals 23; literacy digs 23; photo stories 23
Howard, T. C. 26
Howells, T. 168
Howell, T. 45
Huber, P. 9, 29, 90, 142
Huerta, D. 135

If Dominican Were a Color (Recio, 2020) 98, **166**
Individualized Education Plan (IEP) 112
In My Family/En mi familia (Garza, 2000) 69, 71
Intercultural Training and Resource Center (ITRC) 4
Invernizzi, M. 29
Irizarry, J. G. 122

Isabel and Her Colores Go to School (Alessandri, 2021) 64, **166**
I Sang You Down from the Stars (Spillet-Sumner, 2021) 82, **166**
Islandborn (Díaz, 2018) 96, **166**
I Talk Like a River (Scott, 2020) 135, **166**
Itzhak: A Boy Who Loved the Violin (Newman, 2020) 115, **167**

Jaleel, A. **167**
Jamboard **47**
Jaramillo, N. E. 36
Jasis, P. 111
Javaherbin, M. 80, **168**
Jessner, U. 61
Jiménez, L. 63
Johnson, G. 59
Johnson, P. 25
Johnston, F. 29
José, L. 115
José, S. 115
Juanita, K. **167**, **173**
Julián Is a Mermaid (Love, 2018) 81, **167**
Júnior, O. 98–99, **164**
Just Ask! Be Different, Be Brave, Be You (Sotomayor, 2019) 99, **167**

Kaadan, N. 45, **172**
Kahlo, F. 7
Karl, A. 154
Keelan-Chaffins, J. 114
Keene, E. 29
Kendi, I. X. 149
Kensky, J. 97, **169**
Khan, H. 94
Khorram, A. 46, **170**
Kinloch, V. 24, 103
Krogstad, J. M. 103
Kunkel, A. B. 115–116, **163**

Lachtman, O. D. 50, 53, 55, 57
Ladson-Billings, G. 26
Lareau, A. 90
Larrotta, C. 151
Latham, I. 96–97, **171**
Latour, F. 134, **160**
learning theory 26
Lebeuf, D. 116, **168**
Lee, C. 113, 122
Lessac, F. **173**
The Library Bus (Rahman, 2020) 116, **171**

The Life of/La Vida de Dolores (Rodriguez & Stein, 2021) 135, **171**
Lindstrom, C. 134, **173**
linguistic capital: bilingualism is an asset 52–53; children's literature 57; classroom strategies 59–60; contrastive analysis chart **60**; desire to learn English 53–54; digital tools 64, **64–65**; family strategies 60–61; language brokers 55–56; maintain home languages while learning English 54–55; overview 51–52; and storytelling 57–59
Lintern, T. 130
literacy instruction 18, 28, **29**, 92, 93, 95, 153
Loewus, L. 5
Lomas Garza, C. 142
Loney, A. J. 81, **163**
Long, S. 26
López, R. **163**, **167**, **168**
López-Robertson, J. 8, 9, 23, 26, 50, 51, 70, 74
Lora, L. **168**
Love, J. 81, **167**
Lukoff, K. 80, **173**
Luna, N. A. 50
Lyons, K. S. 80, **165**

Macedo, D. 25, 26
Magaña, A. 75
Magnificent Homespun Brown: A Celebration (Doyon, 2020) 47, **167**
Mahin, M. 114, **174**
Maillard, K. N. 98, **165**
Mapp, K. 19, 24, 90
Martinez, M. 50
Martínez-Neal, J. 79, **159**, **165**
Martínez, R. A. 141
Maryam's Magic (Reid, 2021) 46, **167**
massive open online course (MOOC) 19
Maybe Something Beautiful: How Art Transformed a Neighborhood (Campoy & Howell, 2016) 45, **168**
May Your Life Be Deliciosa (Genhart, 2021) 81, **168**
McCabe, K. 82, **173**
McCarthy, B. **166**
McLaren, P. 36
Medina, M. 98, **164**

The Me I Choose to Be (Tarpley, 2021) 47, **171**
Menjívar, C. 75
Meza, E. **169**
Meza, M. **172**
Michaels, S. 58
Miller, E. T. 23, 28
Minter, D. **165**
Moll, L. C. 22, 51, 56, 70, 76
Monkman, K. 87, 89
Morales, Y. 7, 35, 37, 40, 116, 146–148, **164**
Mora, O. 97, **171**
Morrison, F. **169**
Mr. Sugar Comes to Town/La visita del Señor Azúcar (Rhomer & Gomez, 1989) 4
My City Speaks (Lebeuf, 2021) 116, **168**
My Grandma and Me (Javaherbin, 2019) 80, **168**
My papi has a motorcycle (Quintero, 2019) 104, 110, **168**
My Two Border Towns (Bowles, 2021) 98, **169**

Nash, K. T. 153
National Association for Family, School, and Community Engagement (NAFSCE) 19
navigational capital: children's literature 110; classroom strategies 110–111; communicating in school 109–110; digital tools **117–118**; family strategies 111–113; for healthcare 104–105; libraries' community services 105–108; overview 102; schooling-advanced courses 108–109
Nelson, K. **172**
Nemirovsky, R. 10
Newman, T. 115, **167**
Nieto, S. 26, 36, 103
Nina: A Story of Nina Simone (Todd, 2021) 136, **169**

Oettingen. G. 43
Oliveros, J. 80, **172**
Ordoñez-Jasis, R. 111
Orellana, M. 10, 56, 104, 155

Pacheco, M. 58
Padlet 41, **47**

Páez, M. 61
Palacios, S. **160**
Paley, V. 27
Paris, D. 26, 30, 103
Park, J. J. 142
Passeron, J. 29, 30
Pellicioli, A. 99, **170**
Peña, Z. **168**
The People Remember (Zoboi, 2021) 136, **172**
Pepita Talks Twice/Pepita habla dos veces (Lachtman, 1995) 50, 52, 53, 55, 57
Pérez, W. 105, 115, 127
Perkins, M. 133, **160**
Perlman, I. 115
Phi, B. 114, **158**
PhOLKS (Photographs of Local Knowledge Sources) 23
Pimentel, A. B. 114–115, **159**
Pinnell, G. S. 29
Planting Stories: The Life of Librarian and Storyteller Pura Belpré (Denise, 2019) 114, **169**
preservice teachers 14

Quintero, I. 110, **168**

racism 14n3, 27, 86, 93, 122, 149
Rahman, B. 116, 148, **171**
Ramadan, D. 63, **170**
Ramirez, J. **174**
Ramona, D. 110
Recio, S. 98, **166**
Reid, M. 46, **167**
The Remember Balloons (Oliveros, 2018) 80, **172**
René has Two Last Names/René tiene dos apellidos (Colato Laínez, R.) 129
Rescue & Jessica: A Life-changing Friendship (Kensky, 2018) 97, **169**
resistant capital: because we already know 123–124; children's literature 130; classroom strategies 131–132; cultural assimilation through Día de los Muertos 122–123; cultural assimilation through El Ratón Pérez 124–125; deficit voices 128–129; digital learning community 123; digital tools **137**; family strategies 132; linguistic assimilation 126–127; not giving into the "American" way 129–130; overview 122
RESPECT: Aretha Franklin, the Queen of Soul (Weatherford, 2020) 115, **169**
Reyes, C. **171**
Reyes, I. 56
Reyes, M. D. 50, 103
Reynolds, J. F. 56
Rhomer, H. 4
Rinaldi, C. 61
Robinson, C. **169**
Rodriguez, P. 135, **171**
Roe, B. D. 29
Rogoff, B. 27
Roundtree, D. J. 82, **173**
Rowe, D. 23
Ruiz, C. 79, **159**

Sa'Adeddin, M. A. A. M. 58
Salma the Syrian Chef (Ramadan, 2020) 63, **170**
Sanchez, S. **164**
Santana, C. 114
Schwartz, H. L. 10
Scott, J. 135, **166**
screen recording **118**
Seesaw **117**
self-reflection 141
Seven Special Somethings (Khorram, 2021) 46, **170**
Shamsi-Bashas, K. 96–97, **171**
Sharuko: El Arqueólogo Peruano/Peruvian Archaeologist Julio C. Tello (Brown, 2020) 134, **170**
Sheffield, H. W. 46
Shimizu, Y. **171**
Short, K. G. 2, 12
Shulman, L. S. 10
Simone, N. 136
Slade, S. 116, **164**
Smith, S. **166**
social capital: children's literature 94; classroom strategies 94; digital tools **99**; expectations and responsibilities 90–94; family strategies 95; information networks 89–90; overview 87; societal norms 88–89
social media **137**
Socorro, M. 152

Soldier for Equality: José de la Luz Sáenz and the Great War (Tonatiuh, 2019) 62–63, 146, **170**
Solórzano, D. G. 10, 27, 30, 150, 151
Soñadores (Morales, 2018) 35, 37, 40, 147
Song, M. **158**
Song of the Old City (Pellicioli, 2020) 99, **170**
Sorell, T. 46, 63, 135, 136, **160**, **173**
Söter, A. 58
Sotomayor, S. 99, **167**
Soul Food Sunday (Bingham, 2021) 82, **170**
Spillet-Sumner, T. 82, **166**
The Spirit of Chicano Park/El Espíritu del Parque Chicano (Zamora, 2020) 136, **172**
Starkoff, V. **164**
Stein, A. 135
Steins, A. **171**
Suárez-Orozco, C. 50, 53
Suárez-Orozco, M. M. 50, 53
Sulzby, E. 28
Swords, R. 59

Talking Points **65**
Tarpley, N. A. 47, **171**
Teale, W. H. 28
Tello, J. C. 134, **170**
Templeton, S. **29**
Thank You, Omu! (Mora, 2018) 97, **171**
Tinajero, J. V. 51
Tindle, K. 111
Todd, T. N. 136, **169**
Tomorrow (Kaadan, 2018) 45, **172**
Tonatiuh, D. 62–63, 146, **170**
The Tooth Fairy meets El Ratón Pérez (Colato Laínez, 2010) 124, 130
Trumbull, E. 58
Tse, L. 56
Tyner, M. 12
The Undefeated (Alexander, 2019) 134–135, **172**

Uriarte, M. 109

Valdés, G. 51
Valdez, V. E. 104

Valenzuela, A. 30
Vélez-Ibáñez, C. G. 22
video conferencing platforms **117**
Vilela, F. 81, **160**
Villenas, S. 19, 30, 36, 70, 103
Viva Frida (Morales, 2015) 7
Vogel, S. 55
Vygotsky, L.S. 25

Wakelet **117**
Wang, A. 82, **172**
Watercress (Wang, 2021) 82, **172**
We Are Grateful: Otsaliheliga (Sorell, 2018) 63, **173**
We Are Still Here! Native American Truths Everyone Should Know (Sorell, 2021) 136, **173**
We Are Water Protectors (Lindstrom, 2020) 134, **173**
Weatherford, C. B. 115, **169**
Wei, L. 51, 55
Wells, M. S. 24
We Wait for the Sun (Roundtree & McCabe, 2021) 82, **173**
WhatsApp **99**
Wheeler, R. S. 59
When Aidan Became a Brother (Lukoff, 2019) 80, **173**
When Angels Sing: The Story of Rock Legend Carlos Santana (Mahin, 2018) 114, **174**
Whitney, J. 59
Wise, L. **172**
Woodgate, H. 82, **165**
Wulfekotte, D. **172**
Wu, S. 51, 53

Yamamura, E. K. 151
Yankey, L. **168**
Yosso, T. J. 1, 9, 10, 12, 13, 17, 18, 27, 28, 30, 36, 51, 57, 70, 79, 87, 90, 94, 96, 103, 113, 122, 141

Zamora, B. 136, **172**
Zentella, A. C. 51, 57
Zimmerman, S. **29**
Zoboi, I. 136, **172**
Zubizarreta, R. 54

Made in the USA
Columbia, SC
28 August 2024

41268307R00104